*Translations of Greek Plays
including those referred to in this book
and translated by Gilbert Murray
are available as follows:*

AESCHYLUS

*The Agamemnon
The Choëphoroe
The Eumenides
The Persians
The Seven Against Thebes
The Suppliant Women
The Oresteia
Complete Plays*

EURIPIDES

*Alcestis
The Bacchae
Electra
Hippolytus
Ion
Iphigenia in Tauris
Medea
Rhesus
The Trojan Women
Collected Plays*

SOPHOCLES

*The Antigone
Oedipus at Colonus
Oedipus, King of Thebes
The Wife of Heracles*

ARISTOPHANES

*The Birds
The Frogs
The Knights*

MEANDER

*The Arbitration
The Rape of the Locks*

GREEK CIVILIZATION

BY ANDRÉ BONNARD

Greek Civilization
From the Iliad to the Parthenon

BY A. LYTTON SELLS

The Italian Influence in English Poetry

ANDRÉ BONNARD

◎

GREEK
CIVILIZATION

*From the Antigone
to Socrates*

TRANSLATED BY A. LYTTON SELLS

LONDON: GEORGE ALLEN AND UNWIN LTD
NEW YORK: THE MACMILLAN COMPANY

FIRST PUBLISHED IN 1959

Translated from the French
LA CIVILISATION GRECQUE
(*La Guilde du Livre, Lausanne*)

PRINTED IN GREAT BRITAIN
in 12 point Fournier type
BY ROBERT MACLEHOSE AND CO. LTD
THE UNIVERSITY PRESS, GLASGOW

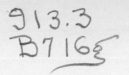
TRANSLATOR'S NOTE

The author's views and interpretations are not
necessarily shared by the translator of this work.

A. L. S. *June*, 1958

ACKNOWLEDGEMENTS

As in the first volume of the present work, the quotations from Greek writers appear in French in the original edition—*Civilisation Grecque: d'Antigone à Socrate*, Lausanne, 1957. For the purpose of the English version, these passages have in general been taken from the following translations into English, and references have been added in footnote:

For Chapter I: *The Dramas of Sophocles*, rendered into English verse by Sir George Young. Everyman Library, London, 1910. Messrs J. M. Dent & Sons, Ltd, and New York: Messrs E. P. Dutton & Co. Inc.

For Chapter IV: *The Tragedies of Sophocles*, a new translation by E. H. Plumptre. London and New York, n.d.

For Chapter V: *The Odes of Pindar, including all the principal fragments*, with an Introduction and an English translation by Sir John Sandys (Loeb Classical Library). London and New York, 1919.

For Chapter VI: *Herodotus*, with an English translation by A. D. Godley (Loeb Classical Library). London and New York, 1931, 3 vols.

For Chapter VII (Aeschylus): *The Prometheus Bound*, edited with Introduction, Commentary and Translation by George Thomson. Cambridge University Press, 1932.
The Medical Works of Hippocrates, a new translation from the original Greek, made . . . by the collaboration of John Chadwick and W. N. Mann. Blackwell Scientific Publications, 1950.

For Chapter VIII: *The Comedies of Aristophanes*, edited, translated and explained by Benjamin Bickley Rogers. London, G. Bell & Sons, Ltd.
The following volumes have been quoted, and in the following order:

The Frogs, 1902.
The Knights, 1910.
The Peace, 1913.
The Acharnians, 1910.
The Revolt of the Women (*Lysistrata*), 1911.
The Birds, 1930.
The Plutus, 1907.

For Chapter IX (Aristophanes): *The Knights*, ed. Rogers, 1910.
The Wasps, ed. Rogers, 1913.

The publishers gratefully acknowledge the cooperation of the following publishers in permitting them to quote from the books in question.

Messrs G. Bell & Sons, Ltd
Blackwell Scientific Publications Ltd
Cambridge University Press
Messrs J. M. Dent & Sons, Ltd
Messrs E. P. Dutton & Co. Inc
The Loeb Classical Library

CONTENTS

ILLUSTRATIONS

The following illustrations are from photographs by Alinari-Giraudon or Anderson-Viollet: Nos. 2, 3, 5, 6, 7, 8, 17, 23, 24, 26, 27. The following from photographs by Madame S. Vautier: Nos. 4, 11, 31, 32. No. 29 is by Madame G. Réal; No. 21 by M. Michel Audrain; No. 28 by M. A. Egger. Nos. 1, 12, and 13 are from Budé negatives.

The following have been borrowed from the works indicated: No. 9 from Max Wegner, *L'Art grec* (Ed. Massin, Paris); Nos. 10, 16 and 18 from *Delphes* (Ed. du Chêne, Paris); Nos. 14 and 15 from Lullies and Hirmer, *Griechische Vasen* (Munich); Nos. 19 and 20 from Max Hirmer, *Die schönsten Griechenmünzen Siziliens* (Leipzig); No. 22 from S. I. Rudenko, *Der zweite Kurgan von Pasyryk* (Berlin); No. 25 from Schefold, *Die Bildnisse der Anticken Dichter* (Bâle); No. 30 from Lechat, *Sculptures grecques antiques* (Hachette, Paris).

CHAPTER ONE

THE PROMISE
OF THE *ANTIGONE*

Tragedies are not written with holy-water, or water sterilized. It is true, if commonplace, to say they are written with blood and tears.

The world of Tragedy is a partly fictional world which Athenian poets created for their countrymen, starting from the hard experience of the reality which these peasants and sailors had been suffering for two centuries past. In Solon's time the Athenians were under the domination of the Eupatridae, after his time under the domination of the rich; and both weighed as heavily on their shoulders as the yoke of a harsh fate. This people was then very near being stripped of its lands and rights, driven into exile or slavery and doomed to the poverty that degrades and kills.

Then, with the second birth of Tragedy at the beginning of the fifth century, came the invasion of the Medes and Persians, accompanied by those mixed and countless hordes who, to feed themselves or simply for the pleasure of destruction, carried off the stores of grain, killed flocks and herds, burned towns and villages, cut down the olive-groves and—supreme sacrilege—overthrew the altars of the gods and broke their statues.

With a sustained effort and then a sudden and powerful jerk, the Athenians freed themselves from the oppression of the Eupatridae and destroyed the Asiatic invader. From the forces that threatened to crush them they wrested the democratic sovereignty and equality of which they were so proud and at the same time they freed their territory and won national independence. The memory of this heroic age when the Athenians triumphantly defied the death that lay in wait, the memory of a battle fought and won with the aid of the gods, remains present, if only dimly reflected, at the heart of every Attic Tragedy. The truth is, that Tragedy was nothing but the poetical response of the Athenian people to the historical pressures which made it what it was: the defender of democracy (however narrow its substructure may then have been) and of the citizens' liberty.

13

The first two of the great tragedians belonged to the aristocracy or the upper class. This does not matter. Before being noble or rich, they were poets of genius, Athenian citizens in the service of the state. Their membership of the community was their surest bond with other men. They felt the inspiration that was in them as a fiery crater kindled by the gods; and their whole art tended to discipline and transform the flames into a sun whose rays would nourish and make fruitful the lives of their fellow citizens.

When Sophocles made his début, some ten years after Salamis and Plataea, a strong movement, born of the victory over the Persians, was carrying the nation towards new achievements and creations. On the plane of Tragedy, the poet's mission is to educate free men. Tragedy is in principle didactic; yet its tone is never that of pedantry. It is by representing an action, much more than by the lyric songs, the words of the chorus-leader or even the speeches which the poet puts into his characters' mouths, that he conveys his message. The dramatic conflict he presents is nearly always the struggle of a hero enamoured of greatness, who is striving—but let him beware that he offend not the gods who have set limits to that greatness!—who is striving to realize that extension of our human powers, that transcendence, that conversion of the man into the hero, which is the proper object of Tragedy. The tragic hero is like the bold aviator who undertakes to break the sound-barrier. He may often crash; but his fall in no way means that we have to condemn him. He is not condemned by the poet: it is for us he has fallen. His death enables us more exactly to mark the invisible wall of flame and gold where the presence of the gods arrests and suddenly breaks man's forward surge to the beyond. It is not the hero's death that is tragic, for we shall all die, but the presence of those inflexible gods which is revealed in his death; for they are there, in the experience of reality which Sophocles and his contemporaries had. Now this presence of the gods seems to oppose man's transcending himself and becoming a hero. Yet every tragedy expresses and reaffirms man's aspiration to transcend himself, and, facing the obstacles he encounters in the world and the society of his time, facing all that is unknown there, to take once again the measure of his greatness; to surpass himself while taking account of those obstacles and while indicating to men in general, whose pioneer and patron and guide the tragic hero is, the barriers which limit our species but which, as soon as they are pointed out, cease to limit us. He will risk losing his life, but who knows whether the man who stumbles forward against an obstacle will not have pushed back the barriers he has at last revealed? Who knows whether, at another time and in another society, the hero's death, which changes to hope in the spectator's heart, will take place in the same way—or even take place at all?

After the sound-barrier has been passed, there will be the heat-barrier or some other, beyond. But thanks to these successive trials, the narrow confines of our lot will gradually grow wider, until the gates open on. . . . The hero's victory and death are alike the pledge of this. Tragedy works always with *continuance*, with that perpetual transformation of the world of men which it expresses and of which it is an agent.

At the end of most Tragedies the mind stands hesitant between horror and hope. At the end? No great Tragedy is ever quite ended; all Tragedies remain open to an immense sky, spangled with new stars and traversed with promises like meteors. In the course of its evolution when it is handled in other forms and in societies that have been relieved of the heavy mortgages that gave birth to it, Tragedy may well take on new meanings, may shine with dazzling beauty and overwhelm us with its greatness. The perennial character of literary masterpieces can, it has been said, be explained in this way. The promise of a new society which such Tragedies have made or sometimes only adumbrated, has been fulfilled in the future in which we are living.

◎

Of all the ancient Tragedies that have been preserved to us, the *Antigone* is doubtless the one which carries the most promises. It is the one which, in its old-time language, conveys the information that is most up-to-date—but also the most difficult exactly to appreciate. Let us start from the facts.

On the eve of the day when the drama opens, Eteocles and Polyneices, the two brothers who are at enmity, legitimate successors, both, of their father Oedipus, have killed each other in the battle under the walls of Thebes. Eteocles was defending the soil of the fatherland; Polyneices, by relying on foreign support in furtherance of his right, was acting as a traitor. Their uncle Creon has inherited the blood-stained throne. He is a man of principle who, at the outset, appears up-right. But he has the limited outlook of those who, on attaining power, think they have reached the peak of their own development. In order to restore the authority of the State which has been shaken by Polyneices' rebellion, in order also to accustom his people, after the recent discords, to respect the established order, Creon, as soon as he has occupied the throne, promulgates a decree which grants funeral honours to the patriot Eteocles but consigns the body of the rebellious Polyneices to be devoured by wild beasts. Whoever infringes this edict will incur the pain of death.

Now Antigone as soon as she hears of the decree decides, at night, to render to Polyneices the honours of which he is being deprived. Piety and fraternal love alike demand it. Antigone does not distinguish between her two unhappy brothers, for death has invested them with a new and unquestionable fraternity.

So, in spite of Creon's interdiction, she will bury Polyneices. She knows that death awaits her at the end; but it will be a 'noble' death, 'after this noble crime'. And so now, under the impulse of faith, she seeks to win over her sister, Ismene, to the enterprise. Ismene replies that it is folly; that they are mere women whose role is to obey the powers that be. She tries to divert Antigone from her foolhardy design. But this obstacle only fortifies Antigone in her resolve. Thus in Sophocles the characters know each other and make themselves known to the audience, and place themselves in sharper focus, in relation to the actions which they engage in or which they refuse. Antigone rejects Ismene and treats her with scorn. But at the moment when she is performing the funeral rites the maiden is arrested by one of the soldiers whom the king has posted to guard the body, her hands are bound and she is led before Creon. She justifies her action; she has obeyed the divine laws, 'laws unwritten', but eternal and revealed to her conscience, laws that must prevail over the decree published by an insensate prince.

Antigone's resistance tears from Creon's face the pompous mask of a ruler devoted to the good of the city, the mask which we have seen him complacently assume in presence of the Chorus of astonished notables of Thebes. She forces the pretentious king to plunge deeper and deeper into arbitrary procedure. He condemns Antigone to death; even more absurdly he condemns Ismene, who has been seen roaming wildly about the palace. Ismene, for her part, wants to die with her sister, and kneeling at Antigone's feet, begs her for permission to share her doom. But Antigone harshly rejects this tardy and inopportune sacrifice, she refuses to Ismene an honour to which the latter is not entitled. She had never, for that matter, asked her sister to die with her or for her, but simply to risk death in burying their dear brother. The heroic sisters fail, again and again, to understand each other, their wills merely come into conflict in this exhausting contretemps.

Exhausting but also fruitful. The scenes between Antigone and Ismene are important not only as showing how, in Sophocles, the characters take shape through the conflict of resemblances but also because they brilliantly display the contagious force of love. But now, in this dark hour when the tragedy seems to be moving to its fatal end, comes a surprising turn of fortune—the first *péripétie* in a Greek play—which, for a time, restores a breath of hope; but which also prepares the blow that is to strike Creon. It does even more: it prepares us to reconcile, in our conscience, Creon and Antigone. Haemon appears before the king his father and asks for the maiden's pardon.

Haemon loves Antigone: the two are indeed affianced. So love once more asserts its contagious power. But what is most striking is that Haemon does not ask for Antigone's pardon in the name of his love. He speaks the only language that befits a man, not the language of sentiment but that of reason enamoured of

1. *Ionian Coré, found on the Acropolis at Athens (Date: c. 520 B.C.)*

1

2

justice. He addresses his father in the most self-controlled and deferential manner. He recalls the father whom he loves but whom he judges to have gone astray, to respect for the divine law; and at the same time strives to enlighten him regarding his true interest which is inseparable from that of the city he rules. He tries, not to soften but to convince him. For Haemon would blush to plead for the life of his betrothed and still more to plead for himself. He pleads only for his father and for justice. There is nothing nobler in Haemon than this filial manliness. The scene is extraordinarily firm. Where the modern stage, so prone to display the passion of love and dilute it in speech and dialogue, would not fail to exploit the situation by an appeal to compassion, the ancient poet refrains from the easy way of senti-ment, he refuses the right to put into Haemon's mouth the slightest allusion to his love. Not that Haemon pretends to deceive anyone as regards his feeling for Antigone. But what kind of man would he be if he dared ask his father to let this feeling override the interests of the community? Honour commands him to con-trol his passion and to speak only the language of reason.

On the other hand the constraint he has thus imposed on his heart allows the scene which has opened in the calm tone of a debate to develop into one of frenzied violence. From the moment when his father accuses him of failing in the honour which, in fact, he has so severely preserved, how can Haemon help rebelling against such injustice, how can he help feeding his rage with the passion he has thus bridled in vain? The explosion of his fury, in the concluding pieces of dialogue, reveals both his love and his sense of honour. As to Creon's anger, it not merely shows us how far he is now involving himself in an unjust course but it informs us of the father's attachment to the son, the kind of attachment that Creon may feel, a paternal love which requires the son to remain the father's property and which makes this sudden resistance to his authority the more intolerable because he guesses that it is supported by another love. Creon's wrath against his son reveals not only a man who has gone astray but one who is defenceless against the blow which the gods are preparing to strike. He still has a heart, and this heart is a vulnerable target.

Meanwhile the altercation between the two men has only fortified Creon in his decision. Once again we know that Antigone is lost. Creon confirms her con-demnation, while withdrawing Ismene's; but to the pain of death he adds the cruellest punishment. Antigone is to be walled up alive in a cavern.

Yet at the moment when Antigone's death appears more certain than ever, this death begins to give us a clearer glimpse of its efficacity. Antigone has been pre-sented from the outset as a light placed before our eyes, a pledge that human life is not doomed to total darkness. Before Haemon's entry, neither the reticent approval of the Elders, nor even the flame of Ismene's devotion, could really

B

2. *Spectators at the Theatre. Detail of a Panathenaic amphora*

assure us that this light will not have burned in vain before the harsh tribunal of the city. If the will of a Creon is enough to extinguish it, then human life will be delivered up to darkness and brutality. Is the drama moving, in our hearts, to this pole of darkness? Yes, at least until the scene with Haemon. Until the moment of this new turn of events, the meaning of Antigone's death remains sterile. We shall have had a promise of joy, but the promise will have been withdrawn. If Antigone is to be given us for all time, dead or living, then her flame must have kindled other flames. Neither the songs of the Chorus, for all their beauty, nor Ismene's frail outburst, have really saved us from despair. It is only Haemon's burning devotion that begins to restore to us Antigone. This is because, without uttering a single word of love, Haemon, by his fidelity to her he loves and also to justice and to the gods, asserts the contagious, nay, the irresistible power of that force which moves the world and human life.

The Chorus is aware of the power of Eros. It has perceived his presence in Haemon. In that half-light (whether of dawn or dusk, we do not yet know) in which the Chorus bears us company, its songs celebrate 'Invincible Eros' and grope towards ennobling truths.

And now, for the last time, Antigone appears before us. The guards are leading her to the place where she must meet her death—a doom blind and earthbound. In this scene we see her fight the last battle, which each of us must fight: alone and naked, her armour of pride laid down, as it should be, back to the wall where destiny lines up its hostages. This scene of Antigone's plaint, these marvellous stanzas in which she tells of her sorrow in departing this life and, in presence of the Elders who are now more inclined to judge than able to understand, experiences and sings of the bitterness of the last and necessary solitude—this scene takes up one of the traditional themes of Greek Tragedy. It is right and just that, before he dies, the hero should bid farewell to the land of the living, and sing his love for the dear light of the sun. He must also measure himself, in his strength and weakness, against the omnipotent destiny that is crushing him.

Some critics have thought that these plaintive songs were out of keeping with Antigone's lofty character. But the opposite is true. The crude light of death which is now directed on Antigone, discovers to us at last the ultimate secret of her nature. Here is the key. We know now that the hard Antigone—hard in combat, hard to herself, hard because she is the daughter of a race of fighters who have been struck down—we know that the harsh Antigone is, in her inner secret and ultimate solitude, all tenderness. She loved the joy of the sunlight, she loved green trees and running water, she loved her own, her parents, and the children she will never have, and the brother who cannot be replaced. How could she have died for that brother, if she had not been all love?

From a theme traditional on the tragic stage Sophocles illustrates by his art the truth that shines out in Antigone: no man has the strength to die save in the love he has had for life. At this moment of Antigone's departure, nothing can avail to save the maiden's life—nothing except the gods. Through the shock of their conflicting passions, men have constructed a web of fatality, a web of which Antigone had woven the first strands—a destiny born of choice and in which the heroine's freedom has been translated into her fate. Humanly speaking, she is lost.

But Tiresias summons us to hear the voice of the gods, silent hitherto, but now suddenly speaking to us. This silence which, almost to the limit of the tragic action, has confined the cries of disputing mortals as in the bottom of a well, suddenly rings out. It speaks clearly; and before closing down once again as the sound of human cries is renewed, it points to the only way along which man's wisdom may find an issue. For a moment the divine voice is loud and distinct; but its clearness is the livid clearness of the immobile heavens in which the thunderbolt hangs ready. We know that Creon may or may not understand, that he may or may not order Antigone's reprieve, or rather that, if he can still understand, it is already too late. As often happens towards the end of the tragic conflict, on the last hundred yards of the track, man and destiny race together, with straining will and straining muscles. The two songs of the Chorus which precede and follow the scene with Tiresias, raise so to speak a fount of groans and a fount of hope, the contrast between which exactly expresses the cleavage of our being in this supreme moment which precedes the climax.

Suddenly, the moment is past; the words: 'Too late' ring in our ears; and disaster breaks upon us in enormous waves. A messenger announces that Antigone has hung herself, he speaks of the tender throat strangled by the scarf, he describes Haemon spitting in the face of his father who has just arrived, raising his sword against Creon but immediately turning it upon himself, and his heart's blood spurting into the face of the maiden as she hangs there, in the cavern. It is not merely disaster, but horror that falls upon us and submerges us. The Greek tragedians were not unaware that horror is one of the permanent features of life, and they looked it firmly in the face.

And now Creon returns, half carrying, half dragging, his son's body. He sobs out his grief, he proclaims his crime. Behind him a door opens, and we see another corpse, another death which, so to speak, strikes him in the back. His wife Eurydice, Haemon's mother, has killed herself through his fault. Between these two bodies which accuse and strike him, Creon is no more than a pitiful creature, a man who has been in error and stands there, sobbing. He prays for Death—Death present in those whom he has loved and killed. Let Death take him too. But there is no reply. And it is at this moment when the world before us is no more than blood and tears, when the circle of human faces which the tragedy has presented to us is a circle of stricken ghosts, when we do not forget the image of Antigone hanging in the cavern, it is in this moment of piled up horrors that our hearts are flooded with an inconceivable joy. For Antigone is within us, radiant and alive; Antigone is blinding and burning truth.

At the same time Creon himself begins to shine in our hearts, like another and fraternal light, Creon smitten by the gods but whom we are forbidden to strike. Haemon's body, outstretched between us and the kneeling father like a lake of pity and tenderness, defends Creon against our blows.

We must now try to understand. It is no intellectual's mania that requires this effort. Our feelings which have been so deeply harrowed, ploughed into the very roots of our understanding, oblige us to seek the meaning of the Tragedy. The poet himself asks us to find an answer to the question put to us by Creon and Antigone. Because the *Antigone* raises a problem of values, the critic is strongly tempted to reduce the play to the level of a *pièce à thèse* and to regard the characters as simply the algebraic signs of the values they represent. Nothing is more likely to warp our judgment of the play than to see in it a conflict of principles; and indeed nothing is more contrary to the poet's creative procedure than the notion that he may be proceeding from abstract to concrete. The *Antigone* is not a conflict of principles, but of human beings strongly characterized and differentiated. The dramatis personae appear before us as solids; and it is even this solidity, in the geometrical sense, the density so to speak of their substance, that allows us—but only afterwards—to project their image on to the screen of ideas.

We must then start from these persons, beings who wound and convince us, if we are to grasp the meaning of Sophocles' play; nor must we forget to weigh in the scales of our judgment the quality of the pleasure we have received. But we must not seek the meaning of the drama in any one character, however important he may be. A great poet never reveals his thought in a selected spokesman: it is, on the contrary, his presence in each of the characters he creates that connects us *with* them, introduces us *into* them and serves to interpret the language of these souls who are at first strangers, dissonant in their utterance, but who at the last speak with but one voice—the poet's voice and now ours. Of all poets the tragedian, precisely because he is a tragedian, make his voice heard only in the concert of these warring children of his brain, creatures struggling inside him and inside us and whom we love because they are at one and the same time the poet and ourselves. The concert is discordant for long enough before it acquires harmony; the movement it follows is slowly and sorrowfully and yet delightfully inscribed in our hearts before it reaches our understanding, through channels of flesh and blood.

Why are Antigone and Creon at daggers drawn? No doubt because there never were two beings at once so different and so alike. Their characters are identical, their souls antithetical. Their wills are inflexible, armed with that hardness and intolerance that are needed by all who are set on prevailing. As one of the Elders says of Antigone:

> *Lo you, the spirit stout*
> *Of her stout father's child—unapt to bend*
> *Beneath misfortune!*[1]

Antigone is called 'intractable'; she is cruel and 'harsh' as Oedipus had been— Oedipus hard to the point of putting out his own eyes, as his daughter is in hanging herself, and as both are hard to others.

But Oedipus' daughter is also Creon's niece. On the pinnacle of greatness where each aspires to stand, the same hardening of the character fixes their rigid outlines. 'A rigid mind, a stiff-necked being,' says Creon of Antigone, not realizing that when he thus defines her he is defining himself. And he flatters himself that these stiff-necked beings are precisely the ones that will break most abruptly, like the fire-hardened iron which one supposed to be the most solid. But when he speaks in this way of the risk Antigone is running, it is his own adventure that he is describing in advance; it is he whose will, stretched to its furthest limit, will be seen to break suddenly in face of the threats of the soothsayer Tiresias.

With regard to others—to those who wish them well—the same defensive reflex is manifest in Antigone as in Creon, the same harsh rejection of the love that intends to save them. Antigone face to face with Ismene, Creon with Haemon, are like symmetrical statues in a pediment in which, under the sign of violence, tower the demons of solitary greatness, trampling under foot any who wish to restrain their impulse. There are in both the same wild and scornful fury, the same insults for those who try to bend them or merely make them think for a moment. They follow a straight course. No matter whether, in our eyes, they are right or wrong. What counts for us, and at first convinces us, is each one's fidelity to himself. Creon is faithful in this: if he yielded to the one who loves and counsels him, he would betray the engagement he has made with himself that, whatever comes of it, he will push on to the goal he has set himself; Antigone is the same. To establish equilibrium in the world which each is obstinately striving to build, this is the

---

[1] *The Dramas of Sophocles,* rendered in English verse by Sir George Young. Everyman edition, London, 1910, Messrs J. M. Dent & Sons, Ltd, New York: Messrs E. P. Dutton & Co. Inc. p. 15.

cost. Let the will falter, even once, and this world will crumble. When Creon gives way, the stability of the universe he has promised us will collapse with him.

This is why Antigone and Creon hate those who love them. The love that turns them away from their task, that refuses to engage itself in that task—such obstinacy is not love, in their eyes, and does not merit love.

A friend in words is not a friend for me,[1]

says Antigone to Ismene; and again:

If you will say it,
I shall detest you soon.[2]

He who is not with them is against them. Creon says to Haemon:

It is for this men pray to breed and rear
In their homes dutiful offspring—to requite
The foe with evil, and their father's friend
Honour, as did their father.[3]

The one imposes on his son, as the other on her sister the same 'everything or nothing'. They demand the same absolute choice that they have made themselves, and Antigone's nature is no less 'tyrannical' than Creon's. One may go as far as to say that they are possessed by the same fanaticism, the same *idée fixe*. One object fascinates them to the point of blinding them to all else. For Antigone it is the un-buried body of Polyneices, for Creon it is his throne in peril. To this they give everything in advance, they sacrifice every good, even life itself. They stake their all, with rapture, on this one card, the possession of which is their highest good. Every fanatic is a gambler who finds delight in the chance of ruin or salvation turning on the luck of a single card. And it is the acute pleasure of a life reduced to the slender chance of the winning card which enables us to appreciate at every moment the conflicting furies of Creon and Antigone. Our whole being aroused not in the service of their 'ideologies' but of their conflicting passions, tastes twice over, as it were, the agony and joy of feeling that life is involved in a struggle against death, involved with the same uncompromising relish and the same scorn of risk.

All greatness aspires to be exclusive. Antigone's fanaticism, and Creon's, explain the mysteries of their nature. Some critics have asked how Antigone could

[1] *Ibid.*, p. 17.
[2] *Ibid.*, p. 4. This is at an earlier point in the play—at the end of the opening scene where Antigone and Ismene are alone (Translator).
[3] *Ibid.*, p. 20.

possibly forget Haemon as entirely as she does. They judge it unlikely that she could brush so closely past the drama of Haemon's life and go through her own without even once mentioning her betrothed. And so some of these tender-hearted critics attribute to Antigone the verse which the manuscripts put in the mouth of Ismene:

> *O dearest Haemon,*
> *How are you slighted by your father!*[1]

This sigh of 'dearest Haemon' seems to them to attenuate the unbearable rigour of Antigone's attitude, and in short to make her more touching.

But, if we are to make Antigone bearable, is it necessary to correct the text? Is her silence regarding Haemon so incomprehensible or, in the last resort, so shocking? This silence is not due to any forgetfulness of him she loves or of the joys which his love promised her. The scene in which the maiden laments that she must die before knowing marriage, before 'giving her breast to a child', proves this well enough. And are we not abundantly satisfied with 'touching' words in the stanzas in which, as she sees Death drawing near, she tells of her great love of life and of life's joys? But if, even at this moment and *à fortiori* in the course of her struggle against Creon, she does not speak of Haemon, her silence can be explained by the deliberate concentration of her thoughts on her brother's misfortune, by the gathering together of all her strength with a view to sisterly affection. Antigone wants to be sisterly and nothing else. If she does not banish from her soul every feeling that would turn her away from simply loving Polyneices, at least she thrusts it into some part of her being where it will have no more power over her conduct.

The same trait of character explains what is obscure in Creon. An intelligent man, he has a clear notion of the aim he has set himself, which is to reign over an orderly state. He loves his son, his wife and the city; selfishly, no doubt, on account of the pleasure, honour and profit he derives from these possessions, but still he loves them on his own plane of affection which is that of a good tyrant. The end of the drama reveals the strength of Creon's attachment for these beings who depended on him.

How then does it come about that this shrewd man, who has decided to use the good things that life offers him, shows himself so limited in the conduct of his life and in the exercise of power? Why is he incapable of grasping a single one of the good reasons his son puts forward, why is he deaf to the voice that clearly predicts his ruin if he insists on governing in a way contrary to the opinions of everyone

---

[1] *Ibid.*, p. 18.

else? The truth is that in this apparent obscurity there is nothing that is not clear. It is in Creon's nature, as in Antigone's, to put himself wholly into any action he undertakes. Having decided to fight against rebellion and anarchy, he will push the struggle to the bitter end, even if the end be fatal. The blindness and obsession of the *idée fixe* can be recognized in the fact that the rebellion he has decided to punish in the person first of Polyneices and then of Antigone, he sees even where it does not exist. It rises up in his path, a phantom of the imagination but one he feels obliged to crush, not only in Antigone but, absurdly enough, in the soldier who arrests the maiden and delivers her up and whom he supposed to have been paid by his enemies; even more absurdly, in Ismene, a gentle creature whom he regards as a sombre *intrigante*. The timid reservations of the Chorus, the sensible advice of his son who is only trying to strengthen his authority, the whisperings of the city and even its silences—all these are rebellion in Creon's eyes. And rebellion, too, are the grave warnings of Tiresias—a greedy soothsayer who has sold himself to the conspirators! Imprisoned by his fanaticism not only in the decision he has taken but in the world of fiction it has built round him and of which it means to retain control, and henceforth admitting no consideration, neither the love of his son, nor common sense, nor pity, nor even the requirements of the situation or an understanding of it—such is Creon, and who or what will destroy the obsession and raise the strange siege or rather blockade that Creon has established against himself? His fanaticism has condemned him to solitude and made him a target for all to shoot at. Even in those who wish to save him he now sees only enemies.

> *Old man, ye all, like archers at a mark,*
> *Are loosing shaft, at me.*[1]

Towards the end of the drama a threat hangs over Creon as over Antigone: the menace of solitude, teacher and snare of those who have given their hearts to the absolute.

But it is not to the same kind of solitude that these two beings are destined by the trenchant nature of their characters. And, besides, one can infer nothing from this close similarity of character against fanaticism in itself. In every combative nature intolerance is the necessary and the only effective way of fighting. But there is something other than character that defines people and counts in the struggle, and that is the quality of their souls. In the shock of their wills in conflict Antigone and Creon reveal not only a striking identity of character, but a quality of soul so dissimilar that one feels suddenly astonished at having been able to compare these two beings. The rigid outlines of their characters are as similar as the nature of

[1] *Ibid.*, p. 31. Creon answering Tiresias.

their souls is different. And this difference will enable Antigone, paradoxically, to find in the solitude of death the means of escaping that solitude to which Creon falls a living victim. So, in these personages, are displayed two wills of equal strength but pointing to opposite poles: equal wills under contrasting signs.

Antigone's is a soul bursting with love. Under the rough bark of this sapling pulses the sweetness—and also the flame—of a loving heart. A deep tenderness, a love ardent and almost absurd, have made this girl what she is, have kindled in her this frenzy of self-sacrifice, this virile energy and hardness and scorn. For gentleness turns to harshness when one loves, and a spirit of humble service turns to scorn and disdain for all but the beloved. And love becomes hate. Antigone hates anyone—and especially Ismene, as tender as she—who refuses to follow her on the road where the impulse of love is taking her.

The dead whom she has loved and continues to love as though still living, those whom she is constantly calling 'my own, my loved ones', are the masters of her soul. And above all 'the beloved brother' who has been refused the peace of the grave, whom she cannot even weep over at ease, the poor body shamefully abandoned to carrion beasts, the 'dear treasure' of her soul. This brother is the master to whom she has given herself, and he alone can make her cherish death, and not so much accept it as embrace it in a movement of joy mingled with tears, but of joy so intense that sorrow turns to song.

Love, like other passions, burns with a devouring fire. In this brazier of her heart all other loves have grown pale and vanished under the intense brightness of this single flame: all other loves—the surest and best tried, her father's and mother's; the most desired, that of the husband that Haemon will never be and of the children he will never give her. All these loves she must now forget, and in the very moment when she weeps over them and proves in so doing that her heart needs them, she must now go to the point of denying them because henceforth a single love occupies the whole field of her soul, and because she must bring to this one unreplaceable brother, by joining him in death, the offering of an undivided heart. The uncompromising tyranny of passion is expressed in an amazing passage which many of the moderns have not understood and of which some, including Goethe, have wished to deny that Sophocles was the author. It is the place where Antigone forcibly declares that what she has done for her brother she would not have done either for a husband or a child. Why? Because, she says, once the parents are dead, only a brother is unreplaceable. But this is nothing but a sophism of the heart, one of those attempts, to which the Greek mind was extremely prone, to create a rational basis for what is really an impulse of the soul. This extravagance of Antigone's clearly reveals the extreme nature of a passion which has led her to err in denying everything but the single object of her love.

Her brother is her all. She clings to him as to a love that can never end. She pursues him beyond the grave as something inseparable from the survival of consciousness.

> *Him will I bury. Death, so met, were honour,*
> *And for that capital crime of piety,*
> *Loving and loved, I will be by his side.*
> *. . . for there*
> *For ever must I be.*[1]

It is never in fact her brain, it is never reason or principle that guide her, but always the heart. It is feeling, exacerbated, that drives her to her doom. Ismene tells her so at the outset:

> *Your heart beats hotly*
> *For chilling work.*

And again:

> *You go on a fool's errand! Lover true*
> *To your beloved none the less are you.*[2]

But Antigone defines her nature most exactly in the brilliant lines in which she proclaims her refusal to hate Polyneices as the enemy of her country:

> *Well, I was made for fellowship in love,*
> *Not fellowship in hate.*[3]

Hers is the purely loving heart that admits no conditions and sets no limits to love. The compression of the construction in Greek makes it difficult to translate. She means that she was born—that it was her nature, her being,—to share love: to give and to receive it, to live in the communion of love.

We must not be deceived. Antigone's action has been commanded by her nature before being prescribed by the gods. Love comes first, it is 'inborn'. If she had not loved her brother, she would not have discovered in herself those laws divine, eternal, unwritten, which enjoin upon her the duty of saving him. These laws do not come to her from without: they are the laws of her own heart; or at least it is through the heart and by an impulse of love that she has access to the divine will, to the exigencies of the spiritual world. A carnal love, if you like, in the sense that it is love of a body, for it is from sisterly love that Antigone draws the strength to rebel against the will of men and wholly to obey the will of God.

We recognize love in its power to sow seeds of discovery and revelation. If an

---

[1] *Ibid.*, p. 3.   [2] *Ibid.*, p. 4.   [3] *Ibid.*, p. 17.

Eros sends Antigone to execution, if this Eros, jealous and exclusive as he always is, appears to shut out everything that is not sisterly love, is it not he also—symbol of the generative principle—who implants in her the loftiest reality in the world of Sophocles, namely the divine word? She carries this word in her heart, she proclaims it with radiant confidence. Death means nothing to her now that she has conceived and ripened this splendid fruit. As she says to Creon:

> ... *nor did I deem*
> *Your ordinance of so much binding force,*
> *As that a mortal man could overbear*
> *The unchangeable unwritten code of Heaven;*
> *This is not of today and yesterday,*
> *But lives for ever. ...*
> *And that I die*
> *Before my hour is due, that I count gain.*
>
> ... *Thus*
> *To me the pain is light to meet this fate;*
> *But had I borne to leave the body of him*
> *My mother bare unburied, then, indeed,*
> *I might feel pain; but, as it is, I cannot.*[1]

The gift of life, the love of her brother, the witness she bears to the divine law, these things are indissoluble in Sophocles' heroine.

Such is her destiny. She assumes its vocation on the plane of life and death, and if she is blinded by it, she also wins from it that lucidity which pierces to the very centre of our being and also the authority with which love invests the noblest beings. Hence the amazing and well-nigh incomprehensible verse we have already cited:

> *Well, I was made for fellowship in love,*
> *Not fellowship in hate.*

It has been said and repeated *ad nauseam* that this verse defines Antigone, but it is clear that it also transcends her. It will be noticed that her actions do not always conform to it. She betrays as much as she remains faithful to this quasi prophetic declaration. It is a declaration wrung from what she will become—something beyond herself—by that which is deep in her nature or rather by an Antigone yet to be, and unknown to the Antigone who still is. The words have perhaps been

---

[1] *Ibid.*, pp. 14–15.

wrung from the poet himself, in the white heat of the tragic conflict. In this matter his creation transcends him as it transcends the ages.

◎

In Antigone all is love, or will become love. In Creon all is self-love. I take this term in the classical sense of love of self.

Creon no doubt loves his wife and his son and his subjects in a certain way; but above all in so far as they display and serve his strength and are the instruments and arguments of his ego. He does not really love them, because he is indifferent to their happiness. He is wounded by their loss, but their real nature is inaccessible to him, and indeed he understands nothing, he understands no one apart from himself. He is occupied wholly with himself and, for all that, can read his own character no more clearly.

Love to him is a closed book. The love that expresses itself in his presence makes him close up; Ismene's for her sister, for example, or Haemon's for Antigone. Love in his eyes is simply nonsense, apart from sex. When he is asked whether he will really send his son's betrothed to her death he answers with a coarseness that betrays his total incomprehension: 'He will find other heifers for his ploughing.'

Creon has no knowledge of love or of his son. If he hates and despises love, he is also afraid of it, because it would force him to open himself to others. For Creon has nourished in his heart the taste for power until it has reversed itself and become impotence: herein he reminds us of a danger to which all are subject. One is struck by the way in which, with all the attributes of power, Creon's conduct is finally revealed as simple powerlessness. The genuine truths which this man represents are rendered sterile by the sterility of a nature rebellious to love. In defending the city which is threatened by the treason of Polyneices and the indiscipline of Antigone, Creon seems for a moment to be devoting himself to an object that transcends him: in struggling to safeguard public order, in combating those whom, with Haemon, he calls anarchists, Creon disposes at the outset of all the arguments proper to convince us. We know that in a moment of extreme peril the community needs to be defended against the Antigones. We are aware that there is no hypocrisy in Creon's public profession of political faith; but there is no love either. The truths of which he is the honest spokesman remain merely cerebral, dead seeds in the barren soil of his nature.

When Creon trembles with anger for the city in peril, is he not rather trembling with fear for himself? At the bottom of this great king's nature is fear, bound up with impotence. Entrenched in fear he sees around him only enemies and conspiracies. When the city speaks to him through the mouth of the Elders, fear emboldens him to brave their warnings. When the gods speak to him, fear drives him to frightful blasphemies, because he suspects these gods of Tiresias of having gone over to his adversaries. As the drama unrolls, the curtain of idealism which he had lowered between his people and himself, when making his speech from the throne, dissolves like a fragile screen. Events now force him to say clearly what he had been hiding from himself. It is not now the city demanding that the traitors be punished, it is terror, growing and at last reigning in Creon's ego. Forced back into the corner in which it hid behind the veil of truths adopted without the saving grace of love, the ego stands out in the nakedness of terror before the eyes of gods and men. And the man who had posed proudly as the exemplary defender of the city is now revealed as a simple individual.

Because he loved only his power, his own self and self-conceit—but was this love?—Creon is doomed to solitude. He loses at one stroke his son, his wife and his power. Now he is reduced to that poor vesture of the self, a skin puffed up in vain with false authority. Antigone too had been alone in the last hour, and no one, not even the Chorus, had shed a tear over her lot as she walked slowly towards the tomb where she was to be buried alive. But Antigone's solitude was only apparent: it was the solitude that every creature faces in the last hour, but not a solitude of the soul. At this very moment Antigone carries in her heart her brother, all the dead she has loved; and love unites her with all that is divine. While Creon, whom the poet exhibits to our pitying gaze as he exhibits every suffering creature to whom his genius has given birth, is reduced to the most barren solitude, the gods whom he claimed to monopolize strike him, the city abandons him, and the wife and son whom he had sacrificed to the hypertrophy of his ego are not even warm and dear presences to comfort his soul: to the eyes of this man, eyes that still seek to appropriate them, they are no more than corpses.

And yet this frightening figure of human error and affliction is made, strangely, by the poet to live in our hearts, not simply as a warning but as a brother. All through the play and most intensely in the last moments, Creon dwells in our consciousness as an authentic part of it: guilty, it is true, but too close to our own errors for us to think of condemning him in the name of some abstract principle. He is part of our tragic experience. In his place and in his way he had been right and he had to act as he did if Sophocles' play was to bear its fruit which was that total knowledge of our dual personality and of the world in which it must act.

We are both Antigone and Creon and the conflict between them. One of the clearest features of Sophocles' art is to make us participate so intimately in the life of each of his characters that we cannot but agree with each of them when he stands and speaks to us. This is because each speaks and lives in us: it is our voice we hear in them, our life we discover. Sophocles is not one of those coarse writers who say: this man is wrong, that man is right. So great is his love for each of the beings he has brought forth that each is right in the place he occupies in the poet's world. We adhere to each as to a being whose truth we have ourselves experienced. Even the young soldier who is glad to have saved his life by capturing Antigone and is also, while announcing it, sorry to be handing her over to the prince who will execute her—this simple-minded boy seems to us entirely right. He is right in saving his skin and being glad about it: we should have done the same. He is right in being true to his nature, which is an important part of our own, on the land where we all live and move. And the changeable Ismene is right in being first a weak and tender woman over against the virile Antigone, she is wise in a weakness she knows and accepts and then suddenly, in the sudden flame of self-sacrifice, as strong as her sister.

And if Antigone is supremely right at the climax, on that peak of pure heroism which her nature enables her to attain and to which she beckons us, Creon is also right in a practical sense, on the plane of politics and under the exigencies of a state at war. Even when the course of the drama leads us to blame Creon for confusing his personal prestige with the good of the State, but only for that reason, we do not, humanly speaking, part company with him. His mistake was too natural, too closely bound up with the perils of political action for us not to admit it as a part of ourselves. We know, moreover, with Creon that when the community is endangered by the 'anarchy' of an Antigone—the anarchy of the Spirit that bloweth dangerously whither it listeth—all is lawful for the State.[1] We also know, though less clearly—and this is the misfortune of political communities—that it is generally the Creons who defend them. They are made for the job, and they manage, more or less. Sometimes the mud sticks, sometimes they come to grief, for there are few tasks that expose even a good workman to more thankless errors. And yet, even amid these errors, the Creons remain true in a way to their nature, which is a low one, for states are not saved by noble thoughts but by rough actions. That the life of action is associated with a certain debasement, we know is a necessary condition of the human lot, and one of the most burdensome. We are made of Creon's heavy clay—why deny it?—before the vase is fired by the keen flame of Antigone. The species of tragic pleasure which is least openly admitted and which requires of the poet an incredible effort of art and affection, is this clear-sighted pity, this brave confession of fraternity with the 'wicked', that he wrests from us. It would be easy to reject them from our souls. But true art

---

[1] *'Tout est légitime au pouvoir.'*

and the pleasure it brings can be had only at the price of confessing them, and this we must.

◎

Sophocles thus awakens, deep within us, beings hitherto asleep. At his touch they find utterance. All that was secret and complex in us is brought to the light of consciousness. All that was seeking to know itself in us, while still lurking shamefully in the darkness, now knows itself and fights in the open. The struggle between the characters in the play is our struggle and imperils us. We tremble for the issue; but we also tremble with joy, we are dazzled by seeing the unexplored riches of the life that may be ours, set out in the light of day. For it is indeed our potential treasures that the poet displays to our eyes; what we may become, shown first in the tumult and disorder of combat. But if the tragic poet brilliantly illuminates the disorder of the world and of our inner life, it is only to bring order out of them. From the tragic conflict he proposes to extract a higher pleasure than from a simple enumeration of our inner riches: the pleasure of showing where they stand and what is their worth. From the clash of those tragic themes which lacerate or sunder us, he at last composes for our delight—but without losing anything of the moral wealth we have recovered—he composes a music of which the magic power expresses the whole of our being and draws us on to new struggles.

The *Antigone* therefore aims at arraying our potential selves in a balance in which our inner world, which is a mirror of the outer world, is presented as a whole, and explained. The tragic experience and the pleasure it furnishes transmute into harmony the conflicting values which the characters represent. Viewed from a broader or narrower angle, these values are all valid, but it is the poet's function to play them one against another, to try or essay them one by means of another, and finally to set them in an ordered hierarchy. Thus we grasp in succession, or rather one with the other, the pleasure of life's complexity, the pleasure of our inner wealth, and also of our unity or 'meaning'; and also the pleasure of grasping the whole of our life with its swarming tendencies and of choosing a direction for it.

The modes of life, valid in themselves, that are proposed seem to examine and try each other until they reach a living equilibrium in us. Creon and Antigone represent two planes of life that seek each other, lean against each other and at last take their place one above the other. In Creon we have an order in which the State is at the summit of human thought and commands all actions. For Creon, the city imposes its service on the living and it is their civic conduct that settles the fate of the dead. To honour Polyneices, says Creon, would be to outrage Eteocles. He believes in gods, but his gods confine themselves to a civic order. Men and gods are engaged in the service of the State. His mind is closed to gods who do not regard their primary function as that of assuring the State's stability and punishing those who rebel against it. When Tiresias speaks the language of gods who are something other than that, he blasphemes. Gods and priests are officials or they are nothing. The gods have been nationalized, like so many in history; they defend frontiers, honour the soldier who falls in defence of the same frontiers, punish whoever, outside or inside the city—whether Polyneices or Antigone—refuses to recognize the supreme authority of the State, which is the order these gods have established and guaranteed.

Over against Creon's world is set the world of Antigone, a universe far more vast. While Creon subjects man and gods and all spiritual values to the political and national order, Antigone limits, without denying, the rights of the State. She says that the decrees of a man who speaks in the name of the State cannot prevail against the eternal laws which are laid up in the conscience. She in no way disputes the validity of human laws, but asserts the existence of a higher reality which has been revealed to her in the love she bore her brother. To this reality which has been written in her conscience, without book or priest—an 'unwritten law', as she specifies—she considers that the political order should submit, at least in the exact circumstances that have been the occasion for her conscience to declare itself.

This declaration of the conscience is an absolute, and in face of it the distinction between good and evil, as defined by the political order, is blotted out.

Antigone.   *All the same, these rites are due*
                   To the underworld.
Creon.   *But not in equal measure*
                   Both for the good man and the bad.
Antigone.   *Who knows*
                   This is not piety there?[1]

It is indeed important to observe that Antigone does not deny Creon's right to put her to death; she is simply contented with manifesting, by a death freely accepted, the primacy of the spiritual order, which she incarnates, over the political—neither more nor less. She has grasped a reality, and bears witness, in dying, to the fact that this reality is superior to life itself.

Thus while Creon's order tends to deny Antigone and strives to abolish her, Antigone does not deny Creon and, if Creon is the State, she does not dispute its legitimacy. She does not deprive Creon of what we have recognized as a portion

[1] Trans. cited.

3. *Antigone led away by the guards. Vase dating from the second half of the 5th Century*

of our own being. Far from abolishing him, she sets him in his true position and asserts her own. Great is our pleasure in feeling that nothing in our nature that asks to live is stifled or mutilated by the progress and *dénouement* of the tragedy, but only adjusted and harmonized. The conflict between Creon and Antigone, supported by the presence of values represented by the other characters, values that are secondary but authentic and precious, does not terminate—for all the suicides and cries of despair—in any destruction of the bonds that unite us to each of these beings. All the characters remain as principles of life in this mutual harmony to which they are subdued by the poet's genius and the sovereignty of Antigone, his elect. For this Antigone, repudiated by all or separated from all, is at length by all confessed as queen and mistress of supreme truth.

In the harmony which Tragedy creates in us, nothing fills us with a deeper joy than Antigone's triumph and the certainty of the truth she represents in relation to Creon. Antigone is liberty and Creon fatality: that is the ultimate meaning of the drama and there lies the pivot of our pleasure. She is the pledge of the free soul's primacy over the enslaving forces that beset it. She is a free soul who has received the gift of liberty by engaging herself in the service of love. At every moment in the play we participate in her irresistible uprush towards an infinity of freedom. She seems essentially anarchical, she *is* anarchical, and Creon is not mistaken in this—at least in a society in which the State does not recognize the limit of its powers: which amounts to saying that Antigone is an 'anarchist' in an anarchical society. For that matter the liberty of the individual has always, in all political communities, come into conflict with authority. There exists a necessity, or fatality, in human societies, and Creon duly reminds us of this. He himself expresses it in respect of what is necessary, severe and sometimes offensive in the maintenance of public order.

In the community in which Antigone was born, and in our communities, Antigone must die. But the joy we experience from this death would be quite inexplicable if it did not mean that the fundamental demand for liberty which it manifests is granted, as Antigone says, to the secret laws that govern the universe. Her death is now no longer a mode of her existence transferred to us. It is the principle by which we are freed from the order of fatality she has fought against. Her death marks the condemnation of the order of things represented by Creon: not the order established by every State, but the kind of order which stifles the free breathing of our personality.[1] We know more or less, thanks to Creon, that the fate of the citizen is bound up with that of the community, that the latter has rights over him, that he must defend it if it deserves to be defended, and that his life, though not his soul, belongs to it in case of need. But thanks to Antigone we

[1] '... tout *État dout l'ordre offusque la libre respiration de notre personne.*'

C

4. *Olympia. Landscape*

also know that, in a State that fails in its task, the individual disposes of an un-limited revolutionary power associated with the secret laws in the universe. If moreover the explosive force of the soul, thwarted in its struggle towards freedom, tends to destroy the fatalities that are oppressing it, its action, far from being purely destructive, may give rise to a new world. If society as it is constituted, still subject to the pressure of tragic forces, can only crush the Antigones, the existence of the Antigones is exactly what constitutes the promise of a new society and the demand for it, a society refashioned in accordance with man's liberty. In such a society the State, reduced to its proper function, will do no more than guarantee the liberties that have come into being; and Creon and Antigone, recon-ciled in history as they are already in our hearts, will by their equilibrium assure the free flowering of our personality within the bosom of a community that is reasonable and just.

The pleasure of Tragedy is deeply rooted in a promise of this kind. The greatest Tragedies, and above all the *Antigone,* contain it and make it clear. The pleasure Tragedy gives us is therefore not simply the relaxation within us of the contrary and conflicting tendencies which the spectacle has laid bare—a conflict appeased by the healthy light of consciousness. It also consists in a new tension, because the vital forces which were thwarting each other within us will henceforth have been brought together by pleasure into a cluster of energies directed towards the winning, and the enjoyment, of the new world promised by the poet.

In the terrible narrative which tells us of Antigone's death, in that supreme moment when Creon collapses on the body of his son, if the horrible vision of the girl hanging by her scarf, if the naked despair of Creon, flood us with joy, this is because a certainty has transfixed us and we stand and face destiny with a strong confidence in ourselves. At this moment in the play we know that a world is coming to birth, in which no Antigone will ever be doomed to execution and no Creon plunged into stupor, because man, grasping the sword that divided him, and equal now to the contest with fatality, will have overcome the tragic forces.

CHAPTER TWO

MARBLE AND BRONZE

The Greeks were as much sculptors as poets. But to understand and do justice to their struggle to extract from marble and bronze those images of man and woman—of the glorious human body which figured in their eyes the manifold face of God—this, in the absence of authentic documents, is no easy task. And indeed, on the threshold of any study of the various aspects of Greek civilization, we can scarcely overemphasize our ignorance.

The museums of Rome, London and Paris, all the museums of classical antiquity that exist, are overflowing with a multitude of statues that disconcert us by abundance, and by absence. The visitor scans, one after the other, the members of this mute and illustrious assemblage. He waits for a sign to be made to him; and yet in room after room his glance is caught by nothing, he sees not the slightest mark of an original style, for such had long since disappeared. It is not simply that these derelicts collected in museums are detached from the function proper to them, which was to present the god to the eyes of the faithful, but especially that in this incredible assemblage the eye discerns only an accumulation of inferior products, half-dead Hellenistic copies of works copied twenty times over so that they are more of counterfeits than ever. Here are those clumsy imitations of classical masterpieces, with which from our childhood upward, the manuals have deafened us; and there is nothing authentic or convincing. Scarcely ever do we come upon an exception. The statues and bas-reliefs of the archaic period were carved by the bold and as yet unskilled hand of the artist who conceived them. But for the art of the classical period (the fifth and fourth centuries B.C.), aside from statues and reliefs in the pediments and friezes of the temples, only one original work of a master, the 'Hermes' of the unique Praxiteles, has survived.[1] But the 'Hermes' is not cited by the ancients as one of the unmatched or exemplary specimens of this artist's style. As to the statues in the pediments and the reliefs in

[1] There is also a bronze head of Apollo by Pythagoras of Rhegium (late fifth century) which was in the collection of the late Duke of Devonshire and was on loan for some time to the Fitzwilliam Museum (Translator).

the friezes of the Parthenon, most of them have grown dull in their confinement in the London fogs; but it was not for those low, cloudy skies that Pheidias shaped in marble the severe and noble likeness of the gods of Olympus and the magistrates and horsemen and maidens of Athens.

Such, very briefly, is the deplorable and disappointing state of the sources for our actual knowledge of ancient statuary. Another circumstance contributes no less to lead us into error: most of the masters of ancient statuary were not workers in stone but in bronze. This is true of three of the greatest artists of the classical age, Myron and Polycleitus in the fifth century and Lysippus in the fourth: none of their bronze statues have survived. If the great museums generally exhibit only marbles and very few bronzes, it is because the original bronzes disappeared at the end of the ancient world. To know and judge the works of these great artists we possess only late copies executed in a different material from that in which they were first made. Rather than preserve these masterpieces in bronze, the centuries following the age of Greek civilization preferred to melt them down to make bells or coins, and, later, cannon.

These few reflexions were needed to explain how far our ignorance in regard to the plastic art of the Greeks (and we shall not even speak of their painting) severely limits the glimpses we are able to obtain of it. We never or almost never, handle anything original, but always or nearly always works at second hand, if not at fourth or fifth.

◎

Yet things appeared very simple at the outset. The Greeks were children of a land composed entirely of rock. It seemed natural that artists should extract from this land the noblest material for sculpture that exists, namely marble, in order to fashion from it the enduring images of the immortal gods.

But things by no means happened so simply. What in effect is shown us by primitive Greek sculpture, by the work of the primitive Greeks? Nothing. And why? Because no work of the ninth or eighth century B.C. has survived. In those days the artists did not carve marble or even soft stone, but simply wood. Now in order to carve wood, and even to cut it, the Greeks needed a long apprenticeship, they needed to be educated generation after generation, and the eye had to be adapted progressively to the objects they wished to reproduce. The education of the hand, the first tool of which the artist must dispose, was a prime necessity.

Without knowing that his successors would tackle stone, the primitive artist carved wood in the manner of a peasant. He shaped out of wood the as yet rude images of the formidable gods he adored. To give them a human form was to exorcise them, to reduce the unknown to the known, to deprive them of their malificent powers. But here, too, he needed an education, and this he got from the society to which he belonged and in the framework of his adopted trade. The social environment allowed him to try his luck, and his vocation required him to try it, in this most perilous venture. Whereas all around him people were mostly adoring 'sticks and stones' and fetishes, he dared to express the divine in terms of the human. He dared to invest with the form of men and women those gods about whom poetry was already relating a multitude of very human stories. It has been said that 'Mythology was not only the arsenal of Greek art, but its cradle'.

In the fifth century, and even later, there was still to be seen in the Erechtheion, the oldest sanctuary in Athens and rebuilt after being burned during the Persian wars, an ancient idol of Athena. It had been carved in wood, long, long ago, and was believed to have fallen from heaven. Although the goddess existed apart from her image, she sometimes at the call of her people came to reside in it. By keeping the goddess in their temple, the Athenians thought her divine power was at their service. All the ancient sanctuaries possessed wooden images of this sort, which had usually 'fallen from heaven'.[1] But their name indicated that they were vaguely known to have been carved by human hands. They were *xoana* (*xoanon* in the singular) The etymology of this word reveals that they were regarded as having been 'wrought', by contrast with the rough stones that had been the fetishes of former times. An ancient historian tells us that the *xoana* had their eyes closed and their arms attached to their sides. Some of them were still adored in certain temples in the time of Pansanias (second century A.D.). They were sacred, carefully preserved and painted in white or vermilion; sometimes they had a wardrobe. Sceptics derided, simple folk venerated them.

From the beginnings down to the classical age, Greek art truly covered a long road, bristling with obstacles of various kinds. Some doubtless were technical, the adaptation of eye and hand, for example; but there were also the obstacles with which the magic beliefs and superstitions of the time filled the artist's brain. For, as Michelangelo says, 'One paints with the brain and not with the hand; and he whose brain is not free, covers himself with shame'. It was by struggling against these obstacles that the artist created something. Every time he overstepped an obstacle, he accomplished something of value. As regards the god whom it was his mission to portray, he was engaged in a series of efforts in which respect for the

---

[1] '. . . what man is there who knoweth not how that the city of the Ephesians is temple-keeper of the great Diana, and of the *image* which fell down from Jupiter?' (*Acts*, XIX, 35.) It may have been a meteorite. 'The Iron Shield', which Numa Pompilius laid up in one of the temples in Rome, almost certainly was. (There is, of course, iron in meteorites.) The palladium of Carthage was the beautifully embroidered cloak that had been made for Alkisthenes of Sybaris. It was supposed to be the mantle of the goddess Tanit; but a fetish of this kind must have been exceptional (Translator).

divine and man's daring in facing the divine—what Greek tragedy called *aidos* and *hubris*—were associated. But the restraints of religious belief were not merely fetters: they incited the artist to efforts of creation capable of turning them aside.

The road was long. We in our turn shall try rapidly to cover it, seeking, with the aid of a few authentic works, to clarify the directions these seem to indicate. Greek art was from the outset profoundly realistic; and it flowered in a classical art. What is the meaning of these two words, realism and classicism, which are so often misrepresented? To answer these questions is the main object of the pages that follow.

◎

Let us start from the *xoana*. To make one, the artist has taken a very straight tree-trunk. He has cut off a length a little longer than the stature of a man. ('The gods are taller than man.') Within the roundness of the trunk he leaves both arms attached horizontally to the body, he confines the legs, which are set firmly on the earth, in their clothing or in a stance that is motionless, and preserves for the whole body a rigorous symmetry. He has scarcely detached from the rest of the body and roughly indicated the principal features of the human structure. In the body of the god, the male organ is clearly indicated; in that of the goddess, the breast is indicated beneath the vesture.

In the second stage of that apprenticeship of the hand which has now grown more supple but also more firm for the struggle with matter, the Greeks tackled limestone—softer than marble. This was towards the middle of the sixth century. Epic poetry had already completed its glorious career, but it was not forgotten. The *Iliad* and the *Odyssey* were recited at civic festivals. The lyric poets had mastered the form of poetry which is associated with song. But sculpture was in its infancy, because here the struggle was harder: a contest of eye, hand and thought against matter.

Consider the *Hera of Samos*, now in the Louvre. It dates from about 560 and is therefore one of the earliest statues that have been preserved. It is certainly not a *xoanon*; in fact no *xoana* have survived. But it quite evidently reproduces the tree-trunk style; its base is circular, thanks to the tunic grooved with a multitude of vertical folds and falling to the ground. The garments that clothe it from feet to shoulders (the head has not been preserved) make it like a tree-trunk which scarcely reveals the female form. The lower part of the body is cylindrical, the legs cannot be divined, the waist and hips are not indicated, and the stomach barely so. Higher up the slight swelling of the breasts can be seen under the raiment. More care, however, has been given to the back of the statue. The sculptor has already begun to see the spinal column and reproduce the lumbar depression. On the other hand the legs and thighs remain enclosed in their sheath. Below, the long tunic is raised to reveal the feet with the ten toes in line so that the worshipper may count them.

This Hera seems more like a trunk which is turning into a woman than the image of a divine being. But the divine is not reproduced: it is simply suggested to the pious heart. Here all that remains of the tree is its way of acquiring life as it grows. The statue rises from the earth and becomes alive. You feel nothing inadequate when you contemplate it. It is splendid in the manner of a birth; and only the dispassionate critic may rightly say that here the weakness of the hand has not equalled the boldness of the eye.

From the sixth century, excavation has by chance restored to us a fairly large number of original statues. In the last centuries before our era their authors did not enjoy the vogue which caused the Alexandrians and Romans to despoil or copy and falsify so many famous works of the classical period. As these archaic statues were not signed by one of the 'great names', their obscurity has been our good fortune.

However, these anonymous masters, whom we generally designate by the name of the place where the boy or girl—the god or goddess—whom they created was discovered, were in their time no less great than Pheidias or Praxiteles. They encountered incredible difficulties in realizing some of their attempts; but they overcame them by building on the long succession of efforts which their predecessors had accomplished—a circumstance that clearly brings out the collective character of artistic creation. To earlier efforts they each time added a new effort in which their own genius shone out. If we place their works in the false perspective which treats archaic art as the preparation of classical art, these works may still appear timid and awkward. But if we take them alone, if we consider each in its originality, we shall see that they are singularly bold and not simply attractive but inspiring. The element of tradition they have assimilated in no way prevents them from giving forcible expression to the novelty of their achievement; because this achievement is not simply theirs: it is that of a people who, while fashioning its gods, is also rising to a clearer consciousness of itself and of its strength.

Greek art is almost exclusively devoted to two and only two types: the naked boy (*couros*) and the girl clothed (*coré*).

The naked boy is in the first place the god in the flower of youth. Most of these statues the archaeologists have baptized as Apollo; but they might as well be called Hermes or even the young Zeus. They could also be images of victorious athletes. There is no great distance between the dwellers on Olympus and the man who has been physically perfected by sport. Heaven is seen in the likeness of earth. When Homer calls the heroes 'godlike', this honours not merely the accomplished hero but also the gods, in whose name the great national games are celebrated at Olympia, Delphi and elsewhere. Did not we see one of them the other day, in the flesh, running along the race-track? It is natural that the gods should be fashioned in the image of young men whose bodies have been made beautiful by exercise in the palaestra.

Greek sculptors learned anatomy by working on the type of the *couros*. In the gymnasium the young men were practically naked obviously. Here in the manners of the time we have one of the fundamental reasons for the rapid progress and the realistic nature of early sculpture. The people who contemplate the statue of a *couros* as it stands in the sanctuary have already seen in the ordeal of the foot-race the play of muscles on the champion's body. In the sixth century, admittedly, the sculptor is far from having properly grasped this play. It is only step by step that he learns the A B C of the musculature. He does not even dare to show the body in movement, to hazard a gesture right or left, or even an inclination of the head. Knowledge of anatomy is still, if you like, in a very rudimentary stage.

The face has some peculiar features. The eyes are slightly protuberant, as though ready to start out from between the heavy eyelids. In the eye, considered alone, there is something fierce as though the gaze were strained in attention. And how can these eyes be reconciled with the smiling mouth? and what are we to say about this smile? It has long been a matter of dispute among historians of ancient art. For some, the archaic smile is merely a mark of technical clumsiness; it is easier, they say, to represent the mouth smiling than in repose. Can we believe them? For others, the smile is 'prophylactic', that is, designed to drive away evil spirits and ward off misfortune. Is it not much simpler to suppose that, since the statue represents a god, it seemed natural to depict in a state of joy those gods whom Homer represented as given up to 'inextinguishable laughter'? The smile of the archaic statues reflects the joy of eternal life, the privilege of the Blessed.

The shoulders of the *couros* are as strong as his waist is slim; the hips are narrow to the point of vanishing. The belly is a flat, smooth surface, broken only by the navel. Two very prominent pectoral muscles furnish the whole musculature of the breast; but the crease of the groins is strongly marked.

The arms, which remain vertical as though supported along the torso, rejoin the body at the top of the thigh; the fists are clenched—a sign of energy in reserve.

The legs support the weight of the body, equally. The statue is not walking, but one leg, always the left, is slightly in advance of the other. This is an indication of the influence of Egyptian sculpture, in which the left leg is advanced for reasons of ritual. It does not appear, however, that any such reason justified the position in

Greek lands. But the forward position of one leg involves no displacement of balance in the rigorous symmetry of the whole body.

The more we consider the *couros*, the more amazed we are by the extraordinary strength at his disposal. The legs are solid, the body narrows and then widens to support the robust barrier of the shoulders. And above them the head laughs with joy, conscious of its strength. This strength is not lacking in attractiveness. Some *couroi* are not satisfied with inspiring fear, they inspire meditation. In the modelling of the muscles there is a gentleness which inclines to pleasure. But, whether we are more aware of strength or of charm, the whole seems rather a promise than an achievement, because the body is motionless and the statue makes no gesture.

Archaic art indeed obeys a law which specialists call a law of frontality. It weighed upon the whole of Egyptian art, but Greek art was to free itself from this handicap towards 500 B.C.

If we cut the body in two halves by a vertical line passing from the top of the head through the base of the nose and of the neck, then through the navel and the bone of the pubis, the two halves of the body will form two strictly symmetrical parts, not counting the left leg. Let us repeat that the advance of this leg involves no repercussion on the muscles of the body. The left leg gives the signal for walking, but the body does not follow it. Walking would in fact destroy the symmetry of the knees, the hips and the shoulders. The whole body seems to be caught in a net of immobility, a net that holds the man prisoner. He wishes to walk, yet he does not move. Is this due only to the extreme technical difficulty? How does one make stone or bronze walk, as if it were living matter? But perhaps this difficulty only reflects another obstacle—a religious obstacle. The god whom the sculptor has undertaken to represent, this god he dare not hurry. More divine appears the god in the immobility which, rather than bending under, he imposes on himself. How have the audacity to set the god in motion? To order him to walk would be to attack his sovereign freedom. Therefore the technical difficulty of representing movement is rooted in the deep respect the artist feels for the god he has shaped out of matter.

On the threshold of classical art this difficulty was to be overcome by Myron. But apart from this, the fact of not walking is not felt as a failure because in presence of the couros-god the sculptor has succeeded in filling us with a sense of his power. In this statue, above all else, we feel the presence of a god swollen with energy, heavy with promise, available for anything in regard to the future which he carries within himself and to which he will give birth—but in a manner unforeseeable, because he is a god.

◎

In archaic times the type of the *coré* corresponded with that of the *couros*; the draped girl and the naked boy; the athlete-god, laughing and formidable, the girl or goddess illuminated with bright colours and magic oriental stripes. Excavation has unearthed fourteen of these *corai* which had been brought from Asia and set up on the Acropolis at Athens a few years before the Persian wars. They were thrown down by the Barbarians in 480 (the year of Salamis), then piously buried by the Athenians on their return home. Huddled close together in their common grave, they served to embank and support the ramparts. The colours were still quite fresh and pleasing, red, ochre and blue being painted, as if at hazard, across the hair and the fine dresses. There was no question in the artist's mind of making a statue resemble a living woman; it was much rather a taste for bright colours that led him to illuminate the bare stone. These saucy little girls have thus belied the opinion of academicians who held that the Greeks never had the bad taste to paint their statues and argued that only the whiteness of marble (and eyes which do not gaze) could express the serenity of Greek art—which indeed was far less serene than it was wild and gay.

These newly unearthed statues are extremely informative. They had been made in Ionia, the Levant of ancient Greece where, one day, all the arts had flowered simultaneously in a mad profusion. Imported or freely imitated, respectfully adorned in severe Attica, they were set up on the Acropolis with their plaited locks of ochre or violet, their many-coloured jewels, and tunics of fine linen whose multitude of irregular folds descended to their ankles; sometimes they were wearing a heavy woollen shawl; and the whole statue was coloured with an un-expected charm and caprice. The body is beginning to appear beneath this double vesture. But the Attic sculptor is better acquainted with the play of muscles on a boy's body than with the more delicate and yet ampler form of a woman. These Ionian girls are standing like men, with one leg advanced as if prepared to walk. Their hips are as narrow as those of the boys. Varying from statue to statue, the breasts are wide apart and allow the drapery to show unforeseen effects. They have, finally, the square shoulders of gymnasts. The truth is that these *corai* are almost like boys in disguise much as, on the stage, young boys were to play the parts of Antigone and Iphigeneia. Their mood is most joyous; they have not failed to adopt the so-called archaic smile which in their case is light, mischievous and well-satisfied, with a glint of humour. They are extremely well pleased with their hair, their dress and everything that adorns them; the smile expresses this pleasure. To draw attention to herself one of them is pouting.

These statues also remind us of the patience, or rather the sprightly emulation, of the sculptors. No two of them are alike, because each artist has introduced amusing variations. There is confusion in the fashions. Sometimes, over an Ionian tunic with its multitudinous pleats, a *coré* is wearing a large rectangle of woollen cloth which, to become a garment, only needs two pins at the shoulder and a belt at the waist; sometimes she wears a long cloak that falls to her ankles, and no tunic; sometimes the tunic has few pleats and clings to the body. Assembled as they are in the museum of the Acropolis, they make you think of a group of mannequins ready to go on parade, mannequins who have been allowed to choose somewhat at hazard the dresses they are going to display. But it is not chance, it is the artist who has chosen. The important thing in his eyes is the complex study of drapery rather than anatomy. The pleats vary infinitely according to the nature of the material, the style of the dress or the part of the body which the garment is to cover: its function is to suggest the human form while appearing to veil it. In Greek sculpture, dress is a marvellous instrument of beauty, whether for the man when he wears it or the woman when she wears scarcely any. Later on, the sculptor plays with it in a most masterly way; even on the *coré* he is executing variations, amusing us and no doubt amusing himself.

It must be remembered that Greek clothes were not as a rule sewn like ours, except for the tunics of which the sleeves were sewn; even so, the sleeves were very wide and the arms very free. Our modern dress, which is sewn and adjusted, has its supporting points on the shoulders and at the hips. Greek dress, on the contrary, was not adjusted but draped. To represent the hundred ways in which garment and body go together, to drape dress and cloak over the shoulders and breast, to make them fall to the legs or spread out by means of a girdle, and fold in every direction—all this was very difficult. The slightest movement of the body or even of a limb modified the direction of the folds. But the sculptor of *corai* faced these obstacles with pleasure because he felt he was on the verge of a discovery.

◎

It was then by slow but converging paths of discovery that the sculptors of the sixth century were moving towards a great achievement, which was the knowledge of the human body, whether naked with its muscular system well covered with flesh; or hidden under garments light or heavy that express or suggest the graceful presence of woman's form. This increasingly firm and sure representation of the human body is very important, the more so as this same body which the sculptor studies with unrelaxed attention is the one he attributes to the gods. The body of man and of woman were in effect the most exact images he could conceive of the divine, and by carving such images he gave visible life to the gods of his people.

The Greek sculptors were moving in the same direction as the poets, who were more advanced than they, and as the scientists, who were less advanced; and all were trying to formulate the laws of nature. By making statues of the gods, the sculptors were explaining the world.

This was an explanation of the divine in terms of the human. No form, in fact, explains the divine presence which is invisible and indubitable in the world, more justly than the human body. The Greeks knew about the Egyptian and Assyrian statues, but they never thought of interpreting the divine by a means of a cow-headed woman or a jackal-headed man. Their myths might indeed borrow certain turns of speech from the Egyptians, certain stories and characters, like Io, the heifer bored into by the gadfly, in Aeschylus' play; but the sculptor's chisel very soon discarded such monstrous shapes, except in the case of creatures who were very near to being forces of nature, like the Centaurs who, in the metopes of the Parthenon, represent the furious attack of the Barbarians. In the eyes of the Greeks the god was the simple naked young man; the goddess was the girl with the noble vesture and the pleasant countenance.

We need not be detained by the interpretation of the *corai* according to which they do not figure the goddess but her worshippers. It is ordinarily said that those on the Acropolis are *orantes*—girls in prayer. Perhaps so, but they are none the less devoted to, and filled with, the spirit of the deity, and in that way goddesses.

This is the precept: *Give the fairest gift to the gods*. What can be fairer than the nakedness of a boy or the grace of a girl clad in embroidered raiment? This was what men offered the gods, and it was thus that they saw them. The gods were like that, and there was no language to express them other than these coloured marble statues. (Like the *corai* the *couroi* had a few touches of colour on their hair, in the eyes and on the lips.) There was no language more appropriate than this, no translation more exact. The statue of the *couros* was the marble word that described the god, and it was the *mot juste*.

The beauty of the human body with its perfect proportions, so regular that later artists were to risk trying to express them in figures,—with its contours gentle or severe, a body so moving and powerful in its quivering tension, so convincing to the soul as well as to the body—all this, in the dazzling youthfulness in which the Greeks represented it, strikes us, even today, as imperishable. Here was the fairest thing man could offer to the immortal gods; and he offered it, every day of his life, by raising towards heaven where the gods dwelt invisible, this visible people of joyous girls and boys bathed in earth's sunlight.

But these gods were not only the work of individual and usually anonymous sculptors, they were also the gods of the city, of the people who ordered the sculptor to make them. Sometimes indeed, as at Delphi, Olympia and elsewhere, they were the gods who protected the whole of the Hellenic community.

This sculpture was civic and popular because it spoke to the people, and national because it was common to all the Greeks. It not only expressed the sculptor's conception of the gods, but also the way in which a community of free men pictured the divine. The god-man, the man who serves as a god; the nicely decked-out young woman, a goddess in prayer, or a goddess painted to resemble a woman—these ambiguous beings in whom are fused the human and divine and whom the cities set up as masters and companions in their daily life—the creation of these beings was one of the boldest enterprises that flowered on the soil of Greece. Nowhere was the divine less separated from the human; the one expressed the other. What indeed other than the human could express the divine? and how should men dare to deprive the god of the beauty of their own form, perishable though it might be? This form they would give the god, a form immortalized even before they knew how to express it in perfection.

Man's love for his god and love for his own flesh were the double goad that urged on the sculptor in stone. One should add: a great love of truth. The increasingly precise knowledge of the structure of bones and muscles, and the increasing precision in representing them, were, finally, the sculptor's first gift, a gift offered to the god in exchange for the progress in work which the sculptor owed him.

◎

But who will impart movement to this man-god? Who, by making him walk, will liberate the energy he is filled with? In these short pages on Greek sculpture, pages that in no way claim to replace a systematic history of Greek art, there can be no question of following step by step the slow birth of movement in the statue. Either we lack documents which would allow us to grasp how it happened, or else there scarcely was any evolution, in this sense, that, like nature sometimes, art has after a few poor efforts proceeded by sudden mutation.

Take Myron's *Discobolus*, which belongs to the mid fifth century, a little before 450 B.C. It is not irrelevant to observe that this is the statue of a man, not of a god. The sculptor, who feels able to make the statue move, has decided to represent the acme of movement in an athlete. The god is for the moment vowed to immobility, owing to the reverence the artist feels for him. We must, however, before analysing this celebrated work which has been copied a hundred times, observe that we possess no original of it. The museums contain only mutilated marble copies. From these which are more or less faithful, the moderns have reconstituted a copy in bronze (the original was in bronze) which is in the museum of the Thermae in Rome. The reflexions on Myron's art which it permits must obviously be hazardous. Yet it is quite evident that this artist, who grew up in an age when the law of frontality still reigned almost unchallenged, conceived an enterprise of extraordinary daring. No doubt there were before Myron some bas-reliefs, a few bronze statuettes, a very few statues, in which the law had been somewhat rough-handled; but such violations were only partial. Thus, in the *Man carrying a Calf*, the arms are no longer as it were stuck to the body but, with strained muscles, are firmly grasping the legs of the calf which is borne on his shoulders. The rest of the body, however, remains inert and as though indifferent to the weight of the burden. In the *Discobolus*, on the other hand, the athlete's body is wholly bent by the movement that possesses him, the movement that, like a streak of fire, seems to traverse him from end to end, from the toes of the left foot which grip the soil to gain a solid purchase for this man so strained and taut in his instability, to the right arm which holds the disk, the arm projected to the rear but a moment later to be released and to hurl the weight; and even to the left arm and the right leg which, while appearing inert, are nevertheless involved in the action. And this action is engaging the whole being; it seems to involve the athlete in an instability in which everything that is not movement is counter-weight; because, if it were not for this balance of opposed masses in which he is caught as in the invisible mesh of a net, the *Discobolus* would fall.

With this statue Myron transports us into a world of action in which movement has suddenly become sovereign, and man knows the intoxication of strength restrained by balance. In this sense he is the founder of statuary, as Aeschylus, his contemporary, is the inventor of dramatic action. Both of them are exploring the limits of human strength. If the sculptor did not respect the laws of balance in movement, the statue as I have said would fall; as perhaps, as soon as the disk has left his hand, the athlete may fall to the ground, in the palaestra.

The *Discobolus* then gives us movement. But are we in presence of a photographic snapshot? It has sometimes been said so—wrongly in my belief. Were it a question of a snapshot, we should not recognize the movement; because the human eye is not like the lens of a camera. The *Discobolus* in fact presents a synthesis of movements which are coordinated in succession. There is no question of fixing on a sensitive plate the image of a man throwing something—as a photograph which, while pretending to record the march of a procession, only shows us a number of gentlemen motionless, with a leg in the air. The movement of a living creature cannot be fixed in a statue—which by definition is formed of inert matter—save by a combination of moments that succeed each other in time. The master of movement is also the master of time.

The archaic Apollos were poised on their two legs outside time, so to speak; and so they might remain to all eternity. The *Discobolus* appears, if you like, to be the image of instantaneous movement; but in fact each part of the bronze statue, which is supported by another part, is caught at a different moment of the action which carries all of them forward. This is how Myron's eye saw it, and the eye of the spectator in the stadium. Myron's realism is already classical in this sense that the sculptor transposes observed reality into a work of art. The function of this work is not only to express the momentary, but the various potentials of the individual and, if one may say so, his *becoming*.

So already, in the *Discobolus*, we may observe that the sculptor's realism, which is founded on an exact knowledge of anatomy and of the play of the muscles, is not a simple copy of reality. Before being reproduced, the object has been thought out anew by the artist. That the figure should be simplified, be stylized according to rules not conformable to those which govern reality—this already informs us that it is ready to submit to a canon, or rule, which is classical.

Realism in sculpture is, properly speaking, the knowledge of the body which the sculptor wishes to represent, as objective reality. Greek sculpture had been tending to this knowledge, and was already in possession of it during the sixth century. The inadequacies in representing the muscles which are a mark of this age are rarely felt by us as inadequacies but rather as simplifications. The sculptor's love of truth, and of the human creature, fills his work with a strength that makes up for all shortcomings.

We must insist that the knowledge he seeks is very rarely that of individuals. It is only by exception that he aims at a portrait. And it is in this passionate realism, in this study of the typical and social rather than the individual model, that fifth-century sculpture is strongly rooted, and particularly the sculpture of the second half of the century. Classical art draws sustenance from the realistic art of the archaic period, and this is the life-blood which gives it such intense vitality.

But once this knowledge of man's body has been acquired—and mainly a knowledge of the muscular system and of the bony structure that supports it, and also, a little later, of the clothing which emphasizes the shape of the body—once this has been acquired, the man, known objectively and presented as god or goddess or athlete, can also be modified, not 'idealized' as people have said, too vaguely, but transformed and corrected with a view to proposing to the community a model which, by an effectual act, can provide the citizens with the virtues they need. As soon as the sculptor realizes that, in the reality he is observing, he can and must choose, he is on the way to classical art; he is a classicist.

The artist therefore chooses the features, forms and attitudes which it then belongs to him to compose. His choice, resting as it does on an authentic realism, is already classical. But by what standard is the choice made? If we say, by that of beauty, the answer is too vague, and inadequate. People have spoken of 'a golden rule', to which the artist presumably conforms. This golden rule is supposed to be an objective law of nature, as manifest in the forms and proportions of leaves as it is in the proportions of the human body, since man is also a part of nature. This notion is not without interest. It would, we are told, explain both Greek classical art and the classical art of China, which antedates it by 2500 years, not to speak of others. But I must say that I greatly object to this personification of nature which, by an objective law, is supposed to fix the most harmonious proportions of the human body—a law that classical art has presumably discovered. A fine effort of imagination, it seems to me, but in reality deriving from an exaggerated mysticism. If, we are told, man has the proportions that nature has fixed for him, then he is harmonious, he is beautiful in the classical sense.

Is it not more accurate to derive this law from the needs of society, and from the tastes that respond to these needs? Should we not be more precise, and more faithful to the nature of things, when it is a question of ancient Greece, if we show that in the classical age beauty cannot be separated from the daily struggle for life and for the good things superior to life, in which the people are engaged? Such a struggle needs men brave and robust. In other words, the Greek artist chooses between those things in society which are destined to decay and those which are made to endure; he chooses what is rising in the direction of life. His realism is constructive. Classical art is nothing less than the law of an art that wills to live in a living society. The energy of man and god is manifest in the muscles of every body that is well adapted to the actions for which they call. Courage is manifest in the impassivity of the face. This impassivity, in which people have generally seen a lack of technique, is really the sign of the mastery man has gained over his individual passions, the sign of that strength of soul and perfect serenity which only the gods possessed of old. The classical impassivity of the countenance corresponds therefore, though in another way, with the archaic smile. This smile had expressed the naïve joy of a living creature. On the other hand, in an epoch that was still full of struggles and very combative, impassivity expresses the control that the will now exercises over the passions and man's consecration to the whole civic community.

This new age is also more human, and no longer wholly impregnated with the divine. It is less the gods whom it represents now in human form, and rather man whom it exalts to divine stature. There is no classical statue in which man does not breathe the noble pride of accomplishing with fidelity his work as a man or a god.

Greek classical art, though founded on realism, is now closely bound up with humanism. It is the expression of a class in the ascendant—the class which by its valour won the Persian wars and which has just entered into possession of the

5. *Hera of Samos: archaic statue* (c. 560)

5

advantages due to its valour. Thus classical art is the culmination of a struggle, and remains prepared for struggle. Not that the strength animating the statues of this age is at all expressed in vehement gestures; it is, on the contrary, immobile, at rest. A strength which gesticulated would be limited to a single action and determined by the gesture peculiar to that action. The strength of the classical statues is indeterminate, a reservoir of strength, a lake of serenity which, we know, would change into a headlong torrent should circumstances demand it. This is what we are shown by, for instance, the statues on the Parthenon, or rather their fragments, which Pheidias carved.

◎

To take a few examples: Polycleitus lived at one of the most decisive moments in the history of Greek art; he was at the summit of realistic perfection and at the same time of classical humanism. Before him, Myron had tended to what appears to us as instantaneous movement. His *Discobolus* was an admirable exercise in virtuosity. But virtuosity is fatiguing, and the instantaneous does not for long hold our attention. Now in the *Lance-bearer* (*Doryphorus*) and other statues, while he does not make his statue walk, Polycleitus none the less gives us the illusion of the continuity of walking. The *Doryphorus* has not been preserved. Polycleitus worked in bronze, and was the greatest of the bronze-statuaries; of his work, we have only marble copies, and what marbles, alas!

The naked man, who carries a spear on his left shoulder and appears to be walking, rests with the whole weight of his body on the right leg which advances, while the left leg trails slightly behind, merely touching the ground with the toes. This attitude reveals a complete break with the archaic symmetry. The lines joining the two shoulders, the two hips, the two knees are no longer horizontal, and moreover they contradict each other. With the lower knee and lower hip on the left, correspond the higher shoulder, and so in reverse. The body, solidly and robustly built of bone and muscle, is perhaps, at least in the copy at Naples which is the least unfaithful, rather heavy. But this body is completely involved in a symmetry of reversals which gives an appearance at once of firmness and suppleness to the fiction of his marching. Others of Polycleitus' statues probably avoided this heaviness. Thus the *Diadumenus* (an athlete binding the insignia of victory round his brows) while reproducing the same rhythm which I have called reversed, lightens the suspicion of heaviness one sees in the *Doryphorus* by having his arms raised and thus removes the excessive weight which the statue seems to display.

It is man liberated from all fear of destiny, man in his lofty strength as master of the natural world, that the *Doryphorus* presents. The proportions of the statue

D

6. *Archaic Couros* (*mid 5th Century*)

might be expressed in figures. Polycleitus had calculated in *palms* (the breadth of the palm of the hand) the dimensions of each part of the body and their inter-relationships. These numbers and ratios are of little moment to us, if they lead—as they did—to the production of a masterpiece. Polycleitus knew no doubt through studying Pythagoras, what is the importance of number in the structure of living things, because he had carefully studied them. He used to say: 'A masterpiece is the result of a number of calculations worked out to a hair's breadth.' And that is why the Greeks proudly called this statue the *canon*.

It is one of the finest images of himself that man has ever produced. Here we have a classical image of the Greek, sure of his physical and moral strength, an image at once true and inspiring. It is optimistic (an ugly word, I should prefer 'ascending'), and expresses in a natural and effortless way the conception of a society that is becoming something more than itself.[1] The image also of a rising social class that has come into power and triumphs in good conscience, imperturb-ably—perhaps too much so; image of a beauty perfectly natural, at once more objective and more subjective than the idealistic aesthetics maintain; inseparable from the objective world of nature, with which its realism connects it, this image can yet only be expressed in terms of beauty by satisfying the human needs it claims to respond to. And finally it is efficacious, because it is the image of a people who would know, if need be, how to defend what it has against all that threatens it. But, for the moment, the *Doryphorus* is not using the spear he carries on his shoulder.

◎

'*Il y a dans l'art un point de perfection et comme de maturité de la nature,*' says La Bruyère. The genius of Pheidias flowered at that exact point of maturity; and this is why his art is more difficult for us to know and understand than archaic sculpture if, as I believe, we have again in a sense become primitives—and let us hope, pre-classicists.

Pheidias had however made images of the gods that were very close to human-ity. He had not been satisfied with representing them under the guise of very handsome mortals; he had started from the human form in order to suggest heroic figures, worthy of Olympus. Like Aeschylus before him, he had lent to his gods the simple perfection of wisdom and goodness. And this perfection he ascribed to the human species as the gift of a society which he desired to be harmonious. This, it seems, was the essential character of his art.

The statement is vouched for by the texts more, alas, than by the sculptor's works. To have any real knowledge of the mutilated pediments, mutilated by man

[1] '... *une société humaine en devenir.*'

far more than by the ravages of time, we are practically reduced to studying the precious drawings of a traveller, James Carey, drawings that preceded by a few years the bursting of that Venetian bomb which damaged the Parthenon, and also preceded Lord Elgin's depredations. Let us also not forget that of the ninety-two metopes, only eighteen remain in good or fairly good condition.

Once this has been said, we may observe, if we are not relying over much on imagination, that Pheidias' art consisted in making humanity flower in divine forms. The brutality of the Centaurs fighting against and crushing men, the graceful charm of the Athenian maidens in the frieze, the quiet immobility of the gods who recline in the angles of the pediments and are waiting for the sun to rise—all speak the same language. Pheidias wishes to convey *that which is*, to express things as they are. Thus there exist in the world brutal forces: the Centaurs in their rutting-time; there also exist beings who in their calm assurance are exempt from accident or misfortune; horsemen riding at ease, others whose mounts are rearing; gods and goddesses in their tranquillity, breasts that the raiment half-covers, half-uncovers with folds so true and fair that they convince us of the presence of the flesh beneath; others, too. Pheidias tells us all this, not because it is required by 'realism', an abstract word unknown to the Greeks, but because it is all in nature. Man is in nature and will always have to do with it. His privilege is to express its strength and beauty, and also to wish to dominate and transform it. And the first mutation, indeed the only path of progress that the sculptor suggests, is for man to be master of himself, to subdue his savage instincts, to behave in such a way that the gods are present on earth, in us. So it was by virtue of justice and benevolence that Pheidias attained that serenity which is an image of happiness.

The gods of Pheidias are also in nature, and are not supernatural. And this is why these gods, who at the end of the frieze represent the completion of human kind, come and mingle with men, not merely to receive their homage but to take part in the popular festival, which is the festival of arts and crafts; and Pheidias was the first who ventured to depict such a thing on a temple, instead of depicting a myth. Now among all the divine figures in the frieze, those of Hephaestus and Athena are characteristic, for the god of metal-workers and the goddess of the industrial arts were the dearest to the Athenian people. Pheidias portrayed them conversing simply and amicably, side by side, like workmen who have relaxed after the day's work. Among all these gods there is nothing supernatural, nothing but humanity at the acme of excellence.

If, in presence of a particular group in the pediments, as for example that of Aphrodite nonchalantly reclining against her mother's breast, we experience a feeling that borders on religious respect, we may at least observe that the generous form of the two women, the breast that distends the garment, all show us that in the fifth century the religious feeling of the Greeks did not separate flesh from spirit. Pheidias felt and expressed it in this way.

The gods are present in frieze and pediments alike, as they were in the very heart of the life of the times. Their presence sheds light on human life and especially on the popular festival represented in the frieze, much as a fine Christmas tree, with all its candles alight in the square of a modern city, does today.

But this sculptor of genius made other statues besides the marbles of the Parthenon, including several isolated images of the gods. Pausanias already called him the 'maker of gods'. I will mention only two. The statue of the *Lemnian Athena* was originally in bronze; but only the fragments of a marble copy still survive. Owing to ill-luck or stupidity, the head of this ancient copy is at Bologna while the body remains at Dresden. It was a work of the master's early years and was consecrated to the goddess by the Athenian colonists before their departure for Lemnos, towards the close of the Persian war. The goddess is not here represented as a warrior: she carries no shield, her head is bare, the aegis unfastened, she is holding her helmet in one hand while the spear, transferred now to the left hand, serves only to support her arm. She is resting after the toils of war, and, with nerves and muscles relaxed, is ready to devote herself to the works of peace. The head with its curls looks very young (for many years it was mistaken for the head of a boy): it is admirable and proud. Pheidias, who at this time may not yet have left the studio where he had had his training in Argos, expressed in this statue his love of peace, the fruit of his people's courage and wisdom.

We may conclude this long study with a few words about the Zeus of Olympia which, in the judgment of the ancients, was his masterpiece. It was a chryselephantine statue. Statuary in gold and ivory was a precious offering that the city made to the gods. It existed during the whole of ancient times, but was generally reserved for very large statues. Ivory bespoke the whiteness of face, arms and bare feet; the clothing was of gold and in different colours, such colours as the gold-dyers knew how to produce.

This Zeus, which had been fashioned for the national temple at Olympia, has naturally been lost. Apart from the gold and ivory, other materials of great value were used in the construction of the throne, ebony in particular and certain precious stones. The seated statue was just over 36 feet high, nearly 46 if you counted the pedestal. These figures and the excessive luxury of the work may startle us; but we must not forget that people saw such statues in perspective, framed between the double colonnade of the *cella* and surrounded by trophies and precious fabrics piled up or hung from the columns. With his vesture and his attributes, and the magnificence of his setting, this Zeus must have been intended by Pheidias, even at the risk of overloading the statue, to convey the greatness of divinity. In a setting of oriental splendour, Zeus appeared as the precious idol of a whole people. But, if we are to believe the ancient writers, what gave the work its unique beauty was the contrast between this triumphal display of vast wealth and the face of the god which was wholly imbued with mildness and good will.

A head which is in the Boston museum apparently reproduces the features. This is not the redoubtable Zeus of the *Iliad* who could make Olympus and the whole world tremble at his frown, it is the father of gods and men, and not only the father but the benefactor.

Dio Chrysostom, a writer of the first century of our era, who saw the original at Olympia, describes it in terms which anticipate Christian language: 'He is the god of peace, supremely gentle, dispenser of being and life and all good things, the common father and saviour and guardian of all men.' It seems therefore that Pheidias tried to combine in his statue the image of a popular Zeus, rich and omnipotent, with the higher conception of God that Socrates or Pericles may have formed about the same time, that is, of a god of providence and goodness. This latter image was revealed in the tender and paternal expression of the face.

Let us recall in this connexion that the ancients said Pheidias had 'added to religion'. Some modern archaeologists think that the Zeus of Pheidias served Christian artists as their first model for the type of the bearded Christ. It is, however, difficult to know whether, on these last points, writers have not been slightly indulging in 'literature'.

One must note at least that the face of Zeus as fashioned by the 'maker of gods' shows that in the course of ages a masterpiece may take on new meanings, provided it has been conceived in accordance with the truth of its time. It is this truth, this classical realism, that has reached us and still speaks to us.

CHAPTER THREE

THE BIRTH OF SCIENCE: THE EXPLANATION
OF THE WORLD: THALES AND DEMOCRITUS

There are moments in the history of mankind when new forms of thought or action appear so abruptly that they seem like explosions. Such was the appearance of science, that is of rational, scientific knowledge in Ionia at the end of the seventh century B.C. with Thales of Miletus and his school. This birth of science, with the appearance of the first scientists or 'philosophers' as our books call them, was if you like spectacular but in no way astonishing or miraculous. It seems, by the way, that the word 'philosopher' only appeared in the age of the sophists and was not in widespread use before the fourth century, when it was popularized by Plato. Of course the scientific attitude to nature was familiar to the most primitive of the Greeks, even to the men most naked and unequipped. Odysseus was typical of this questioning attitude, an attitude which in his case is combined with the most authentic and also the most practical of religious feelings. The poet calls him the man 'of many devices'.

It would in fact be a mistake to treat rational science and myth as if they were contraries that exclude each other; as if both were not for a long time closely intermingled, as if both were not seeking by different paths to surmount the obstacles and difficulties which the cosmos and its unknown laws present to man. All thought, at the outset, took the form of image or story, and we know that towards the end of the classical age Plato frequently uses myth to express his thoughts. He interprets ancient myths in his own way, and he invents myths of his own.

Greek science at its birth was much more like our science than appears at first sight. Naïve as it may be, it knows that man is the product of natural evolution, it holds speech and thought to be the fruit of life in the social state, it regards itself as part of the technique: it is science itself that permits man to master his natural environment. Such a conception of science—an extremely bold one—definitely arose towards the year 600, in the time of Thales; and in the course of two centuries it was to develop with a breadth of outlook and a quest for cohesion which astonish us even today.

We must, however, go back to a much earlier date, long before anything we know about the primitive Greeks, in order to find in man's possession the first tools he invented to defend himself against his environment or to make use of it. The bow was the first 'machine' and it was much older than Odysseus who devised so many things. Its invention dates from about 6000 B.C., towards the close of the palaeolithic epoch. The bow utilizes a reservoir of energy, and is in this sense a machine. Against the outer world which is so foreign to him, so hostile and as we have seen so 'tragic', man is constantly inventing new means of preserving his life. Against destiny he invents morals—a way of living and dying; against hunger he invents new ways of procuring food.

For civilization to be born, it was necessary that man should previously have mastered a certain number of techniques which enabled a being who harvested his food to become a man capable of producing—at least in a large measure. A permanent surplus of foodstuffs is the necessary condition for the birth of any civilization. Techniques of this kind were developed between 6000 and 4000 B.C. in the valleys of the Nile, the Euphrates and the Indus. These two thousand years were of vital importance, because this vast technical revolution constituted the material basis of ancient civilization. Prior to the industrial revolution of the eighteenth century, and until the discovery of atomic fission and nuclear energy, there has been none more important.

So man invents agriculture. This reveals an understanding of the laws of germination, a habit of observing the method of nature, an observation maintained and sharpened by necessity, accompanied by attempts at imitation and by experiments which were no doubt fruitless for long years but at last crowned with success. In any event, there came a time when observation and experiment gave rise to knowledge clear enough to induce primitive men deliberately to sacrifice good food in the hope of harvesting a greater amount in the following year.

Even if there is much magic associated with seed-time or if the harvest is accompanied by religious festivals, the whole operation, which goes from the storing of seed in the silos to the ripening of the young grain which is joyously reaped with the sickle, constitutes a knowledge of natural laws which man has brought into his service. This is a good definition of science, and for the moment an adequate one.

In primitive tribes it was the women who saw to the harvesting, to the preservation of seed-corn, and to the reserves for household use. It is probable that agriculture was invented by women; and for a long time, no doubt until the invention of the hoe, it was woman's work.

The discovery and use of metals was attended with very great difficulties; they proved in the end as useful for agriculture as for war and pillage. Metals had at the outset mainly excited man's curiosity, and they were sought after because they were rare. For a long time bronze and iron served merely for purposes of luxury—as did gold and silver in the Mycenaean age—long before weapons and tools were made from them. Fragments of brass-ore have been found in ancient necklaces. Malachite, which is the easiest of these minerals to smelt, was the object of a considerable trade in Egypt, where it was used in the manufacture of rouge as early as the predynastic epoch.

Brass and tin, which when alloyed make bronze, were found in districts very remote from Greek territory. Tin-ore existed in Colchis, on the eastern shores of the Black Sea, and in Etruria, the modern Tuscany. These circumstances had a great deal to do with the progress of shipbuilding and the technique of navigation. For the sailor to steer by the stars or the position of the sun, a map of the heavens had to be made.

Thus, long before the birth of science properly so-called, that is, of astronomy and geometry in the time of Thales and his successors, many other examples could be cited of man's scientific attitude, of his application in observing phenomena and patience in trying to imitate and make use of natural laws. As early as the neolithic epoch this attitude had resulted in some of the most remarkable inventions ever made. Not only were there the invention of agriculture and the discovery of metals, but the domestication of animals, first as a reserve of food and later as beasts of burden. There were the inventions of the wheel and the cart, and later on, of the lunar calendar and the solar calendar. All these inventions form part of the history of science, at least if science should be defined as the mass of knowledge and methods of proceeding which enable man to increase his mastery over nature. All the inventions we have enumerated were made much earlier than the appearance of the Greeks on the stage of history; but the Greeks kept them in memory as a treasure accumulated by earlier generations; and they usually attributed them to beneficent gods.

The sciences then were born of the most elementary needs of men and of the techniques, such as tillage and navigation, which satisfied those needs. They were also born of the needs of luxury in the ruling class. Men need to eat and to be clothed. They must perfect the instruments of labour. They must build ships and know how to build them, they must be able to steer at sea and for that purpose they must know the movements of the stars. A knowledge of the movements of the stars is equally necessary for the ordering of ploughing and sowing according to the proper dates of which the peasant is informed by the rising of such and such a star in the sky.

Now what was happening in Ionia in the seventh and sixth centuries? A population of mixed blood, Carian, Greek and Phoenician, was engaged in a long and severe class-war. Which blood, or bloods, flowed in the veins of Thales? and in what proportions? We do not know. But it was very active, very political and inventive. He proposed, we are told, that this restless and divided population of the Ionian seaboard should create a new kind of political organization, a federated state governed by a federal council. The proposal was very judicious and also very novel for the Greek world; but Thales was not listened to.

The class-war which raged in the Ionian cities, the same kind of war as that which ravaged Attica in Solon's time, was the motive force behind all the inventions of this land of inventions. Owners of vineyards or corn-lands; iron-workers, wool-workers, carpet-makers, dyers, manufacturers of luxury weapons; merchants, shipowners and sailors—these three classes which were struggling one against the other for the possession of political rights were drawn along in the movement that was leading them to produce constantly renewed inventions. But it was the merchants supported by the seamen who soon led in the race. It was they who, in extending their relations from the Black Sea to Egypt, and in the west as far as southern Italy, collected the knowledge which had been accumulating for centuries in the old world and proceeded to organize it into a single system. Ionia therefore had invented and was still inventing, in the field of the arts, of economics, of politics and of science, very many things which only appear disparate to the unattentive eye.

Let us recall the Homeric poems which acquired the form in which we know them at the time of the birth of the middle class. Neither the *Iliad* nor the *Odyssey* were written by nobles, or even for the service of the nobility or with the nobility in view. There are signal indications informing us that these poems were composed and written by the rising class of 'new men' who, to consolidate their political gains, began by appropriating the culture of the class they were engaged in dispossessing. The virtues of the heroes were henceforth to be celebrated by the people and placed at the disposal of the creative enthusiasm of the free citizens.

With Archilochus, who was the son of a noble and a slave girl, the victory of the despised social class is more open: it declares itself. He is the inventor of lyrical poetry, military, amorous and especially satiric. This poetry he forges out of his personal adventures, as a weapon, as the sword and buckler of his status as soldier-citizen engaged in the service of the city that his father has founded and that he is defending. And now, round Archilochus, lyrical verse flowers suddenly and in abundance, taking on the most unexpected forms, but forms always singular and fresh. To the apathetic youth of Ephesus, now under menace of attack, Callinus addresses a vigorous appeal:

How long will ye be idle? When, young man, will ye show a stout heart? Have ye no shame of your sloth before them that dwell round about you? Purpose ye to sit in peace though the land is full of war? . . . and let every man cast his javelin once more as he dies. For 'tis an honourable thing and a glorious to a man to fight the foe for land and children and wedded wife; . . . Oftentime, it may be, he returneth safe from the conflict of battle and the thud of spears, and the doom of death cometh upon him at home; yet such is not dear to the people nor regretted, whereas if aught happen to the other sort he is bewailed of small and great . . . in their eyes he is a tower. . . .[1]

The hero is no longer a legendary Hector, but the mobilized citizen or rather the young man who has volunteered to defend the motherland.

Meanwhile in nearby Colophon, Mimnermus sings the pleasures of youth and love. His elegies speak in melancholy accents of the flight of time and the sad approach of eld, carnal image of approaching death:

But what life would there be, what joy, without golden Aphrodite? May I die when I be no more concerned with secret love and suasive gifts and the bed, such things as are the very flowers of youth. . . . And when dolorous Age cometh, that maketh a man both foul without and evil within, ill cares do wear and wear his heart, he hath no more the joy of looking on the sunlight, to children he is hateful, to women contemptible, so grievous hath God made Age.[2]

This lyricism is elegiac, in the modern sense of the word. There were other poets too.

From Ionia also came those fascinating, gaily-robed girls whom we have already encountered on the Athenian Acropolis and whose smile is at once attractive and modest.

It was in Ionia that the massive severity of the Doric temple with its squat columns that seem strong enough to support the sky, its capitals as sharply outlined as knife-blades, its solidity like that of a tree-trunk swollen with sap which appears as the defiance of inert stone to man's living flesh—it was in Ionia that the haughty massiveness of Doric architecture suddenly becomes elegant, graceful, smiling and inviting. The lengthening slimness of the Ionic column is like the body of a growing boy. It bears aloft its capital like a delicate flower whose petals are scrolls wound round upon themselves in a double spiral, gentle yet firm, and living as the human hand.

Nor, among the inventions of Ionia, should we forget coined money, and banking, and bills of exchange. All these were inventions or devices renewed by the new use assigned to them by this changing people who were eager to discover

[1] *Elegy and Iambus . . .* edited and translated by J. M. Edmonds, London and New York, 1931, Vol. I, pp. 45–7.

[2] *Elegy and Iambus,* ed. cit. (trans. J. M. Edmonds), I, 89, 91.

and possess life in its brilliant complexity. One is dumbfounded by the profusion of Ionian genius.

Of all these inventions, the most prodigious, the most fruitful and the most enduring—an invention that will endure to our remotest posterity—was that of science. It would seem at first sight as though there were little connexion between the verses of Archilochus, the Ionian *corai* and the thoughts of men like Thales and his disciples. But these inventions were the product of the same social climate, which was one of intellectual liberty achieved at the cost of a hard struggle. It was not merely liberty of thought but liberty of action. This the cities of Ionia won and defended during the whole period of their activity. It was a freedom to reject the world, or simply to travel over it, especially to explain and modify it. Applied in different fields, the action of Archilochus and the action of Thales were not different in nature; because both found their liberty in an action that was practical. Both claimed to wrest positive advantages from the span of life allotted to them. The spirit of their social class[1] and of their quest was materialistic. They did not deny the gods. Perhaps God was nothing other than the eternal matter that pressed in on them from all sides. But they did not constantly refer to the gods because they were not satisfied with explaining the unknown by another unknown. They wished to know the world and man's place in it. 'Learn to know the rhythm of human life,' said old Archilochus, who was thus anticipating what would be the language of science and philosophy.

Thales dealt with very simple things and his object was entirely practical. His fellow-citizens called him one of the Seven Sages; but how bold and at the same time modest was his wisdom! Among the maxims that are ascribed exclusively to him, the one no doubt most characteristic of his genius was this: 'Ignorance is a heavy burden.' Anxious to understand the world we live in, he began by studying what takes place between heaven and earth, and what the Greeks called 'meteors', that is to say, meteorology. This was because he lived in a city of merchants. His researches were dictated by considerations of utility. As he desired that the ships should bring their cargo safely to port, he desired to know why rain falls, what the winds are, which are the stars by which the steersman should be guided, which of them move more rapidly and which less rapidly.[2]

---

[1] Thales belonged to one of the great families and pretended to Cadmaean descent. This family was probably that of the Thelids, who may have had Phoenician forbears. The other great family was the Neleids, the royal clan, who had originally come from Pylos in the Peloponnese. The races were even more mixed in Miletus than elsewhere, but class-distinctions were more tenacious than race-distinctions. It is clear that Thales considered himself of noble origin. See Glotz, *Histoire grecque*, I, 276–8, 547 (Translator).

[2] '*Lesquels sort les plus mouvants et lesquels les plus fixes*', that is, in relation to a point fixed by agreement or convention—say our planet, or better still, Miletus (Translator).

Thus the origin of science is simply the practical: its object, as someone has put it, is to discover 'that the thing works'. Science is born of contact with things, and depends on the witness of the senses. Even if it should happen to depart from sensory evidence, it must always return to it. This is the first condition of its development. It requires logic and the elaboration of a theory, but its strictest logic and most audacious theory must be put to trial by practice. Practical science is the necessary foundation of speculative.

Thales was a man of great initiative. In earlier times the city of Miletus had twice taken to seafaring in order to discover metals and corn-lands. She had founded ninety colonies and trading-posts. Now Thales himself was a great traveller; he wandered over Egypt and the interior of Asia Minor and Chaldea and in these countries collected what remained of ancient knowledge, notably great numbers of facts concerning the earth and the heavens; and he planned to assemble these facts in an original way. In the course of his travels he had been a military engineer in the service of Croesus,[1] and now had to solve practical problems. But his was also a boldly speculative mind. Many facts he owed either to the observations of the Egyptians and Chaldeans, or to the practise of his profession; and from this collection he was to formulate something new.

Many currents of thought, many interests and enquiries encountered each other in Ionia, which might be called the Babel of the Greek world. Thales lived at the centre where these multiple currents converged. For him and his fellow-citizens the problem of living resided in an unknown domain, which they had to know if they were to live in it. So they formulated new questions. Thales puts these questions in accordance with a method which is his own and in a language still unusual in such matters—in fact, in the language in which merchants transacted their business. He was a merchant and an engineer, and if he dealt with 'meteors', it was in any event not in order to tell himself 'stories', but to assign 'reasons' to phenomena, to know how things happen as they do with the elements with which he was acquainted, namely, air, earth, water and fire.

The rational science which was appearing and the character of demonstration which the whole of Greek science was to assume, seem to have been the result of a multitude of actions and gestures made by these observant sailors in steering their

[1] Croesus was King of Lydia, the great state of the interior. He became master of the whole western coast of Asia Minor. He had compelled rebellious Ephesus (in spite of Callinus' appeals) to resume, and accept, her regular situation as a client or dependent of Sardes, while Miletus now became for the first time a protectorate of the Lydian kingdom. (See Herodotus, *History*, Vol. I; also Glotz, op. cit., I, 268.) It must be added that the yoke of Croesus was easy and pleasant; it did not affect the internal autonomy of the Greek cities, or their commercial prosperity. Croesus was a great statesman, and also a devout admirer of Greek culture. He offered splendid gifts to Sparta, Corinth and Delphi, and was made a member of the Panhellenic community. He was of course very conscious of the impending menace from Persia. See Glotz, I, 268-9 (Translator).

ships, when they observed, at every movement of their arms, that this movement was followed by a certain effect, and when they sought to establish a rigorous connexion between cause and effect, without leaving to chance the part that belongs to it.

The results obtained by Thales in his research were no doubt slight, problematical and often erroneous; but his way of observing the world, and his way of thinking, were those of a true scientist.[1] Not perhaps in the modern sense of the word, according to which the scientist practises a science closely bound up with experiment or experience, but in the simple sense of practising a science that is wholly one of observation, the sense in which he takes account of what he observes without using myths and with the greatest possible amount of exactness. On the basis of his observations he constructs hypotheses that seem to him plausible; he builds up a theory which, in the course of time, will be subjected to experience.

So, instead of regarding the stars as gods—which they were before him and were to remain long after his time, for Plato and others—Thales was the first to treat them as natural objects. In his view, their nature was earthy or fiery. He was the first to say that when the moon, which is of earthy nature, was placed in a straight line between the sun and the earth, the sun was eclipsed. Did he really predict an eclipse of the sun, the eclipse of 610, or 585, or some other, as Greek tradition asserts? Perhaps, by relying on the calculations of the Babylonians, he indicated the year of a probable eclipse; his knowledge of astronomy would scarcely permit of greater precision. Much more important than the results was the method of his research. Neither when treating of the stars, nor when treating of water, did Thales invoke gods or myths. He spoke of those phenomena as of purely physical and material things. When the modern chemist puts the question: 'Whence comes water?' he replies: 'from a combination of hydrogen and oxygen.' Thales' reply could not be identical; ignorance weighed on him as too 'heavy a burden'; he was conscious of this and said so. But when he puts the question of the origin of water, he does not answer with a myth, but in an objective way, that is, by seeking to formulate a law of nature that will correspond to the reality of nature and may one day be verified by experience.

This form of thought, which is so novel, is sometimes extremely audacious in its enterprises, so audacious as to appear naïve. Thales and the first Ionian scientists were trying to discover what matter the world is made of. It seemed to them that there must be a material element from which the other elements are engendered by a process not mythical, as in the old cosmogonies, but physical. For Thales, water was primitive, and from this primordial water was born earth which is, so to

[1] 'Un vrai savant.'

speak, its residue, and also air and fire which are vapours or exhalations from water. Everything is born of water and returns to water.

It was probably the techniques of fire that suggested to these scientists the notion of a transformation of one element into another, which other takes on another appearance while remaining identical. They had observed the various effects produced by the action of fire. Fire changes water into steam; it changes other matter into ash; in the foundry, it liquefies metal; in the processes of metallurgy it separates and purifies it. Conversely, it unites in the processes of alloying and soldering. Thus, by observing his own techniques, man arrives at the notion of a transformation of elements or of the appearance of these elements. But these observations entail a share of suffering. Fire is not only a great educator, but also a pitiless despot who demands blood, sweat and tears. 'I have seen the blacksmith working at his furnace-mouth', wrote a satirical poet of Egypt. 'His fingers are like crocodile-skin; he stinks like fish-roe.' An observation of this kind, while implying a share of pain, also implies, in the formation of the theory, a share of error.

His conception of water as the origin of the other elements may have been suggested to Thales by simple facts of nature. The fact that water deposits mud or alluvium, for example in the flooding of the Nile and the formation of the Delta, or again the formation of sea-fogs, or perhaps the appearance of will-o'-the-wisps floating over ponds—all these things roused the scientist's attention. The important point is that the scientist began to observe nature or human techniques, while freeing himself from any supernatural explanations. In this process of observing and of verifying his observations, for example in the very important technique of casting statues in bronze, the scientist was taking the first steps in what was to deserve, much later, the name of the experimental method. It was as yet only the stammering of a beginner, but of one who is inventing a new language.

About the same time the same scientists and, notably, Thales himself, discovered another scientific method, which men mastered from the outset better than any other. This was the mathematical method, in the form of geometry. In the eighth century the vases of Dipylon had already displayed the passion which the Greeks felt for the plain, bare style of geometry. The men and horses who move round the linear decoration of the vases are themselves geometry: they are like angles and segments of circles that have been assembled.

But, as always, the Greeks, whose imaginations had been filled with geometrical figures, invented this science by starting from precise techniques. The Egyptians and Assyrians, it is true, had already established the foundations of what was to become mathematical science. For example, when they wanted to re-establish the boundaries of their fields after they had been flooded by the Nile which buried them under a layer of mud, the Egyptians knew certain methods of land-surveying which might initiate the discovery of certain theorems. Thus they knew that, for a right-angled triangle of which the shorter sides measure 3 and 4, while the hypotenuse measures 5, the squares of 3 and 4 together have the same area as the square of the hypotenuse. They knew this and measured it out on the ground, because they knew that $3 \times 3 = 9$, plus $4 \times 4 = 16$, is the same thing as $5 \times 5 = 25$. But they did not know that this proposition is true of any right-angled triangle and they were incapable of demonstrating it. Their geometry was not yet strictly a science.

For centuries what was to become the mathematical method was only a collection of rules. These were already sometimes very complicated and in certain cases, for example, allowed one to predict the position of the stars. But this collection of rules did not constitute a science. They were not all related to each other, they were valid only for particular cases and no one thought of demonstrating that they derived from certain simple principles which are imposed on the mind by experience; as, for example: 'A straight line is the shortest distance between two points.' No one demonstrated that these rules are laws of nature and are necessarily what they are. Now the Greeks needed to develop their geometry for two main purposes: navigation—and no doubt shipbuilding, because in this period their ships had ceased to be mere canoes or primitive barges—and temple-building.

One day, we are told, Thales made a geometrical discovery which seems to relate exactly to the construction of the drums on temple-columns. He showed not only that the angle inscribed in a semi-circle is a right angle, but that it must necessarily be so, that is to say that, if you join the extremities of a half-circumference to any other point on the circumference, the two lines must always contain a right angle. In the same way Pythagoras, or some member of his school, but at an early date, showed that the square on the hypotenuse of a right-angled triangle is necessarily equal to the sum of the squares on the other sides, whatever the dimensions of the triangle. Thus the particular cases known to the Orientals became the universal properties of geometrical figures. The Greeks therefore invented a science of geometry, which is ours, a science in which the properties of straight lines, circles and a few other curves could be demonstrated by reasoning and verified by the application of technique. And I am thinking especially of architecture which, by this means, they raised to a high degree of solidity and beauty.

In this way the Greeks built up a science of geometry closely connected with navigation and the art of building. The whole tradition relating to Thales ascribes to him a quite concrete knowledge of the distance of a ship in the open sea from a raised point on the shore; the same tradition ascribes to him the geometrical knowledge, abstract and rational, of the properties of figures whose construction alone allows one to measure this distance.

This science is the work of merchants who wanted boats to sail on long voyages, and also temples to set forth the glory of their city at the same time and as much as the glory of the gods. Science founded under these conditions is clearly humanistic. Thanks to it, men can read in the apparent disorder of nature rigorous laws which are present in nature; they wish to do so in order to make use of these laws. Science at its birth was therefore utilitarian, both in principle and purpose, and people took hold of it as a tool.

Thales' greatness did not fundamentally consist in his having been the first of the 'philosophers', unless of course the word be taken in a general sense: the boundary between philosophy and science was still very vague in his time. He was first of all a physicist, too much attached to nature, the 'physis', to add anything whatever to nature or seek anything beyond nature, that is, to be a 'metaphysician'. He thought in terms of matter, he was a materialist. No doubt Greek thinkers had not yet separated or distinguished between matter and spirit. But matter was so precious to Thales and his school that they confused it with life: all matter was in their eyes living. We may therefore say that these scientists were not materialists in the modern sense, because for them the difference between the material and the non-material did not exist. But it is significant that Aristotle, an idealist, presented them as materialists. They were primitive materialists. Later on, the Greeks called these old Ionians 'hylozoïsts', that is, 'men who think that matter is alive', or men who think that life, or the soul, did not come into the world from anything but matter, but that it is inherent in matter and is the very way in which matter behaves.

So these thinkers spoke of matter and forgot the gods. Very near them in time and space, the creation of the world was explained by the union of Ouranos (the Sky) with Gé (the Earth). All that had followed from this, the birth of gods and men, remained myth and mythology, something 'too human'. For Thales the sky was the three-dimensional space in which he made ships sail or raised the columns of temples. The earth was the primitive clay that water had deposited and now sustained, and which returned to water.

This explanation in terms of earth and water (the earth separated from the waters) appears to have been borrowed from a Sumerian tale, and seems like a history of the creation or the flood. All countries were once seas, according to the Babylonian cosmologies. Marduk, the Creator, laid on the waters a carpet of reeds that he covered with mud. Thales also declared that at the outset everything had been water, but he supposed that the earth and all living things had been formed, starting from water, by a natural process. Perhaps he owed his conjecture to a primitive oriental mythology, the one which is also reflected in *Genesis*. But, in

7. *The Diadumenus of Polycleitus.* (*The work was conceived between 445 and 420*). *An ancient copy*

becoming Greek, the myth has been decanted. What has become of the spirit of God moving upon the face of the waters, in the still uncreated world of the first chapter in the Bible? What has become of Marduk? Of the Creator? Of the voice of God which spoke to Noah in the story of the flood? All this has dissolved like a metaphysical dream.

The rational and also the universal character of Thales' propositions make him the second founder of science, at least if we must this time understand by science an ensemble of propositions linked together by logical connexions and constituting laws valid in all times. Aristotle was to define the notion in the words: 'There is no science save of the general.' This is a narrower definition than the one mentioned above, but it allows us better to situate Thales in the history of human knowledge. With him the chain of myths is interrupted for a time, and a new history begins: the history of men inventing sciences—inventing science as conceived in its universal character and under a rigorous and rational aspect.

One may finally mention the view that certain modern historians have ascribed to Thales, a view according to which nature is at once intelligent and unconscious. One can see how such a reflexion could have been turned to account in the next century by Hippocrates and his school. Observing the connexion, the close analogy between the human organism and nature taken as a whole, the doctors noted in fact that the human organism must necessarily do things better without having learned them and by remaining unconscious of them. This is what doctors observe in the healing of wounds, the formation of the bony callus and the phenomena of salutary reactions which are not the effect of art but the automatic work of nature. In this way medical science may also have derived partly from Thales.

◎

Thales' researches were not isolated. Science only advances through the collaboration of enquirers. These enquirers, who owed their impetus to Thales, were like him called physicists. They observed nature in a positive and practical spirit, and they were fairly prompt in subjecting their observations to experiment. A few of their names may be cited.

Anaximander, younger than Thales by scarcely one generation, was in one aspect of his work a minute technician. He drew up the first maps. He was also the first to use the gnomon, which the Babylonians had invented, by making a sundial of it. The gnomon is an iron rod which, if planted vertically in level ground, can, by the variations of its shadow, mark the true south, the solstices and equinoxes, and also the intermediate hours and dates. From it Anaximander made a *polos* which was the first clock.

E

8. *Marble copy of the head of a chryselephantine statue*

Xenophanes, who was exiled from Ionia when the Persians conquered that country, went to Italy. He wandered from town to town, declaiming in the market-places his poem *Of Nature*; in this he criticized the traditional mythology and mocked at the anthropomorphic conception of the divine. He wrote these astonishing lines: 'If oxen, horses and lions had hands and could paint pictures and carve statues, they would represent the gods under the guise of oxen, horses and lions, in the manner of men who represent them in their own image.' This Xenophanes was a scientist whose curiosity looked to the most diverse horizons. It led him to make discoveries of great significance, as for example in recognizing the presence of sea-shells on mountains and the imprint left by fishes on stones on Malta, on Paros and in the quarries at Syracuse.

In the fifth century scientists like Anaxagoras and Empedocles seem to have gone still further in this direction. The former was interested in all kinds of astronomical and biological phenomena. He observed the existence of parhelia, those strange luminous phenomena over the Black Sea, and tried to explain them. He also considered the cause for the flooding of the Nile. Empedocles has recently been described as a 'real forerunner of Bacon'. He devised original experiments in order to account, by analogy, for several phenomena that are natural, or that he believed to be. These attempts of his, revealing as they do a great deal of ingenuity, mark the birth of scientific experimentation.

All these efforts on the part of Thales' successors, efforts which, in the absence of adequate documents, are insufficiently known to us, led up to the two great discoveries in physics which were made in the fifth century. One was the exact knowledge of the annual movement of the sun in the heavens, on a plane which is oblique in relation to the plane in which the sun accomplishes, or appears to accomplish, its movement in a day. The other was the determining of the mathematical value of musical intervals, a value already familiar to one or two scientists at the end of the fifth century.

Such then is a rough summary of the scientific achievements of the successors of Thales.

◎

Popular tradition exposed this man of genius to the sarcasm of passers-by and servant-girls on such occasions as when, being occupied every evening in following the course of the stars, he happened by mischance to fall into a well. This mischievous story is in Aesop, and also in Plato. Montaigne writes:

I am grateful to that Milesian wench who, seeing the philosopher Thales perpetually beguiling himself with the contemplation of the firmament . . . , set in his path something that would make him stumble, to warn him that it would be time to beguile his thoughts over things that were in the clouds when he should have provided for those that were at his feet.

La Fontaine warns him too:

> *Pauvre bête,*
> *Tandis qu'à peine à tes pieds tu peux voir,*
> *Penses-tu lire au-dessus de ta tête?*

Poor, glorious Thales! Whoever had his feet more firmly planted on earth than you? Science, hard achievement of mankind; defiance to commonsense, and object of its derision.

◎

The Ionians of the school of Thales had directed their efforts towards a dynamic conception of the world, based and hinged on material elements in continual and mutual transformation. Their materialism proceeds from an exact but naïve intuition of nature conceived as a mass of matter, eternal and infinite and perpetually moving and changing. This intuition (and it could then only be a question of intuition and not of demonstrated scientific knowledge) was taken up and rendered more exact, though still intuitively, by Democritus in the fifth century before our era. The materialism of Democritus acquired a greater force, historically speaking irresistible, from the fact that during the century that separated him from Thales it had been contested by the school of Parmenides, for whom nothing exists save in stability and the absence of movement, and by Heracleitus for whom everything is in change and flux. It was by replying to Parmenides and Heracleitus, by going beyond both stability and change, that Democritus found his answer and developed his system of nature. Leaving aside the details of these disputes, let us try to explain Democritus' system.

This is very difficult, because the writings of Democritus are missing to an incredible extent. His work was extremely vast, extending to every field of human knowledge. Today we do not possess a single work of his *in extenso*, whereas the whole of Plato's work, which was no less but not more vast, has been preserved without the loss of a single book. We even have rather more, because a few unauthentic writings have been mixed with the authentic ones.

It is difficult to see the hand of chance in the difference of treatment accorded by tradition to the writings of these two men; nor should we allow ourselves blindly to believe what the ancients tell us in this matter. They babble to the effect that Plato did not conceal his desire to consign, if he could, the whole of Democritus' works to the flames. Let us suppose that they are ascribing to Plato an intention that remained a secret wish, and let us not go as far as reading in people's hearts. But the surprising thing is that this wish, whether or not it was expressed, was in fact realized in the course of the ages. As early as the third century of our era, the traces of Democritus' works became harder to detect. Later on, we may suppose that the persecutions of which the ancient manuscripts were the object, on the part of the Christian Church—persecutions that lasted for three centuries, the sixth, the seventh and the eighth—were particularly severe as regards a writer already denounced as the father of materialism. The same persecutions of the Church were, on the contrary, to be very indulgent to the founder of the idealistic tradition from which that Church was to borrow a whole part of its theology.

This then is the result. Of Democritus we have only some very scanty and sometimes obscure quotations, which in certain cases we can even regard as falsified. We scarcely hear this great philosopher spoken of except by his adversaries or, by chance, by Aristotle and Theophrastus who as naturalists were more inclined to do justice to the material world.

Democritus was born about the year 460 at Abdera, a Greek colony on the coast of Thrace, a circumstance which allowed Cicero to play the wag when declaring that what Democritus said of the gods was worthier of his country than of himself. Abdera, in the eyes of the ancients, was the capital of the kingdom of fools. It was at Abdera that he followed the teaching of Leucippus, the almost unknown father of the sensationalism that Democritus was to develop. We have practically no surviving text of Leucippus. Like all the great Greek thinkers, Democritus travelled far and wide. We need not shrug our shoulders if told that he conversed with the gymnosophists in India. These quaint witnesses to eastern wisdom always greatly intrigued the Greeks. He talked with priests in Egypt, and also visited Ethiopia. Plato did scarcely less. The Greek sages always travelled widely and profited from their wanderings, except for Socrates who boasted of not travelling. In Egypt this man of encyclopaedic learning collected empirical formulae in chemistry, and an abundance of information, true or false, on natural history. From the Chaldeans, or again from the Egyptians, he acquired a mass of elementary notions in mathematics and astronomy. The information we are given regarding these journeys may be false; but it is impossible to glance at most of the fragments of Democritus that have been preserved without being struck by the extreme openness of his views on the world and the future of mankind. A keen and biting air, like the air that blows at dawn over Alpine summits, icy to the skin, exciting to the heart, blows through the works of Democritus as through the works of Epicurus and Lucretius, those other 'cursed' thinkers. Truly, these materialists pierce our souls in the most cutting way, and the wound is fruitful.

Democritus, as the ancients say, had 'written about everything'. If we do not possess his works, we at any rate have a list of their titles, and they confirm the assertion. He had written remarkable treatises on mathematics, according to Archimedes who gives examples of Democritus' discoveries in that art. He had written on biology, on which he spoke as a scientist who had practised dissection, a fact almost unique at that time. He had written on physics, ethics, philology, literary history and music. Above all, he had formulated his own system of nature.

He lived to a great age, over ninety, and he even, according to those who like records, reached his hundredth year. These figures show him as surviving into the second quarter of the fourth century.

Democritus launched the great word 'atom'—as an hypothesis. But because this hypothesis answered the problems raised by his predecessors and by his age better than any other, the word he launched was destined to traverse the centuries. Modern science has taken it up; and if modern science uses it in a less narrow sense, if it is in a position to reveal the internal structure of the atom, it none the less derives from that spontaneous intuition of Democritus: the existence of atoms. J. C. Feinberg, a modern physicist, shows the striking parallelism between Democritus' atomic forecasts, if we may so call them, and Einstein's. He writes:

In 1905, merely with paper, a pencil and his brain, and many years before anyone succeeded in disintegrating an atom and destroying matter, Einstein predicted that matter could be destroyed and that, when it was, it would liberate terrifying quantities of energy.

In the fifth century before our era, merely with a wax tablet, a stylet and his brain, many centuries before science learned how to explore the interior of a substance, Democritus predicted that all substance was made of atoms.

Democritus therefore admits only two primordial realities in his system: atoms and vacuum. With regard to the vacuum we may note that the hypothesis of its existence in nature has today been entirely demonstrated. For a long time both philosophers and scientists declared in a peremptory manner that 'Nature abhors the vacuum'. But they were really attributing to nature a horror they felt themselves. Today it is admitted and has been demonstrated that there is vacuum inside the atom as there is also between atoms. Professor Joliot-Curie writes: 'There are great empty spaces in matter. When account is taken of the dimensions of the particles that constitute matter, these empty spaces are comparable to interplanetary spaces.'

Democritus defines atoms as solid corpuscles, indivisible and indissoluble (their name means 'insecable': Democritus contested the possibility of splitting the atom). They are infinite in number, and eternal. They move in the void. This movement is not external to them, but coexists with matter and, like matter, **is** primordial. Atoms have no qualities other than a certain form, differing from one to another, and a weight connected with their dimensions.

The qualities we perceive in things by means of our senses are for Democritus purely subjective and do not exist in atoms. He had the merit of trying to found a science of nature, starting from the notion of quantity and then deducing from it sensible (or perceptible) qualities. The atoms are then like points, not mathematical but material, extremely small and which completely escape our sensory perception. They still escape it, today, in their structure, although they are decomposed and utilized by scientists. These atoms move about, 'they jostle each other in every direction', without there being in the universe either top or bottom or middle or end. This affirmation of Democritus contains one of the clearest signs of the soundness of his spontaneous intuition. Nature for him is a 'splashing of atoms in all directions'. Their trajectories cannot fail to 'cross each other', so that there are produced 'grazings, shocks, reboundings, blows and collisions and also interlacings'; lastly, 'formations of masses'.   .

Such is the starting-point of Democritus' system of nature: a materialism at once ingenuous and deliberate, a doctrine by which the author makes an immense effort to explain the world in the most objective way, without any divine intervention. Following on the work of the old Ionian materialists, it is in fact the first really atheistic doctrine in the ancient Greek world.

It was in this way then that the world we live in formed a spherical mass in which the heavier atoms occupy the centre of the sphere while the more tenuous ones are rejected to the upper edges.[1] The heavier atoms formed the early mass, but in this mass atoms less heavy formed the waters that remain lodged in the hollows of the earth's surface. Other atoms, still lighter, have formed the atmosphere we breathe.

It must be added that the world we live in, the earth, is only one of the worlds which, according to Democritus, has formed itself in the limitless extension of space. There exist others, infinitely numerous, which may have their suns and planets, or which may be forming or disappearing. Such an explanation of the world implies no idea of creation, no supernatural intervention in the birth and conservation of the world. There exist only matter and movement.

We are not, with Democritus, in presence of a mechanistic doctrine, although certain modern writers maintain that we are. Mechanistic conceptions akin to those of certain seventeenth-century and eighteenth-century philosophers have been too lightly ascribed to him. In the first place, Democritus on occasion uses explanations which are in no way mechanistic, such as the principle of the simple attraction

---

[1] '. . . *tandis que les plus subtils sont rejetés dans les hauteurs de celle-ci* (*la sphère*).'

of like by like; in the second, the mechanistic knowledge of his time was in an embryonic state and could furnish no scientific foundation for his notion of the world. His materialism was intuitive, it was a physicist's hypothesis, and not at all a metaphysical materialism. He launched his system of nature to defend his thesis of the objective reality of the surrounding world and of the indestructability of matter, in opposition to the philosophers of the time who either disputed the proposition that movement was compatible with existence or, like the sophists, plunged into the contradictions of relativism.

His atomic hypothesis has proved sound; but he was not in a position to place it on a scientific foundation. Viewed from one angle, Democritus' materialism, because it was not adequately supported by the science of his time and was, besides, unprovided with the instruments of observation used by modern scientists, incredibly poor also in facts objectively established, remained in itself very inadequate for accomplishing the task it had set itself, namely, to explain the world. Engels, however, who makes a reflexion of this kind, adds: 'Therein also lies its superiority (the superiority of Greek philosophy) over all its subsequent metaphysical opponents. If metaphysics was right in regard to the Greeks, in detail, the Greeks were right in regard to metaphysics, in general.'

If we pass now to the appearance in our world of vegetable and animal life, and then of human beings, we shall see that Democritus admits that science should seek the explanation in the laws of the attraction and aggregation of atoms of the same form: a purely material explanation. Moreover, the life or the soul are not in his eyes a force superadded to matter. Life is eternally present in matter and is of the same nature as matter. It consists of fiery atoms, very subtle, round, smooth and extremely mobile. Thus they move the bodies in which they are found and life is maintained as long as they are in sufficient number. The atmosphere contains a great number, and it is breathing which maintains the lives of beings up to their normal term.

Living creatures are therefore considered as aggregations of atoms which have reached the state in which we see them as the result of long evolution. Regarding man, Democritus advanced the conjecture 'that he was a child of chance who had come to birth in water and mud'.

As to religion one must insist on the fact that in the atomic system in which nature and man are explained by natural and material principles, and in which life after death is categorically denied, the religious problem is totally deprived of the substance that nourishes it. Democritus touches on this question mainly to affirm that the belief in the existence of gods is caused by the fright with which men are seized in face of natural phenomena, which they do not understand, and particularly in face of death.

In another passage, however, Democritus makes a reservation regarding the gods which may seem strange but which was inspired by his scientific mind open to all hypotheses. He admits that there might exist beings formed of atoms more subtle than those of which we are formed; beings who, without being immortal, might live for an extremely long time. But these beings have no power either over things or men; and so their hypothetical existence implies no duty on our part. Democritus speaks neither of prayer, nor piety, nor worship, nor sacrifice. He makes fun of those who implore the gods to give them health, when they are themselves ruining their health by intemperance and debauchery.

The way in which Democritus treated the religious problem furnishes a striking proof of his mental liberty in respect of popular beliefs.

The way in which he explained how man takes cognizance of the outer world is also very interesting to take up, the more so as it has given rise to various interpretations. Man knows the world through his senses and in a wholly material fashion. Auditory sensations for example are due to currents of atoms that are projected to our ears from the resonant object. These currents set in motion the particles of air which are like them and enter our organism by way of the ear. In the same fashion, visual sensations are produced by images, called *simulacra*, which are detached from external objects and enter the eyes, or rather the brain through the eyes.

These explanations are false and seem childish. However, the state of physics in the fifth century and especially the non-existence in the ancient world of the anatomy and physiology of the sensory organs made it difficult to go further and conjecture more accurately. The notion that knowledge of the world is given us by our senses and by means of currents (we say, waves) which, coming from outer objects, strike our sensory organs—this is still the manner in which modern science and also a whole part of modern philosophy represent things.

Democritus' position in the theory of knowledge is a form of sensationalism. But, in his explanations, he ran against difficulties and even contradictions. His consciousness of the difficulties in the way of knowledge does not mean that we should class him among the sceptics: he was not a sceptic but a mind conscious of the immensity of the task lying before the scientific enquirer. He therefore at times expresses feelings of doubt and reservation, feelings which, in any age, every honest seeker inevitably experiences when he compares the results attained with what remains to be attained. In one of such moments he declares that the vocation of a seeker is the finest of vocations and that to devote oneself to giving a causal explanation of natural phenomena is better suited to make a man happy than the possession of a king's throne.

Here, as an example, is a passage in which we see Democritus involved in one of the contradictions which his system, as he invented it, led up to. The great physician, Galen, wrote:

After discrediting the appearance of things by saying: 'Colour is a convention, the sweet is a convention, the bitter is a convention, there are in reality only atoms and vacuum', Democritus makes the senses speak as follows to reason: 'Poor reason, after depriving us of the means of proof, you want to beat us down. Your victory is also your defeat.'

The mere fact that the admitted contradiction leads to a dialogue is a sign of the robust vitality of the thinker who seeks only one solution, the truth.

Democritus' system, as one sees, is remarkable for the variety of problems it strives to solve and for the solidity of the principles on which it rests. As M. Robin in his conclusion on Democritus, observes: 'This original and coherent solution . . . might, had the philosophy of Ideas not prevailed, have furnished the science of nature . . . with a methodological hypothesis suited for the organization of its researches.'

Certainly, we must not deceive ourselves as to the resemblances between ancient atomic theory and that of modern science. In consequence of the immense progress that has been realized in experimental techniques and in mathematics, the atom is today no longer the indivisible unit which Democritus envisaged. It is a system formed of a certain number of corpuscles of negative electricity—the electrons—gravitating round a nucleus with a positive charge, exactly as planets gravitate round the sun. To quote the conclusion of M. Solovine's work on Democritus:

And yet, in the last analysis, the picture of the universe is the same for us as it was for Democritus: an inconceivable number of corpuscles disseminated in limitless space and moving eternally.

Let us admire the lucidity and courage of the great thinker Democritus. At the expense of his reputation, he achieved something immense in restoring dignity to matter; that is to say, that he reconciled us, body and soul together, with ourselves. If we can hear him aright, he assures us of the greatness of our vocation as men. Without letting us exalt ourselves over much, since he connects men with the primitive clay of which they are fashioned, he none the less sets us in the van of a progress of which we are the result and, from now onward, the artisans.

In spite of or because of this, Democritus was one of the scientists most vilified by the ancient world. To love and praise matter, to bring our soul back to matter, was to be a 'tool of Satan', as would be said later.

Democritus in this way lost his reputation and, as I have observed, his work.

'He's a madman,' said his fellow citizens. Always reading and writing. 'Reading was his ruin.' La Fontaine summarized the talk of the Abderitans and then made mock of Democritus' teaching:

> *Aucun nombre, dit-il, les mondes ne limite.*
> *Peut-être même ils sont remplis*
> *De Démocrites infinis.*

His fellow-citizens decided to ask Hippocrates, the great contemporary physician, for a consultation. The discussion between these two men of genius turned, we are told—for the anecdote is fictional—into a dialogue between science and friendship. '*Aucun n'est prophète chez soi*,' comments the fabulist.

◎

If, however, as someone has said, 'the brain of Democritus was not differently constituted from the brain of Einstein', then it is clear that the birth of science which proceeded from his researches, from those also of his predecessors like the old Ionians or his successors like Aristarchus of Samos or Archimedes, is one of the most salient facts of ancient civilization and, through its distant consequences, doubtless the most important.

For reasons which will be explained later, Greek science could not progress or even endure in ancient societies. But its well-nigh total disappearance in the Roman epoch and its long period of semi-slumber in the middle ages were but appearance. Men had not lost confidence in themselves, in their power to understand the world with their reason and to make it better and more just. That was the great hope of Greek science and its most certain justification. The Renaissance deserves its name. It was to take its departure exactly from the point where ancient science had fallen by the way, and without forgetting the fact.

CHAPTER FOUR

SOPHOCLES AND OEDIPUS:
THE REPLY TO DESTINY

Let us return now to that other method of deciphering human life and the world. Greek Tragedy, as much as science and philosophy, presents itself as a mode of explaining the world and knowing it. It was indeed such during the second half of the fifth century, a still quite religious era in Greek thought. Rare indeed in that age were thinkers and poets who, in trying to solve life's problems, did not present them in the iridescent light of heaven and entrust them to the imperious will of the gods.

Sophocles was as much a believer as any of them, or more—a believer in despite of winds and tides, in despite of the evidence of morals and the ambiguity of destiny. His long and green old age seems to have been haunted by a myth: the myth of Oedipus, more fearful than any other, a story that wounds the human sense of justice as it appears to wound religious faith. At an interval of fifteen years, the poet twice grappled with this myth. In 420 B.C. he wrote *Oedipus Rex*; he was then 75. In 405, at the age of 90, he took up almost the same subject in a new form, as if still hesitant as to the *dénouement* he had given it. He then wrote *Oedipus at Colonus*. He wished to think out the subject thoroughly, he wished to know whether, in the last resort, the gods could punish an innocent man; to know what becomes of man in a world governed by such gods.

The theme is well known. A man kills his father without knowing it is his father; and he marries his mother without knowing it is his mother. The gods punish him for these crimes, to which they had destined him even before his birth. Oedipus accuses himself of these sins, for which we do not judge him responsible; he proclaims the wisdom of the deity. We are in presence of a strange religion, shocking ethics, unlikely situations and arbitrary psychology. Sophocles wants to explain to the people this absurd and scandalous story; and, without stripping it of its character of inevitability, he wants to insert in it a man's reply, which completely modifies its meaning.

75

I

'Behold, O spectator, this machine, wound up so that the spring will unwind through the whole course of a man's life—one of the most perfect machines devised by the infernal gods for the systematic destruction of a mortal.' It is on these words that, with Jean Cocteau, the curtain rises on the modern drama of Oedipus which the author has so justly named *The Infernal Machine*. The title would apply to the ancient drama; it would at least express both its most apparent meaning and its movement. Sophocles has in effect constructed the action of his drama as one constructs a machine. The success of the construction rivals in skill the success of him who has set the trap. The technical perfection of the drama suggests, by its rigorous advance, the mechanical progress of the catastrophe so cleverly devised by one knows not whom. A machine, infernal or divine, for disintegrating and ruining the inner structure of a man's happiness—it is a pleasure to see all the elements of the action, all the release-triggers of the psychology, working together so as to produce the necessary result. To the inflexible march of events all the characters, and Oedipus first of all, unconsciously contribute. They are themselves pieces of the machine, driving-belts and wheels in the action which could not advance without their help. They are ignorant of everything in the function assigned to them. They are ignorant of the goal to which the mechanism in which they are engaged is moving. They feel themselves to be free agents, unrelated to this machine of which they vaguely perceive the distant approach. They are men busied with their own affairs, busied with the happiness they have bravely won in the honest exercise of their human function— in the exercise of virtue. And suddenly, a few yards from them, they perceive this kind of enormous tank which they have set in motion at unawares, and which is their own life marching upon them to crush them.

The first scene in the drama presents the picture of a man at the peak of human greatness. King Oedipus is on the steps of his palace. The people on their knees are supplicating him through the mouth of a priest. A misfortune has descended on Thebes, an epidemic is destroying the very seeds of life. Oedipus had once delivered the city from the Sphinx: it is for him to save the country once again. In the eyes of his subjects he is 'the first of men and the best'. He carries with him the splendid memory of his acts, his exploits and good deeds. Of this great king, Sophocles has not made a haughty prince or hard master, drunk with success, but has lent him only feelings of goodness and obliging gestures for his people. Even before they had come to beseech him, he had reflected and acted. He had sent his brother-in-law, Creon, to consult the oracle at Delphi, displaying by this his usual spirit of decision. And now, in response to the appeal, he is deeply moved, declaring that he suffers more than any of the Thebans because he suffers for the whole city. We know that this is true. He feels responsible for the country he governs and loves. So, from the opening of the play, Oedipus incarnates the highest virtues of man and ruler. The gods could not take advantage of his pride or his insolence in order to strike him down. Everything about him is authentic, everything in his high estate is deserved. This is the first image fixed in our memory. On the same spot, at the head of the steps, will appear in the last scene the outcast with bleeding eyes—image of a man fallen from the pinnacle of greatness into the depth of misery.

Knowing the outcome of his destiny, we await this reversal of fortune. From the beginning we hear touches of the tragic irony that gives its tone to the play, colouring the words, unknown to those who speak them, and warning us of what is to come. The characters themselves, ignorant of the ancient drama in which they had played their part, a drama really complete and waiting only to reveal its horror in the light of day, pronounce now and then a word which for them has only a commonplace and reassuring sense, a word they even confidently insist on. Now for the spectator who knows the past and the future, the same word has a sense entirely different and full of menace. The poet plays in this way on the double register of the character's ignorance and the spectator's knowledge. The two meanings simultaneously heard are like two notes fused in frightful dissonance. This is not merely a trick of style. These ironical words are felt by us as though they had been formed unconsciously on the characters' lips by the action of the mysterious power hidden behind the course of events. A god is making mock of man's false sense of assurance.

The rest of the drama shows a succession of four 'episodes', in each of which destiny strikes Oedipus a further blow. The last fells him to the earth. The composition is so clear that the spectator at once perceives its direction and conclusion. He sees the four steps that destiny takes against the tragic hero. He cannot imagine in what way the god will strike the man, because each time the poet has invented a situation unknown to the legend. But from the outset he grasps the connexion between the episodes, the coherence of the four scenes by which the action advances like the movement of clockwork. For Oedipus on the other hand, all that which, in the spectator's eyes, is logical sequence and methodical execution of a plan concerted by the god, presents itself as a series of incidents or chances of which he cannot perceive the connexion and which, in his eyes, merely interrupt him or turn him aside from the straightforward advance he thinks he is following in his search for the murderer of Laius. Oedipus is being led by an iron hand, and indeed in a straight line, toward a goal he does not perceive, toward a guilty man who is himself, and at the same time he is led astray along diverging paths. Each incident turns him in a new direction; each blow stuns him, sometimes with joy; and nothing warns him. There are therefore, in the progress of the action, two distinct movements which we follow simultaneously: on the one hand, the implacable advance of a ray of light in the heart of the darkness, on the other, the groping advance of a being who turns this way and that, who strikes against invisible obstacles in the dark, but who is progressively and yet unsuspectingly being drawn toward the source of the light. Suddenly the two lines intersect: the insect has been caught in the flame. And in a moment all is over. Or perhaps it only seems to be. For is it still from this unknown beacon, or not rather from the stricken mortal, that the light will now come?

The first instrument that destiny uses to strike Oedipus is the soothsayer Tiresias. Oedipus has sent for the blind old man to help in throwing light on the murder of Laius. As the price for the salvation of Thebes Apollo has decreed the expulsion of the murderer. Tiresias knows everything; the blind man is the seer. He knows who has killed Laius, he knows it is Oedipus and that Oedipus is the son of Laius. But how could he reveal this, and who would believe him? He recoils before the storm which truth would raise, and he naturally refuses to reply. It is equally natural that this should irritate Oedipus. Here before him is a man who need only say one word to save Thebes, and he is silent. What could be more scandalous in the eyes of a good citizen like Oedipus? And what could be more suspect? Only one explanation suggests itself, that Tiresias had been the accomplice of the guilty man whom his silence is now trying to cover. Now who could have profited from the crime? Creon, the heir of Laius. Conclusion: Creon is the assassin. Oedipus suddenly believes that his enquiry is near its goal, and he loses his temper with Tiresias whose obstinate silence blocks the way and who—no doubt because he had been involved in the plot—refuses to divulge the clues that are needed.

This accusation of the priest by the king creates, in turn and by a similar necessity, a new situation. The play of character, thus rigorously conducted, causes the infernal machine to advance. Tiresias, who feels outraged, can only proclaim the truth: 'The murderer thou seekest, 'tis thyself.' The first blow has been struck, and Oedipus is now faced with the truth he has been seeking, but which he cannot understand. In the part of the scene that follows, in the rising flood of anger, the soothsayer half uncovers an even more terrifying abyss of truth: 'The murderer of Laius is a Theban. He killed his sire, he polluted his mother's bed.' But Oedipus cannot really grasp the truth that Tiresias offers him. He knows that he has not killed Laius, he knows he is the son of a king of Corinth and that he never had to do with the land of Thebes prior to the day when, as a young man, he saved it from the Sphinx. He returns to the palace dazed but not shaken, and prepares with his usual ardour to follow the false scent that destiny has put him on to—the imaginary plot of Creon.

Jocasta is the instrument chosen by the deity to strike the second blow. The queen intervenes in the dispute between her husband and her brother, wishing, as she does, to calm the king and reassure him respecting Tiresias' statements. She thinks to succeed in this by offering a striking proof of the inanity of oracles. A soothsayer had once told Laius that he would perish by the hand of his son. Now that king had been assassinated by brigands, at a cross-roads, when he was going on a journey abroad; and the only son he ever had—that son had been exposed on the mountain to die, three days after his birth. All of which shows how much credit one need give soothsayers.

The words of Jocasta, which are calculated to reassure Oedipus, are precisely what for the first time will shake his certainty of innocence. There was in the infernal machine a little spring which could change assurance into doubt and security into dread; and Jocasta has touched this spring unwittingly. When speaking of the death of Laius she has furnished one of those insignificant details that one puts into a narrative without thinking, she has said in passing that Laius had been assassinated 'at a cross-roads'. This detail has sunk into the subconscious mind of Oedipus and stirred a whole mass of forgotten memories. Suddenly the king sees, in his mind's eye, a journey of long ago, the cross-roads, the quarrel with the driver of a carriage, the old man who had lashed him with his whip, his own youthful fit of anger and the blow he had struck. Could Tiresias have spoken the truth? Not that Oedipus has as yet the slightest suspicion of the chain of events that had led him to the cross-roads. Once he has heard Jocasta speak of 'the crossing of three roads', Oedipus, plunged into memories of the past, has paid no heed to her next words, about the child who had been exposed, words that would have risked engaging his thoughts in a far more dreadful direction. It is impossible for him to suppose he could have killed his father, but he is forced to admit that he may have killed Laius.

So he harasses Jocasta with questions. In the murder which she has been relating he hopes to find a circumstance which does not agree with the murder he now remembers having committed:

> *I thought I heard thee say that Laius fell,*
> *Smitten to death, where meet the three great roads. . . .*
> *Where was the spot?*[1]

---

[1] This and the following passages from the *Oedipus Rex* and the *Oedipus at Colonus* are quoted from *The Tragedies of Sophocles*, a new translation . . . by E. H. Plumptre, London and New York, see p. 28.

The place was the same.

> *And what the interval of time since then?*

The times agree also. Oedipus continues to question:

> *. . . but Laius, tell of him,*
> *His build, his features, and his years of life.*

Jocasta replies:

> *Tall was he, and the white hairs snowed his head.*

And then, as if she had thought of it for the first time:

> *And in his form not much unlike to thee.*[1]

Here one grasps the power of the tragic irony and the meaning, unknown to Jocasta, which the spectators now associate with this resemblance. And yet there is one detail which does not fit in. The only serving-man who had escaped from the massacre at the cross-roads had declared (we guess, however, that he had been lying in order to excuse himself) that his master and his master's companions had been killed by a band of brigands. Oedipus knows that he himself had been alone. He sends for the servant; he clings to the false detail, while from the coming encounter the spectator awaits the catastrophe.

Now we have the third attack of destiny: the messenger from Corinth. In the course of the previous scene Oedipus had spoken to Jocasta of an oracle that had been delivered him when he was a young man. He was to kill his father and marry his mother. It was for that reason that he had left Corinth and come to Thebes. A messenger now arrives with news of the death of king Polybos, the father whom he was to assassinate. Jocasta is in triumph.

> *Now, oracles of Gods,*
> *Where are ye now?*[2]

Oedipus shares her joy; but he refuses to return to Corinth for fear of exposing himself to the second menace of the oracle. The messenger however undertakes to reassure him, and like Jocasta a little earlier, and with the best intentions, he is about to bring into play a part of the machine that will precipitate the catastrophe.

Messenger. *Who is this woman about whom ye fear?*
Oedipus.   *'Tis Merope, old sir, who lives with Polybos.*
Messenger. *And what leads you to think of her with fear?*
Oedipus.   *A fearful oracle. . . .*

[1] *Ibid.*, p. 29.   [2] *Ibid.*, p. 35.

9. *Amphora in geometric style (height c. 4 feet 8 inches) 8th Century*

9

Messenger. *And know'st thou not there is no cause for fear?*
Oedipus.   *Is there no cause if I was born their son? . . .*
        What say'st thou? Did not Polybos beget me?
Messenger. *No more than he thou speak'st to . . .*[1]

Here is a new track, suddenly opening up and perfidiously inviting Oedipus to follow: he rushes blindly along it. His mind is now far away from the slaying of Laius, and in his glad excitement he thinks only of unravelling the secret of his birth. He presses the messenger with questions. The latter tells Oedipus that he had handed him, as a baby, to the king of Corinth; that he had received the child from a shepherd of Cithaeron,[2] one of Laius' servants.

In a flash Jocasta links up the two lying oracles, which are now seen to have been a true prophecy. She immediately understands. She is the mother of the child who had been exposed, she had never forgotten the fate of the unhappy little creature. And this is why, on hearing this other story of a child exposed—really the same story—she is the first to see the truth. Oedipus, on the other hand, had paid scant attention to the fate of Laius' child, even if he had heard what little Jocasta had told him of it. Besides, it is the enigma of his birth that is wholly occupying him at the moment and diverting his mind from all other thoughts. In vain Jocasta implores him not to force the secret:

Ah, by the Gods, if that thou valuest life,
Inquire no more. My misery is enough.[3]

Oedipus puts her request down to a movement of female vanity. No doubt the queen fears having to blush for the obscure birth of her consort. He himself glories in it:

. . . but I, who count
Myself the child of Fortune, fear no shame:
My mother she, and she has prospered me.
And so the months that span my life have made me
Both low and high. . . .[4]

This is true, he has been great. But the greatness which is his own achievement, the Destiny to which he acribes it, has conceded this greatness only to withdraw it and make mock of him.

And now Destiny deals the final blow. All that is needed is for the messenger

[1] *Ibid.*, pp. 37–8.
[2] The sinews of the child's feet had been pierced before he was left exposed in a 'shrub-grown hollow' on the mountain-side. This is the last, fearful clue to the identification: the name 'Oedipus' means swollen-footed. Laius had had his son exposed because the oracle of Delphi had warned him that if he had a son, by that son's hand he would die (Translator).
[3] Trans. cited, p. 39.   [4] *Ibid.*, p. 40.

F

10. *Column and polygonal structure. The supporting wall of the temple of Apollo at Delphi.* (*End of the 6th Century*)

from Corinth to be confronted, in Oedipus' presence, with the shepherd of Cithaeron who had consigned the unknown child to the Corinthian. By a skilful contrivance of the poet, this shepherd is the same person as the serving-man who had escaped from the tragedy at the cross-roads. The care for economy shown by Sophocles in this instance is in keeping with the sobriety of the composition. A drama in which blow follows blow so exactly and so rapidly cannot tolerate any superfluous feature. Apart from this, the poet desires that Oedipus should learn the whole truth at once and from a single word. Not, first, that he was the murderer of Laius, and then, that Laius was his father. A catastrophe in two stages would have lacked the dramatic intensity of the *dénouement* which—from the fact that one man possesses the key to the whole truth—is to descend in a single and terrible thunderbolt on the head of Oedipus. When the king learns from his father's servant that he is the son of Laius, he has no need to ask now who has killed Laius. The truth is suddenly only too blinding. He rushes away to put out his eyes.

Jocasta has hanged herself. And now we have the spectacle of him who had been 'the first among men': a face with blind eyes. What will it tell us?

After the frightful description[1] of the golden clasps, piercing his eyeballs with redoubled blows, the last part of the drama is the slow finale of a poem of which the movement had not, hitherto, ceased to rush onward. Destiny, now appeased, suspends its course and we take breath. The headlong movement of the action suddenly comes to a halt: we have lyric plaints, farewells, and regrets, and recollections. The action, however, has not really ceased, but, in these last moments of the drama, has become inner: it is taking place in the hero's heart. Lyricism is now action, while Oedipus meditates on the meaning of his life, and readjusts his soul to the universe which the *dénouement* has revealed to him. If the 'infernal machine' has now accomplished 'the mathematical annihilation' of a human being, it is precisely in this annihilated being that, athwart our terror, we see the action resuming its advance, following the path of tears and, contrary to our expectation, opening out in fraternal pity and flowering in courage.

For the moderns, every Tragedy ends in catastrophe, and to them *Oedipus Rex* appears as the masterpiece of the tragic genre because the hero seems to be engulfed in horror. But this is a false interpretation; it takes no account of this so-called lyrical conclusion which is to contain Oedipus' response. As long as this conclusion, which is so magnificent on the stage, has not been satisfactorily explained, the critic will have simply misrepresented the meaning of the poem; he will not have understood the *Oedipus Rex*.

[1] The 'Second Messenger' describes how Oedipus, rushing into the bed chamber, had found Jocasta hanging 'by twisted cords suspended'. He had loosened the body, then, tearing the clasps from her dress, had repeatedly stabbed himself in the eyes (Translator).

Let us contemplate this being who advances tottering and gropingly. Has he really been destroyed? Shall we complacently regard in him the horror of a nameless destiny?

Ye mortal men, resign yourselves:
The world to destiny belongs.

No Greek Tragedy, not even this one, ever suggested such resignation to the Athenians; it would have been like running up the white flag of surrender. Beyond what seem to be cries of despair and protests against abandonment, we shall discover that 'strength of soul' which is the hard core of unbreakable resistance on the part of this old man (Sophocles—Oedipus) and his people. We feel already that in this being doomed to annihilation life is still throbbing and that it will resume its advance. Oedipus will pick up the stones that Destiny has thrown at him as if they were new weapons. He lives to fight again, but as seeing himself now in better focus. It is this new focus that he discovers in the last part of the play.

Therefore, in the last quarter of the drama, the *Oedipus Rex* opens to our eyes horizons of which we had not even suspected the existence at the beginning. From the first moment the drama had fallaciously led us to await the anguish of the time when Oedipus would discover the meaning of his past life: it seemed to be wholly designed to produce this cunning murder concerted by the gods, the real crime of the play, the murder of an innocent man.

'It seemed'—but this is not so. In this conclusion, the poet, by means of the very beautiful lyric development that crowns his drama, shows us that the real goal of the work was not the destruction of Oedipus. We slowly become aware that, however severe a hold the action has taken on us, it was not leading us to the hero's ruin but that, right through the play and in the depths of our consciousness, it was causing us to await something unknown, something at once dreaded and hoped for—the response that Oedipus, struck down by the gods, would have to make to them, a response that we must now examine.

II

To shed tragic tears is to reflect; and yet no great poetic work was written with a view to making us think. The object of Tragedy is to move the emotions and to please. It is dangerous to ask oneself about the meaning of a poetical work and to formulate the meaning in terms of intellect. However, unless our mind is divided into water-tight compartments, every work that moves us echoes in the intelligence and seizes the whole of our being. And it was indeed with his whole being that the poet had composed his drama. He reaches our thoughts by way of the strange pleasure we feel in the suffering we share with the children of his soul. It is the terror, pity, admiration and love we feel for the tragic hero that compel us to ask ourselves: 'What is happening to this man? What means this destiny?' The poet therefore obliges us to seek the meaning of his work as a natural reaction of our understanding to the emotional state into which he has thrown us.

As regards the *Oedipus Rex* I seem to distinguish three reactions of this kind, three meanings which our mind ascribes to the tragedy as it unrolls and advances in our consciousness, three mental stages leading to its full significance. The first stage is one of revolt. We see a man caught in a diabolical trap. He is an honourable man. The trap has been laid by gods whom he respects, by a god who has imposed on him a crime that he imputes to him. Who is guilty and who innocent? We answer: Oedipus is innocent, the god is criminal. Oedipus is innocent because, in the first state of our feelings, we see no fault in him apart from a free will which has chosen the wrong course.[1]

Aeschylus when treating the same subject had represented the oracle as forbidding Laius to have a son. Hence the begetting of this child was an act of disobedience to the gods. Oedipus was paying for his father's fault, though not without adding, during his life, a further fault of his own. The god of Aeschylus was just when punishing.

But Sophocles does not follow this interpretation of the myth. He presents the oracle delivered by Apollo to Laius as a pure and simple prediction of what will take place. No human fault or act of imprudence justifies the divine wrath. Laius and Jocasta do all they possibly can to stay the course of the crime. Similarly Oedipus, when he hears the second oracle, leaves his parents.[2] Neither his good intentions nor his faith falter in any circumstance. He desires only one thing, to save his country, and he counts, for success, on the support of the gods. If all actions should be judged by the intention, then Oedipus is innocent of a parricide and incest which he neither desired nor was conscious of.

Who then is guilty? The god. He alone without a shadow of reason, has launched the series of events that lead to the crime. The part he plays is the more revolting in that he only intervenes personally in circumstances where the man, by dint of good will, would risk escaping from destiny. Thus, in delivering the second oracle to Oedipus, he knows that this oracle will be misinterpreted. Speculating on the filial love and the piety of his victim, he reveals just what is needed of the

---

[1] '. . . *en dehors d'une volanté libre qui a choisi le mal.*' I do not think that the author means 'which has chosen evil', because this would seem to attribute to Oedipus a consciousness of doing wrong, at the time he was doing it. He had, on the contrary, tried to escape from situations that would involve him in evil. It is only in the *dénouement* that he discovers he has taken the wrong course unwittingly (Translator).

[2] That is, Polybus and Merope whom he believes to be his parents (Translator).

future for this to come true with the assistance of virtue. His revelation causes those elements of freedom in the human soul to act precisely in the same direction as the mechanism of destiny. These little thrusts and pushes given by the god are revolting.

But they amuse the god. The words of tragic irony echo his laughter in the wings. It is for this derision, though less than for his other actions, that we cannot forgive the deity. If the gods make mock of Oedipus, a man innocent or guilty only through their fault, how can we not feel the hero's fate as an outrage to our humanity? Hence, in the feeling of our wounded dignity, we take hold of the Tragedy as a ground of accusation against the god, a document in the plea of an injustice which has been done us.

This reaction is healthy. Sophocles himself experienced a feeling of legitimate revolt, and the hard structure of his drama inspires it in us. But Sophocles did not stop at this movement of anger against our hostile masters. There are throughout the play signs that warn us, there are obstacles that thwart this feeling of rebellion and prevent us from adopting it and suggest that we should go beyond this first meaning of the drama and interrogate it anew.

The first obstacle is provided by the Chorus. The importance in all ancient Tragedies of the lyrical Chorus is well known. Closely associated with the action, as is manner with matter, the lyric songs elucidate the meaning of the drama. In the *Oedipus Rex* after each of the episodes that increase our indignation against the gods, the songs of the Chorus come as astonishing professions of faith in the deity. Unchanging is the Chorus's attachment to the king, unchanging its love and loyalty to the benefactor of Thebes, but unchanging too its confidence in the deity's wisdom. Never does the Chorus set Oedipus and the gods in opposition. Where we seek an innocent and a guilty person, a victim and an executioner, the Chorus associates the king and the god in one and the same sentiment of love and veneration. In the centre of this drama where we see the man with his work and his fortune engulfed in nothingness, the Chorus firmly assures us that there exist enduring things; it affirms that beyond the world of appearances there is a splendid and unknown reality which asks of us something other than a rebellious denial.

Yet at the very moment when the Chorus asserts its faith, we feel the passage of trembling doubts which make this faith more authentic. How this opposition, which at times seems to separate Oedipus from the gods, will be solved, neither the Chorus nor even Sophocles yet fully know. In order that these apparent and fugitive contradictions should be removed and the antinomies resolved in a statement of truth, fifteen years would be needed: it would be necessary for Sophocles to write *Oedipus at Colonus*.

There is, however, another character who diverts our mind from rebellion, though in an opposite manner. Jocasta's is a strange figure. She is herself a negation. She denies the validity of oracles, denying what she fears and does not understand. She believes herself a woman of experience, whereas she is really a limited and sceptical mind. She thinks she is afraid of nothing, and, to reassure herself, declares that, in the heart of being, there is nothing but chance.

> *Why should we fear, when chance rules everything?*
> *...'Tis best to live at random as one can.*
> *But thou, fear not that marriage with thy mother:*
> *Many ere now have dreamt of things like this,*
> *But who cares least about them bears life best.*[1]

This fashion of leaving it to chance to remove all meaning from our actions, this flatly rationalistic or Freudian explanation of the oracle that is frightening Oedipus is a poor sort of philosophy: it estranges us from Jocasta and prevents us from following a path on which our disquiet regarding the gods would be calmed by a refusal to pay heed to their obscure language. In the arguments of this woman we feel the presence of a rather low, limited outlook which suddenly prevents our forming any light judgment of the gods or of the mystery in which they dwell. Her false philosophy obliges us to put our finger on our own ignorance.

When the truth comes out, Jocasta hangs herself. Her suicide fills us with horror; but we shed no tears for this soul of a reprobate.

Finally, at the moment of the catastrophe, a last and quite unforeseen obstacle forbids us to condemn the gods. Oedipus does not condemn them. We accuse them of having struck an innocent man; but now the innocent man proclaims himself guilty. The whole conclusion of the tragedy—the long scene in which, now that the catastrophe has burst upon Oedipus and struck him in the face, we contemplate the hero and his destiny as a sea of suffering spreads before us—all this end of the drama is, as I have indicated, essential to its meaning. Oedipus now knows the source of the blow that has struck him down. He cries:

> *Apollo, oh my friends, the god, Apollo,*
> *Who worketh out all these, my bitter woes....*

He knows he is 'hateful to the gods';[2] he says so, and repeats it. And yet he is not moved to hate them. His greatest grief is to be deprived of them, because he feels himself separated from them: 'now all godless.'[3]

How is he, the guilty criminal, to enter again into communion with the deity? He frames no accusation and proffers no blasphemy; indeed his entire respect for the action of the gods, his submission to their authority in the ordeal into which

---

[1] Trans. cited, p. 37.   [2] Trans. cited, p. 49.   [3] *Ibid.*, p. 50.

they have thrown him, inform us that he has a glimpse of the meaning of his destiny and suggest that we, after him, should seek that meaning. By what right should we rebel, if Oedipus does not? We wish, with him, to learn of the divine order, that order which, beyond the order of justice, imposes itself on men.

Knowledge is then the second stage in our reflexions. Every Tragedy, and this one more than any other, opens a perspective on the human lot. The *Oedipus Rex* is the Tragedy of man: not of a particular man with his distinct character and the personal problem he debates with himself. Indeed no ancient Tragedy is less psychological or more 'philosophical' than this one. This is the Tragedy of man in full possession of all human power and clashing with that which in the universe rejects man.

The poet represents Oedipus as human perfection. He possesses all human perspicacity: sagacity, judgment, power to choose the better part in every matter. He also possesses all human 'action' (I am translating the Greek word)—spirit of decision, energy, power to incorporate the thought in the act. He is, as the Greeks would say, master of the *logos* and the *ergon,* that is of thought and act. He is the man who reflects, explains and acts.

Oedipus has, moreover, always devoted this thoughtful action to the service of the community; and this is an essential aspect of man's perfection. His vocation is that of a citizen and head of state, and this he realizes not as a 'tyrant' (in spite of the false Greek title of the play) but in clear-sighted submission to the good of the community. His 'fault' has nothing to do with a bad use of his gifts or an evil will, trying to cause private interest to prevail over the public good. At every moment he is ready to devote himself entirely to the city. When Tiresias thinks to frighten him by saying:

> *And yet this same success has worked thy fall.*

Oedipus answers:

> *I little care, if I have saved the state.*[1]

Action inspired by thought and action devoted to the good of the community, these were the marks of the ideal man, for the ancients. But what hold could such a man offer to destiny? Only this, that he is a man, and that human action is subject to the universal laws that govern our lot. We must not ascribe Oedipus' fault to his will. The universe is not concerned with that, it cares nothing for our intentions whether good or bad, or for the moral system we have devised on the human level. The universe is concerned only with the act in itself in order to

---

[1] *Ibid.,* p. 19.

prevent that act from deranging the universal order, an order into which our lives do indeed enter but which remains foreign to us.

Reality is a whole, and every action produces repercussions in it. Sophocles is profoundly conscious of the law of solidarity which, whether a man wishes it or not, binds him to the world. Whoever acts detaches from himself, so to speak, a new being, his act, which, though separated from its author, continues to operate in the world in a way which its author cannot possibly foresee. The first author of the event none the less remains—not in justice but in fact—responsible for its ultimate repercussions. This responsibility ought only, in justice, to attach to him if he knew all the consequences of his action. But he does not know them, he is not omniscient—and he must act. Therein lies his tragedy. Every act exposes us. Oedipus, who is supremely a man, is supremely exposed.

We have thus an indication of a singularly hard, and from a certain angle, a very modern notion of responsibility. A man is not merely responsible for what he has willed but for what he turns out to have done in the light of the outcome which his actions have given birth to, without his having disposed of any means of calculating and, *à fortiori*, of preventing this result.

To be treated by the universe as if we were omniscient, this is the muffled threat that hangs over every destiny if our knowledge always remains mingled with ignorance and if the world in which we are obliged to act in order to subsist is still, as regards the secret play of its forces, almost entirely obscure. Sophocles is warning us. Man does not know the ensemble of forces whose equilibrium constitutes the life of the world. His good will, being the prisoner of his natural blindness, therefore remains ineffectual in preserving him from misfortune.

Such is the knowledge that the poet reveals to us in his tragedy. It is hard; but it corresponds so exactly with a whole part of our experience that we are dazzled by its truth; and the pleasure we receive from truth delivers us from rebellion. The destiny of Oedipus, even if his case is only a boundary-case,[1] suddenly appears to us as exemplary of every human destiny; and even more so than if he were expiating a fault in the ordinary sense of the word. If he were behaving like a brutal and iniquitous master, like the tyrant in the *Antigone* for example, we should no doubt be affected by his fall, but less acutely, because we should think we could avoid his fate. One can avoid being a wicked man. But how can one avoid being a man? Oedipus is simply man—a man who has made a success of his career as no other man has. His life is wholly made up of good works; and now suddenly, in its conclusion, displays his impotence and reveals the vanity of works when facing the tribunal of the universe.

Not that his example discourages us from acting. There emanates from his

---

[1] *'Un cas-limite.'* Or 'boundary-situation'—one of the Existentialist formulae.

person, even when plunged in the abyss from which he speaks to us, a vitality too powerful. But thanks to him, we know—yes, we know: this at least has been gained—the price we must pay for every action, and also that the outcome of the action sometimes does not belong to us. The world which used to seem deceptively clear to us when we thought that by dint of wisdom and virtue we could build in it a happiness entirely exempt from the blows that the world had in store for us, the reality we supposed to be tractable—this world and reality suddenly reveal themselves as opaque, resistant, full of things, presences and laws which do not love us, and which exist not for our use and service, but in their unknown being. We know that it is so and that our life is immersed in a life more vast, which is perhaps condemning us. We know that when we looked on things with clear eyes, then we were blind. We know that our knowledge is a very small thing, or rather that, of the intentions of the universe regarding us, only one remains certain; the condemnation pronounced against us by the laws of biology.

Sophocles uses the blindness of Oedipus as an excellent symbol, packed with suggestions. By blinding himself Oedipus renders visible the ignorance of man. But he does more: he not only presents the nothingness of human knowledge, he reaches another light in the darkness, he wins access to other knowledge, which is that of the presence around us of a dark, obscure world. This knowledge of the obscure is now no more blindness, but contemplation.[1]

The same theme had been initiated in the dialogue between the king and Tiresias: the blind saw with the gaze of the Invisible, while the man with sight remained plunged in darkness. At the end of the drama, by destroying his human eyes, Oedipus not only makes it plain that only the god is a seer, but he comes into possession of a light which is his own, a light which permits him to bear the sight of the world as it is and, contrary to expectation, still to affirm his liberty.

Oedipus' action in putting out his eyes enables us in fact to reach, in the astonishing conclusion of the tragedy, the highest meaning it contains. Why should our contemplation of the bleeding face, as soon as it appears on the stage, instead of simply filling us with horror, inspire in us, the spectators, a kind of trembling joy? The reason is that in these blinded eyes we have, not at all something to gorge us with horror, but Oedipus' reply to destiny. It is he who has blinded himself, as he loudly proclaims:

[1] Cf. Milton on his blindness, in *Paradise Lost, III*, 51 et seq.:
> *So much the rather thou, celestial light,*
> *Shine inward, and the mind through all her powers*
> *Irradiate, there plant eyes, all mists from thence*
> *Purge and disperse, that I may see and tell*
> *Of things invisible to mortal sight.* (Translator's note.)

Chorus.　*O man of fearful deeds, how could'st thou bear*
　　　　　Thine eyes to outrage? What Power stirred thee to it?
Oedipus.　*Apollo, oh, my friends, the god, Apollo,*
　　　　　Who worketh out all these, my bitter woes;
　　　　　Yet no man's hand but mine has smitten them.[1]

So he claims and even chooses the chastisement that destiny was reserving for him. This he makes his first gesture as a free man whom the gods will not reject. Not passively but from the depths of his being, Oedipus stoutly adheres to the world as now revealed to him. In his act, his energy is singular and frightening, and truly as fierce as the hostility of the world to himself.

But what is the meaning of this powerful impulse which rises like sap from the roots of his being and drives him to put the crown on his misfortune unless it be this, that in the last trial of strength in the rivalry between himself and the world, Oedipus is now leading in the race and that, having resolved to accept his destiny, he catches up with it, overtakes it, and at last leaves it behind? Now he is free.

So the final meaning of the play is both adhesion and liberation.

It is adhesion. Oedipus wills what the god has willed. Not that his soul unites in mystic joy with the divine being. The Greek tragedian very rarely emerges into mysticism, if he does so at all. Oedipus' attitude is founded on an objective recognition that there exist in the world forces which are still unknown to man but which govern his action. This unknown region of Being, this divine mystery, this world separated from the world of men by a deep gulf—all this divinity is felt by Oedipus as another and foreign world. It will perhaps one day be taken possession of and explained in human language; but for the moment, Sophocles' moment, it is fundamentally foreign, almost a foreign body to be expelled from man's consciousness. It is not, as with the mystic, a world with which the soul is to unite, but, in reality, a world to be humanized.

To win freedom in respect of this world, Oedipus has thrown himself into the gulf that separates it from ours. By an act of unheard of courage, he has gone to seek in the world of the gods an act of theirs which has been prepared for his punishment; and this act, a blow which was to be delivered to wound him, he has applied to himself, 'with his own hand'; he has made it an act of the human world, which means a free act.

Yet to this Stranger who, man is forced to admit, is capable of assuming the direction of man's life, without man's being aware of it, the tragic hero can finally accord a place in his thought, can agree to regulate his conduct according to the

[1] Trans. cited, p. 49.

experience he has of him, only if he is persuaded that this Master is, in his un-known being, in some way worthy of being loved.[1] By choosing to live sightless, Oedipus adapts his own life to the knowledge of the divine action in the world which he owes to his misfortune. In that sense he wills what the god has willed. But this adhesion to the divine, which is above all an act of well considered courage, would be impossible if it did not imply an element of love: a love that proceeds from two impulses in man's nature: first, respect for reality and for the conditions it imposes on those who wish to live fully, and secondly, the impulse that carries every living thing towards life.

In order to agree to pay the penalty for an offence he has committed without knowing how, Oedipus must admit the existence of a reality whose equilibrium he has disturbed; he must, if only confusedly, perceive in the mystery he has clashed with, an order, harmony and fullness of existence with which he is impelled to associate by the ardent love which he has always had for life and action, and which he will have henceforward in full awareness of the threats they reserve for the man who wishes to live in greatness.

Oedipus adheres to the world that has broken him because, whatever it under-takes in respect of our world, it is the receptacle of the living God. His is a religious act which demands of him clear-sighted courage and complete detachment, since the order which he feels to be existing behind the veil of appearances is not one that his human mind can clearly grasp, and in any case not an order that concerns him, a divine plane in which man is the end or object, a providence that judges him and seeks to promote his good according to human morals.

What then is this universal order? How is one to apprehend these indiscernible laws? There exists, says the poet, in the heart of the universe, 'an awful purity.'[2] It subsists of itself and in order to subsist has no need of man's cooperation. Should some imprudent mortal happen to disturb it by mistake, the universe will re-establish its sacred order at the expense of the guilty one. It will bring its law into operation, and what is false will be corrected, as it were automatically. If the hero of Sophocles' drama appears to us to have been crushed by a machine, this is because the world, whose harmony has been deranged by parricide and incest, has spontaneously and mechanically restored its equilibrium by crushing Oedipus. The punishment of the guilty man has no other meaning: it is a 'correction' in the sense of rectification of an error. But, in the passage of a catastrophe that devastates his life, Oedipus recognizes that the life of the universe has manifested its presence.

[1] This is a complex sentence in the French text, and I have followed its structure as closely as possible. It appears to mean that the tragic hero agrees to accept and in some sort cooperate with the divine power ('cet Étranger') only if he is sure that it deserves his love (Translator).

[2] Trans. cited, p. 32.

He loves this pure source of Being; and this distant love he unexpectedly bears 'the Stranger' nourishes and regenerates his own life from the moment that he has accepted the re-establishment, by way of his own chastisement, of the inviolable holiness of the world that is crushing him.

The god who strikes Oedipus is a hard god and not a god of love. A god of love would certainly have appeared to Sophocles as too subjective, made in the image of man and of his illusions, tarnished both with anthropomorphic and anthropocentric feeling. Nothing in Oedipus' experience suggests such a god. The divine is mystery and order. It has its own laws. It is omniscience and omnipotence. And there is nothing else to be said about it. If, however, it is difficult to suppose that this divinity loves us, it is at least possible for man, in all dignity, to conclude a pact with the unknown wisdom.

God reigns, unknowable. Oracles, presentiments and dreams—the vague language in which he addresses us—are like bubbles that float up from the abyss into the region of the perceptible. Signs of his presence, they yet in no way permit us to understand and judge him, and they have not so much the meaning of a predestination as they afford man a glimpse of God's omniscience and an opportunity of contemplating Necessity and Law. The view he takes of them will henceforward guide his behaviour as a creature puny no doubt, but resolved to live in harmony with the severe laws of the Cosmos. As soon as Oedipus hears the call of the Universe, uttered in the obscure language used by these laws, he hastens towards his destiny in an *élan* like that of love. *Amor fati,* the ancients (or rather Nietzsche, condensing their thought) used to say, in order to express this very noble form of the religious sentiment—this forgetting of trespasses, this pardoning of the world by man; or rather, in man's divided heart, this reconciliation of his destiny, which is to be crushed by the world, with his vocation, which is to love and to complete the world.

Adhesion, therefore, in love which is creation. And at the same time, Liberation. Oedipus seems suddenly to stand erect:

> *. . . no soul save me*
> *Can bear the burden of my countless ills.*[1]

Oedipus has in fact broken out of the circle of fatality from the moment that he cooperates in his own misfortune and pushes it to its zenith, when, by a deliberate act, he completes the absolute image of woe which the gods have been pleased to fashion in him. He has crossed to the far side of the wall, beyond reach of the god, from the moment that he has known and admitted his woe as a fact indubitable

---

[1] Trans. cited, p. 51.

though not strictly definable, when he has experienced it in the disaster of his life and when he now takes it up in his office as justicer, substitutes himself for it, and in some sort evicts it.

And does he not rival it even in his creative function, if the masterpiece of that woe that the divine artist had conceived, is really the clasp which the hand of Oedipus has raised against himself and which is to seek and bring to the light of day the last drop of woe hidden behind the eyeballs?

And now the greatness of Oedipus, his lofty human stature, stands once more erect. We see it reversed, not in the sense that we imagined at the beginning of the drama when we thought that his greatness would be overthrown and annihilated, but in the sense that it has changed into a contrary kind of greatness. Before this happened, it had been a greatness founded on good fortune, contingent and as it were borrowed, measurable by external standards, by the throne he has won, by his many great exploits, a greatness compact of what man may wrest from fate as it were by surprise. Now it is a greatness of misfortune, of ordeals duly borne, not of catastrophes which have remained external but of suffering that has been assumed and fully accepted, in the flesh and in the mind, and measurable henceforth only by man's infinite woe, by the sorrow that Oedipus has made his own. Sharing in the immensity of our native misery, this greatness renders him who submits to making amends, at the price of his suffering, for the evil he had not willed, equal to Him who had invented it in order to consummate his ruin.[1]

The greatness which the gods refused him in the light of the sun, Oedipus restores in a state of peace not nocturnal but illumined with the constellations of the soul; a peace unsullied by their gifts, their grace and their service, nurtured on their malediction and on the blows and wounds they have inflicted, a peace compounded of lucidity, resolution and self-possession.

Thus man makes reply to destiny. He turns the enterprise of his enslavement into the instrument of his liberation.

III

The *Oedipus Rex* showed us that in every circumstance and even when subject to the most rigorous offensive on the part of Destiny, man is in a position to maintain his greatness and prestige. The menace of tragedy can do everything against his life, but nothing against his strength of soul. This firmness we find intact in the hero of *Oedipus at Colonus*. In the opening verses of the play he

---

[1] 'Participant de l'immensité de notre misère native, cette grandeur égale enfin celui qui accepte de réparer au prix de sa souffrance le mal qu'il n'avait pa voulu à Celui qui l'avait inventé pour consommer sa perte.'

affirms it as the supreme virtue that sustains him in the terrible ordeal he has been facing for years in his wanderings.

When Sophocles wrote *Oedipus at Colonus* he had exceeded the normal years of man's life. He had thought much about Oedipus, lived much with him in imagination. The hero's reply to destiny in the last part of *Oedipus Rex* did not appear quite satisfying now that Sophocles himself was near his end. The reply was still valid for the moment in Oedipus' life when it was given. But Oedipus has gone on living. And now have not the gods resumed the dialogue? Perhaps the offensive? *Oedipus at Colonus* is a sequel to the debate between Oedipus and the gods, a sequel composed in the light of the myth but also in the light of Sophocles' experience of extreme old age. It seems as though the poet, himself near the point of death, is trying to throw a bridge, a mere gangway, from the human condition to the divine. *Oedipus at Colonus* is the only Greek tragedy that crosses the abyss between man and deity, between Life and Death. It is the story of the death of Oedipus, a death which is not really death but the passage on to another plane of a man chosen by the gods, no one knows why, to be a hero.

The heroes were very powerful beings in Greek religion, sometimes churlishly benevolent, sometimes frankly malevolent. The hero Oedipus was patron of the village of Colonus where Sophocles had been born and grown up; where as child and boy he had prospered under the eyes of this capricious 'daemon' who dwelt in the depths of the earth. In *Oedipus at Colonus* Sophocles is seeking to fill in the gap which, for the Greeks, for the Athenian public and for himself, separated the criminal monarch driven from Thebes, the outlaw condemned to wander far and wide over the earth, on the one hand, from, on the other, the beneficent being who is leading a strange after-life on Attic soil, the god in whose shadow the poet's genius had first flowered.

The subject, then, is the death of Oedipus or, more exactly, his passage from the human plane to the divine. But because of the implicit reference to the youth of Sophocles—a peasant boyhood spent amid olive and laurel groves, with the song of nightingales and the pleasures of boating and riding—and because of the other reference to the poet's old age, heavy with conflicts and cruel griefs but bright and calm in its final serenity, this unique tragedy is the transposition into a marvellous poem of all we can perceive of the hopes that Sophocles in his last days placed in death and in the gods.

Oedipus attains his death in three stages: in the struggle with the old peasants of Colonus, in the struggle with Creon and in the struggle with his son Polyneices. In each struggle with people who want to deprive him of death, he displays an energy singular in an old man, a passion and violence which, in the last struggle— with his son—attains a well-nigh intolerable intensity.

Yet these scenes of struggle which lead us to the moment of death as to a benefit that is to be won, take place in a contrary current of joy, tenderness, friendship and confident expectation of death. The scenes of struggle are therefore connected and prepared for by scenes in which the old man gathers his strength in the midst of those he loves, Antigone, Ismene, Theseus, the king of Athens and amid the peace of nature tastes of the last joys of life while preparing himself for the death he hopes for and is waiting for. He reviews in memory the sorrows of his life, sorrows which will soon cease to hurt him. And this current of peaceful emotions leads us towards the serene end which has been promised him. Thus his death comes magnificently as the crown to his drama.

The death of Oedipus comes therefore at the end of two alternating currents of tranquillity and struggle. It is the prize of combat and the fulfilment of expectation. We are moving towards what I may call a sort of knowledge of death, if these words could have a meaning; thanks to Sophocles' art, everything happens as if they had one.

The first scene of the tragedy is full of familiar poetry and pathetic beauty. The blind old man and the barefooted girl are advancing along a stony highway. We do not know for how many years they have been wandering. The old man is weary and wants to sit down; he asks where he is. How often has this scene been enacted? Antigone describes the landscape: she sees it for her father and for us. No doubt, when the play was performed, there were trees painted on a back-cloth. Sophocles invented and used stage-scenery. But the poetry that flows from Antigone's lips gives us the true background. The girl describes the sacred wood with its laurels and wild olives and vineyard; she makes us hear the song of nightingales; we see the rocky seat by the wayside and in the distance the high walls of the citadel of Athens.

The old man sits, or rather Antigone seats him on the rock. He recovers breath. All this is indicated in the text in poignant detail. Three things, Oedipus tells his daughter, have sustained him in his ordeal: patience, or what he describes with a word that also means 'to love'; resignation, a quality that blends with the love of things and beings; and, most efficacious of all, 'firmness of soul', a nobility and generosity of nature which misfortune has not been able to mar.

A stranger now appearing on the road is questioned. He answers:

> *Man comes not here, nor dwells. The Goddesses,*
> *Dread daughters of the Earth and Darkness claim it.*

Oedipus. *What solemn name should I invoke them with?*
Stranger. *Eumenides, the Gentle Ones, all seeing—*[1]

[1] Trans. cited, pp. 60-1.

The old man starts, for in these words he recognizes the place that the oracle had promised as the scene of his death. With all the energy of the former Oedipus he declares he will not be dragged away from the spot. He claims death, which will grant him peace. The stranger goes to warn Theseus. Alone now with Antigone, Oedipus prays to the dread goddesses to have pity on him and grant him the peace of his last sleep. His body is now utterly wasted; he will quit this withered frame and die.

The sound of footsteps is now heard. It is a band of peasants of Colonus, who have been warned that strangers have entered the sacred wood and are angered at the sacrilege. Oedipus' first motion is to withdraw into the heart of the wood, and not let himself be robbed of death. The peasants watch for him at the wood's edge. But suddenly Oedipus, who is not a man to hide for long, comes out. He will defend his right to die. In response to pressing and prying questions, he proclaims his horrible identity. The Chorus of peasants tremble with horror and, forgetting their promise that they would not use violence, they cry out: 'Depart ye from our land!'[1] Oedipus is a polluted being, whom they will expel.

In this first struggle Oedipus proclaims and pleads his innocence—an attitude contrary to that of the earlier play. It seems as though, through his long sufferings and in the course of slow and sorrowful wandering, he has become conscious of it. Not that this new feeling raises him up against the gods who have smitten him; but simply that he knows two things: the gods are gods, and he is innocent. And moreover, because the gods have touched him, because each day they load him with misery, he is invested with a sacred character. Oedipus feels and says confusedly that a being smitten by the gods is beyond the reach of human hands—of the threatening hands that the peasants stretch out to seize him. His sacred body must rest in the grove of the Eumenides. Labouring under the burden of divine malediction, of pollutions unknowingly contracted, his body which is both impure and sacred (these were the same thing for primitive peoples) henceforth disposes of a new power. He is like a relic, a permanent source of blessings for those who preserve it. Oedipus proudly announces it to the peasants: by bringing his body to the dwellers in Attica, he is offering a benefit to the whole country, and to the city of Athens whose greatness he will assure.

The peasants draw back: Oedipus has won his first contest; and the drama pursues its way with numerous *péripéties*.

The most heartrending and decisive scene is that of Polyneices' supplication and his father's grim refusal to hear him. The son is now before the father— the son who had driven him out and doomed him to misery and exile. Polyneices is at first paralyzed by what he sees. This old man who drags himself along the

Ibid., p. 68.

11. *Cnossus. (Second millenium)*
12. (Overleaf, left) *Wood-carver. Cup dating from the 5th Century*
13. (Overleaf, right) *Sphinx's head. Archaic earthenware (Beginning of 6th Century)*

11

13

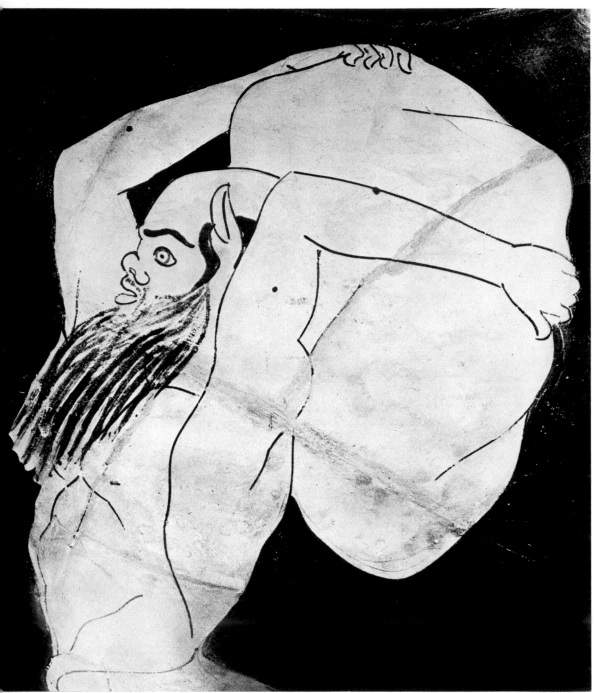

14

highways bereft of eyesight, his cheeks hollow with hunger, his hair unkempt, clad in a dirty cloak of which the filth is sticking to the filth of his old body, this wreck of a man is his father. The man whom he was proposing to supplicate, perhaps to abduct, in any case to take with him to save him from his enemies and restore him to his throne—he can no longer ask him anything: he can only confess his fault and seek pardon. He does it with a simplicity which excludes any suspicion of hypocrisy: everything in his words bears the mark of sincerity. Oedipus listens but does not reply a word. He hates this son. Polyneices, faced with this block of hatred, asks Antigone what he should do. She says: Begin again and continue. So he resumes his story, telling of the quarrel his younger brother, Eteocles, had picked with him. He is speaking not only for himself, but for his sisters and his father, whom he promises to reinstate in the palace.

But he is still confronted with the same wall of implacable rancour: Oedipus remains motionless and untamed. Finally, however, the herald asks him to reply out of deference to Theseus who had sent Polyneices. Now this malignant and unsociable being is courteous, and he replies but only out of regard for his host, and his reply is to burst into horrible imprecations. This old man so near the gates of death, so desirous of the peace of the last long sleep, does not yield an inch from his inexpiable hatred, even at this moment when he sees his prodigal and repentant son for the last time.

In numerous scenes of this long drama we see an Oedipus pacified, an Oedipus at peace conversing in happy friendship with Theseus or in the sweetness of affection with Ismene and Antigone. This appeasement of his wrath was always due to the long apprenticeship in suffering which his wretched condition has imposed on him. He has learned, while wandering on the highways, to bear his lot and adapt himself to his miserable existence. But forgiveness and forgetfulness of offences, he has not learned. He does not know how to forgive his enemies. His sons have treated him as an enemy: he returns blow for blow. He curses his sons, and of all imprecations a father's are the most terrible:

> *It may not be*
> *That thou shalt ever lay that city waste,*
> *But thou thyself shalt fall, with blood defiled;*
> *And so shall fall thy brother! Once before*
> *I breathed these curses deep upon you both....*[1]

He repeats the regular formulae so that the maledictions he has called down may act of themselves:

[1] Trans. cited, p. 110.

G

14. *Centaur. Vase-painting* (c. 480)

> *. . . but die*
> *Slain by a brother's hand, and slaying him*
> *Who drove thee forth to exile. So I curse*
> *And call on that drear dark of Tartaros,*
> *My father's home, to snatch thee from the earth,*
> *And call on these dread Powers, and I invoke*
> *Ares who stirred this fearful hate in you.*
> *Hear this and go thy way! And then proclaim*
> *. . . that Oedipus has left*
> *To both his sons such legacies as these.*

After cursing his son, the old man suddenly falls silent, he withdraws again into his stony silence, while Antigone and Polyneices weep long together. The young man at length sets out again towards his destiny. Never in the course of the play has the old man been so terrible, or perhaps further from us. He has ferociously settled his accounts with life. And now the gods are going to glorify him.

A thunderclap is heard. Oedipus recognizes the voice of Zeus who is calling him. He asks that Theseus may be brought, as Theseus alone must be present at his death and receive from him a secret he will transmit to his descendants.

Oedipus is free of all fear. As the solemn moment approaches, we feel as though he has been delivered from the weight of his wretched mortal body. His blindness is no longer an obstacle in his path: as he says to Theseus:

> *And I myself, with none to guide my steps,*
> *Will show the spot where I am doomed to die.*[1]

He feels in his limbs a light that is touching him.[2] Guided by the invisible light he makes his way into the sacred grove, followed by his daughters and Theseus. The Chorus sings of eternal sleep. And now a messenger returns. 'Is he then dead?' asks the Chorus. The man does not know how to reply. He relates the last words of Oedipus and how he had bade farewell to his daughters. The old man had then plunged further into the wood, accompanied only by Theseus. A voice had resounded in the sky, the thunder had rolled once more. The others had moved away. When they came back,

> *. . . lo! we saw*
> *The man no more; but he, the king, was there,*
> *Holding his hand to shade his eyes, as one*
> *To whom there comes a vision drear and dread*

---

[1] Trans. cited, p. 115.
[2] 'O Light! to me all dark, thou once wast mine,
    And now this body feels thy ray's last touch,
    Now, and no more' (p. 116).

He may not bear to look on. Yet awhile,
But little, and we see him bowed to earth,
Adoring it, and in the self-same prayer
Olympos, home of Gods.[1]

How has Oedipus died? None know. Is he dead? And what is death? Is there a connexion between Oedipus' life and this extraordinary death? And if so, what? Though we cannot answer all these questions, we have the feeling that, in this strange death by which the hero vanishes in a light too dazzling for mortal eyes, the gods have on behalf of Oedipus broken the course of natural law. The death of Oedipus seems, for example to Nietzche, to found a new world, one in which there would be no more destiny.

To interpret the *Oedipus at Colonus* is a difficult task. We must first recall the important difference between this tragedy and the *Oedipus Rex*. In the older play, Oedipus had confessed his fault and assumed the whole responsibility. Throughout the second play and in face of most of the characters, he protests his innocence. He claims that this case is one of fair self-defence, which, before an Athenian court, would entail a verdict of acquittal.

But this contradiction between the two dramas, apart from the fact that it can be justified by the space of time in Oedipus' life that separates the actions, is only one of appearance. For this there are several reasons. The most important is that the Oedipus of the second drama is defending his innocence only from the point of view of human logic and human law. He is speaking to men who have to make a ruling as to his fate; he wants to obtain justice and protection. He asserts that just men have no right to condemn him, and that he is humanly innocent. His innocence therefore is envisaged in relation to the laws of human society: he is 'innocent according to the law'. But it is not affirmed in an absolute way; if it were, the new consciousness that Oedipus would have of it would be expressed in a reversal of his attitude toward the gods. His respect for their action in his own life, that mixture of terror and adoration which he experiences in the *Oedipus Rex* at having been chosen to illustrate the divine omnipotence, would give place to a feeling of rebellion at having been smitten in spite of his innocence. But nothing of the kind appears in the second drama. Here, exactly as in the *Oedipus Rex*, he proclaims the intervention of the gods in his life, and he does so with simplicity, in the same passages as those which maintain his human innocence. ('For so the gods have willed', or, 'The gods have guided all things.') There is no acrimony in Oedipus, in either play. In the *Oedipus at Colonus* as in the *Oedipus Rex* he displays the same detachment with the same objective attitude.

[1] Trans. cited, p. 120.

I come as I have come, yet knowing naught.
The gods, who knew, have brought about my fall.

The words 'innocent' or 'guilty' are too human. The fall of Oedipus simply proves his own ignorance and the gods' omniscience.

But, at the end of the *Oedipus Rex* as throughout the *Oedipus at Colonus*, it is only from the gods and never from his own merits, that the stricken king awaits his deliverance. His salvation depends on a free decision of the gods. The concept of salvation that is manifest in our drama confirms, therefore, and presents in a wholly new way the concept of fault and punishment as manifested in the first tragedy. Oedipus no more deserves his salvation than he had desired his fault or deserved his punishment. It is quite evident that the apotheosis which completes the drama and sets a crown on the destiny of Oedipus can in no way be interpreted as reward for a moral attitude.

So it is not the king's innocence, or his repentance or his pardoning his sons, that determine the benevolent intervention of the gods. One circumstance alone seems to have decided them: the extent of his misfortunes.

One may now try to define the religious meaning of the *Oedipus at Colonus* without forgetting that of the *Oedipus Rex*. In the *Oedipus Rex* the king was smitten not for a personal fault but as a man who is ignorant but who acts, by virtue of the law which is encountered by every active being. His only fault lay in his existence, in the necessity in which man finds himself of acting in a world whose laws he does not know. The condemnation that smote him, a condemnation divested of any punitive character, smote only the active man. The *Oedipus at Colonus* shows us that there exists in the universe another law, of which the gods are guardians, and which is complementary to the preceding one: the law which serves the suffering man. The elevation of Oedipus to the rank of the heroes is not granted him personally as a reward for his merits and virtue: it is given by an act of grace to the sufferer. As in the first drama Oedipus had been perfection in action, he has, as we see him at Colonus, reached the extreme point of human suffering. I have no need to enumerate his woes or establish the details of his suffering. A single line in the first scene is enough to remind us of the abyss of misery into which this man born to act and rule has fallen. In his exhaustion he says to Antigone: 'Place me then here, and o'er the blind man watch.'[1] The contrast of this image of the old man weaker than a child is of a piece with the image of the king, protector and saviour of his people, that was offered us at the beginning of *Oedipus Rex*.

Now it is this old man overwhelmed by fate, this sufferer, whom the gods are

---

[1] Trans. cited, p. 60.

going to save, whom they have chosen to glorify, not so much on account of the way he has endured his woes as in order to manifest their signal power. Not only will he be saved, but himself will become a saviour. His polluted body will be invested with a singular virtue: he will give victory to the people and prosperity to the land. Why has he been chosen? We do not exactly know, unless it is because he was suffering. Once again the gods are gods, and their grace is freely given.

Scarcely do we perceive that in the mystery of the universe there exists for Sophocles a kind of law of compensation. If the gods smite Oedipus without reason, if they raise him again without reason, it is still the same man who is now smitten, now raised. When Oedipus is astonished at hearing from Ismene of the oracle that confers this salutary power on his body, Ismene replies: 'The Gods did vex thee once, they prosper now.'[1] Ismene does not formulate this remark as law; but it seems that Sophocles wishes to enable us just to perceive that in the heart of the universe there is not only the hard indifference of the gods, but also a clemency, and that the same man may in the course of his life encounter both. The messenger says of Oedipus:

> *What form of death*
> *He died knows no man, but our Theseus only.*
>
> .   .   .   .
>
> *But either someone whom the Gods had sent,*
> *To guide his steps, or else the abyss of earth*
> *In friendly mood had opened wide its jaws*
> *Without one pang. . . .*[2]

The death of Oedipus represents neither the purification of the guilty nor the justification of the innocent. It is simply the peace that follows life's combats, the repose to which some god guides our steps.

Sophocles knows, without being disturbed by the knowledge, that death is the only possible fulfilment of a human life. Man is born for suffering. Oedipus says: 'In suffering was I born.' To live is to risk suffering. But the temporal nature which exposes us to it also accomplishes our liberation. Oedipus prays to the goddesses in the sacred grove:

> *But, O ye Powers,*
> *Grant me, according to Apollo's voice,*
> *An issue and completion of my life;*
> *Unless it chance I seem too low for this,*
> *Of all mankind the most enslaved to ills.*[3]

[1] *Ibid.*, p. 73.   [2] *Ibid.*, p. 120.   [3] *Ibid.*, p. 63.

Oedipus speaks as a good servant who has well accomplished his task of suffering. He claims his wages, which are the peace of death.

Sophocles seems to ask nothing more of death than this peace which is the hidden source of life. No personal immortality seems to him necessary, simply he does not speak of it. The meaning he gives to Oedipus' death appears to him sufficient because the gods will that it should be so. Once again we are brought back to the rock of Sophocles' faith: to admit what is.

The poet, however, here turns our attention to another aspect of Being. If the gods are perfidious or indifferent enough to human life and happiness to allow one of them to set the abominable trap which we see in Oedipus' life, their varying indifference also comprises goodness, among its many choices. They have changed their mood as a woman changes her dress: after the dress coloured with blood and conflagrations, the dress which has the colour of Time.

The colour is perhaps less tragic but more human; and after all we are men, which is why the whole drama interests and holds us by a more tender cord. The sky has changed, and has taken on, for once, a human aspect. Hence, in the play, so many quiet moments of calm intercourse, so many friendly presences, so much attentive serenity; hence too the bright beauty of trees and horses, of birds singing or on the wing, of cooing doves. And then there is the long, long life of Oedipus, and of Sophocles, a life which, in spite of everything, has flowed on day by day and been breathed in as one drinks when thirsty.

Every mark of friendship or intention to reassure, in the *Oedipus Rex,* had an ironical background and only a mortal meaning. In the *Oedipus at Colonus* the slow preparation for the hero's death is at moments so full of kindly friendship that these human attentions, which unite by chance with the divine goodness, at last impart to the drama as a whole, the drama of Oedipus' death, a sense of life.

This sense of life is present throughout the tragedy. It is woven constantly into the fabric of the play, like the scarlet thread woven into the white sails of the old-time English ships, which, in case of shipwreck, enabled searchers to reach the scene of disaster. Thus this drama of death contains a precious and constant value of life; but all this culminates at the end in the signal gift which the gods grant to Oedipus' mortal remains.

He has been chosen by the gods to become, after death, an exemplary image of human life, woeful and courageous, a kind of life-force that will defend the soil of Attica for ever. As he has been, so he will remain. He had been vindictive to the point of pronouncing malediction on his son. But this feature is in harmony with his new character as a hero. Of heroes, a certain scholar has written: 'These superior beings are eminently injurious powers. When they assist they at the same time hurt, and they lend their aid only on condition of doing harm.'

The immortality of the hero Oedipus is in no way his personal immortality in a distant beyond, but on the contrary the duration, on the very spot where he finished his course, of an exceptional power granted by the gods to his mortal body in its tomb, and to his anger against the enemies of the Athenian community. Oedipus no longer exists, his personal and historic existence is over; but the warm blood of his enemies, flowing on this soil of Colonus, will one day warm his icy corpse with passion. He desires it, he declares it in the very heart of the drama. His personal destiny is henceforth at an end; but his tomb subsists in a place where the active power of the gods manifests itself on Attic soil.

If he has, again, any human existence, this is far less personal than collective. He will exist to the extent in which Theseus, his people and their descendants remember and make use of him. His existence is therefore closely bound up with that of the community of which the gods have made him the protector. This public meaning in the death of Oedipus comes out very clearly in the last instructions the old man gives his daughters. He insists strongly that they shall not be present at his death; only Theseus, the head of the State, will be present and will transmit to his successors the secret that Oedipus will confide to his keeping. Thus the death of Oedipus is no longer his own, any more than it belongs to those he has loved more than anyone in the world will ever love them. It is not a private affair, but one that belongs to Athens and the Athenian king. And lastly, its meaning is one of life and of Athenian public life. It is not the end of Oedipus' story, but a pledge of duration for the people who will venerate him.

And now Oedipus has joined the company of heroes who protect and defend Athens and Greece: heroes consecrated by genius, Homer, Hesiod, Archilochus, Sappho, Aeschylus. Very soon Sophocles too will take his place in this constellation of bright presences that watch over the Athenian people. Men sometimes contrive to force the hand of destiny and install themselves in the heroic heavens by dint of genius or misfortune. Oedipus and Sophocles have equal right to a place there.

Such is the poet's last reply to the question which the legend of Oedipus had set before him in childhood and which he only solved at the end of his life, when he was facing the gates of death, now open to receive him.

CHAPTER FIVE

PINDAR, PRINCE OF POETS
AND POET OF PRINCES

P indar, I fear, will soon be accessible only to a few specialists in Greek studies. This 'singer of coachmen and boxing-matches', as Voltaire called him—insultingly and very inaccurately, choosing the meanest words that he thought could be applied to him—this great lyricist whose imagination was fired by victories in sport and athletics, could scarcely today raise the enthusiasms of the crowd, even if 'hands and the virtue of feet' have recaptured the place they had long since lost in popular favour.

In this work in which everything proceeds by choice, as a matter of chance or calculation, I might have 'forgotten' Pindar, as I shall forget many other spirits of an amplitude equal to his. But many reasons have stayed my hand. I did not wish to limit this work almost entirely to certain aspects of Ionian or Athenian civilization. I wished also to touch on those high poetical values produced by the rest of Greece and notably by the countries which had remained faithful to an aristocratic régime; and I wished also to do justice to Dorian Greece, of which Sparta and Thebes were the head. Apart from that I could not agree to refuse my readers the keen pleasure of loving Pindar's brilliant verse in the enthusiastic way in which Ronsard loved it. With Aeschylus and Aristophanes this dazzling singer is one of the three masters of the Greek poetical language, which is naturally untranslatable. Lastly, this poet whose strange profession consisted in the celebration of sporting victories by means of choral song was, by this very profession, placed in touch with very great personages, such as Hieron tyrant of Syracuse, Theron tyrant of Acragas and Arcesilas king of Cyrene. He lived at the court of one or other of them and became their counsellor and friend: an unusually independent counsellor even when warmly praising, a friend capable of speaking the truth to the prince he is celebrating. There is greatness in such a man.

How should we acquaint ourselves with his work? We have no other means of understanding him than by accosting him directly in the exercise of his profession in a few selected odes, and by seeing how he mingles in a 'fine' but only apparent 'disorder',[1] which is but a paradoxical and calculated order, the mythical themes of epic poetry which he treats in his own way, the themes he borrows from Hesiod's didactic writing or from that of other old poets, and those he draws from the lyrical effusions in which he speaks of himself and his verses. To understand him means, in fact, approaching him, as far as that is possible in a French commentary,[2] in his strange expressions which are at once very indirect and the most direct that can be, in the prodigiously but naturally metaphorical style in which he writes.

Here then are a few of his odes. It will be seen that they are composed and, if one may say so, deduced from a few simple propositions which are rigorously but subtly linked together.

◎

The first of his triumphal odes, the Tenth Pythian, though not one of his masterpieces, deserves special study because in it we see the whole of Pindar. The main features of his thought, his unshakeable religious faith, his devotion to Apollo, his admiration for Sparta and the aristocratic régimes, his praise of inherited virtue, the primacy he sees in the felicity of great athletes, lastly the calculated disorder of the composition and the brightly flashing density of the style—here are the essentials of the ode and here the whole of Pindar is, so to speak, announced.

He had been born at Thebes, and in 498 B.C.—the moment in question—he was twenty years old. Thanks no doubt to the connexions of his noble family—an old family of priests of Apollo and colonizers—he was commissioned to write an epinician ode to celebrate a friend of the Aleuadae, princes of Thessaly. The victor, whose name was Hippocleas, had won the prize in the double-stadium foot-race for boys at Delphi—in that stadium which is still intact and where it is so good to walk in the bracing air. Pindar travelled to Thessaly, was entertained by the prince and directed the performance of his Chorus.

The ode opens with words that might serve as epigraph for a large portion of Pindar's work: 'Happy is Lacedaemon!'[3] The poet insists here on the kinship between Sparta and Thessaly, both governed by descendants of Heracles, of the great Theban whom he is constantly celebrating as the model of heroic virtue. Then he goes on to eulogize the young runner; and in this connexion he develops one of his favourite themes, namely that, as in other noble families, 'his inborn

---

[1] *'Un beau désordre est souvent un effet de l'art'* is a remark of Boileau's (Translator).

[2] Or rather 'English' in these circumstances (Translator).

[3] *The Odes of Pindar* . . . with an Introduction and an English Translation by Sir John Sandys. London and Cambridge, Mass., The Loeb Classical Library, 1937, p. 289. The passages from Pindar that follow are also quoted from this version.

valour hath trodden in the foot prints of his father',[1] that is to say that physical exploits as well as moral virtue are part of what one inherits from one's ancestors. Then comes the theme of the athlete's happiness. He who is victorious in the games, he who sees his son victorious—'The brazen heaven he cannot climb; but, as for all the bright achievements which we mortals attain, he reacheth the utmost limit of that voyage.'[2] The myth, which occupies the centre of the ode, now emerges abruptly; the word 'happiness'[3] has been enough to release it. The myth is that of the happy Hyperboreans: it was an old popular belief that beyond the northern mountains, whence comes Boreas, there dwell a blessed people: it is with them that Apollo, the god dear to Pindar, sojourns in winter, and from thence he returns in spring, flying on his winged tripod.

The myth, without being related, is simply suggested in lively images and by fleeting but striking allusions. It seems like a dream unfinished yet open to the imagination, and in which visions in armfuls carry the dreamer in every direction. Thus we suddenly see Perseus appearing at a banquet of the Hyperboreans. He finds them sacrificing prodigious hecatombs of asses to Apollo, who, the poet tells us, is pleased by the sacrifice of these lewd beasts. In his abrupt manner, Pindar writes: 'Apollo . . . laugheth as he looketh on the brute beasts in their rampant lewdness.'[4] It may be observed that this kind of sacrifice was an exotic feature; the Greeks never made such offerings to their gods. At this point however the poet immediately adds that from the copious feasts of this happy people 'the Muse is not banished, but, on every side, the dances of maidens and the sounds of the lyre and the notes of the flute are ever circling'.[5]

Other features provide a contrast. This Perseus, who makes his appearance among the Hyperboreans, is the hero who aforetime had slain the Gorgon: he still holds in his hand that 'head that glittered with serpent-locks, to slay the islanders by turning them into stone'.[6] But, adds the poet, 'as for me, in the handi-work of the gods, nothing ever seemeth too incredible for wonder'.[7]

---

[1] *Ibid.* The father of Hippocleas, whose name is unknown (unless it was Phricias—though Phricias ('Bristler') was probably his horse—had previously won the foot-race in armour on two occasions at Olympia (Sandys, p. 291, note 1).

[2] *Ibid.,* p. 291.

[3] By speaking of 'the utmost limit' of mortal happiness, Pindar prepares his hearers to think of the utmost northern limit of the world—the country of the 'happy' Hyperboreans—a daring and unexpected transition (Translator).

[4] Trans. cited, p. 291.   [5] *Ibid.,* p. 293.

[6] *Ibid.* These islanders were dwellers on Seriphus, whose king, Polydectes, tried to deceive the chieftains into making him presents for a marriage he did not intend to arrange. When Perseus offered him the head of Medusa, the Gorgon, he accepted it and was turned into stone (Translator).

[7] P. 293.

The poet leaves the myth at this point, and, by means of another image, defines his own art of composition: 'For the blossom of these hymns of praise flitteth, like a bee, from theme to theme.' He adds a word for Hippocleas. 'I may, with my strains of minstrelsy, cause Hippocleas . . . to be looked upon with a sweet care by the young maidens.'[1]

◎

There is another work of Pindar's youth—he was thirty at the time—an ode that contains no myth but is a simple prayer to deities who were very near the poet's heart. This is the Fourteenth Olympian in which he also celebrates the victory of a boy, this time in the short foot-race. The ode, brief as it is, reveals the deep source of the poet's inspiration, in his love of the Graces. He begins by designating the three types of men whom they have favoured: 'For, by your aid, all things pleasant and sweet are accomplished for mortals, if any man be skilled in song, or be fair to look upon, or hath won renown.' Now these three blessings— genius, beauty, glory—are but gifts of the Graces. They direct all things:

Yea, not even the gods order the dance or the banquet, without the aid of the holy Graces . . . their thrones are set beside the Lord of the golden bow, the Pythian Apollo, and . . . they adore the everflowing honour of the Olympian Father.[2]

The poet now names the Graces: 'O queen Aglaia' (Aglaia dispenses glory) 'and Euphrosyne, that lovest the dance and song' (Euphrosyne means wisdom; and in Pindar's eyes all wisdom is poetry) . . . 'and thou Thalia, that art enamoured of the song and dance,' (Thalia is the Grace who gives Beauty, Youth and Joy) 'when thou hast looked upon this triumphant chorus, as it lightly steppeth along. . . . For I have come to sing the praise of Asopichus . . . because, thanks to thee, the house of the Minyae is victorious in Olympia.'[3] The young athlete is an orphan, so the poet invokes the nymph Echo in these words:

Now! hie thee, Echo, to the dark-walled home of Persephone, and bear the glorious tidings to the father, so that . . . thou mayest tell him that, beside the famous vale of Pisa, his son hath crowned his youthful locks with garlands won from the ennobling games.[4]

Thus everything in the event that is being celebrated is presented as the work of the Graces. Pindar's kingdom is not that of sensual pleasure. He never paid the

---

[1] *Ibid.*
[2] Trans. cited, p. 147.
[3] *Ibid.*, pp. 147, 149. Asopichus came from Orchemonus, where the worship of the Graces had long been established (see Sir John Sandys' introductory note, p. 145).
[4] P. 149.

slightest tribute to the kind of man the Greeks called the 'epaphroditon', which means the 'seductive' man. He celebrated the graceful or 'epichari': his kingdom was that of Grace.

◎

The last years of Pindar's youth were marked by a grave crisis in the history of the Greek people, the crisis that opened in 490 B.C. and recurred in 480 and 479, that of the Persian Wars. It must be clearly stated that Pindar did not understand the meaning of these wars in Greek history, or he only understood afterwards and with difficulty. He was nearly thirty in the year of Marathon, and nearly forty at the time of Salamis and Plataea. Of the first Persian war there is no echo in his surviving work, important as the latter is. It is not that the name of Marathon is absent; it recurs several times but is always connected with the mention of some sporting victory that has been won by an athlete whom the poet is celebrating. Marathon for him is not the scene of a victory for liberty, but the name of a sports' ground. As for many Parisians no doubt the names of battles and even French poets are only métro-stations.

To grasp the meaning of Pindar's odes one must understand that in his eyes the value of a sporting victory was at least equal to that of a military victory, especially to that of Marathon where the Athenian people saved a democratic liberty which for him had a very mediocre value. Man's freedom and dignity consist, first, in the possession of his body. For him, the 'fair limbs of youth' are one of the essential attainments of human life, they are attained at the cost of a continuous act of will, of an unflagging moral and physical asceticism.

We now come to the year of Salamis, when Pindar was approaching the age of forty. We know the decision that was taken by Thebes: she hastened to the service of the occupying power. The Greek historians, from Herodotus to Polybius, are unanimous: Thebes betrayed Greece. Polybius writes that 'the Thebans refused to go to war in the cause of the Greeks and took the side of the Persians' and that 'there is no reason to praise the poet Pindar who made it known in a poem that it was necessary to maintain peace'.[1] Thus, at the moment when other Greek cities were demanding of their populations the sternest sacrifices—evacuation of the territory which was abandoned to fire and devastation, and the conduct of war far from their own people—Pindar was preaching non-resistance to his compatriots. The words he uses in two of the verses of this poem that have been preserved seem to indicate that he was addressing the people who wished to fight, in order to

---

[1] This may be fragment 109 (ed. Sandys, pp. 578, 579). It is an appeal for peace and internal unity (Translator).

persuade them to accept the aristocrats' policy, the assiduous reception offered by the oligarchy to the Persians.

There is truly something strange in the spectacle of Pindar, the singer of athletes and old-time heroes, remaining insensible, at this time of catastrophe, to the drama of liberty that was being enacted before his eyes. Did a victory in boxing or in the pancratium stir him more deeply than Salamis?

Later on, Pindar certainly had fits of repentance; but always, when speaking of Salamis, in a tone of embarrassment. This tone subsists in the Eighth Isthmian ode which he addressed, a few years after the victory, to one of his Aeginetan friends. He speaks insistently of the 'ordeal' of Greece. He claims the right to invoke the Muse:

Yet, now that we are set free from mighty woes, let us not fall into any lack of festal garlands, nor do thou brood over sorrows.

But the peril has passed:

. . . inasmuch as the trouble that Hellas could not brook, the stone of Tantalus above our head, hath now been turned aside for us by one of the gods . . . man has hanging over him a treacherous time that maketh crooked the path of life. Yet even this may be healed for mortals, if only they have freedom.

The passage as a whole is far from constituting a eulogy of the victors of Salamis. It is not a question of victory and glory, but of trial and mourning. Only towards the end does the poet speak the language of those who had saved Greece. He recognizes, implicitly not explicitly, that the freedom he retains he owes to those who have fought for her. The trial, he says by way of excuse, was beyond the courage of the Greeks;[1] which is true of the Thebans' courage but not of the Athenians'. Pindar in fact renders thanks to God, and to God alone, for the happy outcome. Herodotus, who was scarcely less pious than Pindar, puts things in their right place when he says: 'It would not be departing from truth to say that the Athenians were the liberators of Hellas: it was they who, at least after the gods, repulsed the Great King.'

Let us leave aside other marks of repentance.[2] Pindar who praised the bravery of

---

[1] If, as I presume, this refers to verse 11: 'ἀτόλματον Ἑλλάδι μόχθον', then the plain meaning of the words is: 'a toil unendurable for Hellas'. This is the *first* meaning of ἀτόλματος given by Liddell and Scott. Sandys also interprets it in this sense—'the trouble that Hellas could not brook'. It *could* mean a trouble 'not to be dared', but this sense does not fit the context, because he is praising Aegina, and the Aeginetans *had* dared it. Everything suggests that Pindar meant 'a trouble that Hellas could not endure (but resisted and threw off)'—Translator.

[2] One should not forget the great passage in the Fifth Isthmian (for Phylacidas of Aegina), *Full many an arrow hath my . . . tongue to ring out in praise of those heroes; and even now could the land of Aias (Aegina) attest in war that she was saved from falling by her sailors, yes, Salamis, in*

the Aeginetans at Salamis, always neglected to praise the eminent Panhellenic part played by Athens during these decisive years in the formation of Greek genius.[1] Nothing in his education or in his genius prepared him to understand the city which was already become the seat of scientific research, of 'philosophy'.

In this first half of the fifth century the intellectual climate of Athens, as compared with Thebes, was one of 'wisdom', a climate in which religion did not fear the approach of reason. Pindar always detested that. The problems that Ionian and Athenian scientists set themselves appeared to him the vainest thing in the world; they were people who, according to him, 'gather the unripe fruit of wisdom'. Pindar—and this explains his lack of friendship for Athens—was a man who, even in the middle of the fifth century, remained untouched by philosophy. The problems considered by the Ionian scientists (what is the world made of? What produces eclipses of the sun?), such problems had been long since solved by a poet of his own country, Hesiod, and by the religion of Apollo. The phenomena examined by the scientist were, in his eyes, miracles of the gods: there was no question to be asked about them.

◎

Let us now take some of our poet's major odes, the Sixth Olympian, for example. It was written for the Syracusan Hagesias, one of Hieron's principal officers, a very great personage.

The family of Hagesias were Iamids: they claimed descent from Apollo and from Euadné, a Peloponnesian nymph who was herself the daughter of Poseidon and Pitané, a nymph of the Eurotas. The Iamids were therefore descended from two great gods, and they exercised priestly functions at Olympia. But Hagesias, who had gone to try his luck in Syracuse, had had a brilliant career at the court of Hieron. Pindar's epinician ode celebrated his victory in the mule chariot-race at Olympia. The ode was first presented not far from Olympia, at Stymphalus in Arcadia, the home of Hagesias' mother, and a second time at Syracuse.

The ode is divided into three unequal parts. The first is a eulogy of the victory. This is supported by a splendid image which serves as overture to the whole poem. We see a magnificent palace being built; the porch dazzles us with its golden

the ruinous, heaven-sent storm . . . (verses 46–50: Trans. cited, p. 477).
Here he renders honour for the victory to the Aeginetan navy. It is true that he adds that one should not boast, as 'Zeus giveth _this_, and giveth _that_ . . .'. See also the First Pythian, verse 77 (Translator).

[1] This overlooks the great Dithyramb (Fragments 76, 77, 78: ed. Sandys, pp. 556–7) in honour of Athens, 'bulwark of Hellas . . . city divine', in recognition of which the Athenians presented him with a handsome gift, set up his statue in the city, and appointed him _proxenus_, or consul, at Thebes (Translator).

pillars that shine to the horizon. Now the palace is the ode, and the colonnade is the glory of Hagesias who is both seer and Olympic champion. This opening portion of the ode is full of brilliant allusions, including the one to another warrior-seer, a hero whom Zeus honoured by causing the earth to open and swallow up him and his mares: he was a popular Theban hero, and later Pan-hellenic hero. The opening of the poem is like a dense grove of mingled images, illumined by the sun's rays.

To reach the second and most important part of the hymn, namely the myth, Pindar asks the driver of Hagesias' chariot to

yoke me the sturdy mules with all good speed, that so we may set our car in the clear and open path of song, and that I may at last arrive at the theme of the descent of our heroes. . . .

Therefore is it meet for us to ope for them the portals of song. . . .[1]

We shall now learn from the poet, a believer, the story of two seductions effected by gods. On the banks of Eurotas there once lived the young nymph, Pitanó. Mingled with Poseidon, she 'is said to have borne Euadné of the violet tresses. But she, with the folds of her robe, concealed the fruit of her unwedded love.' Thereafter she sent the child, conceived of the god, to the banks of another river, the Alpheüs; and here Euadné grew up 'and first tasted the sweets of love in the arms of Apollo'.[2] The father[3] went to consult the oracle about this intolerable and splendid disaster.

Meanwhile, she laid down her crimson zone and her silver pitcher, and 'neath the blue brake was about to bear a boy inspired of heaven; and the Lord of the golden hair sent to her aid the gentle goddess of birth, and the Fates; and from her womb, and amid sweet sorrow, forthwith came Iamus to the light of day. And she, though sore distressed, was fain to leave him there upon the ground; but, by the will of the gods, two grey-eyed serpents tended the babe with the bane, the harmless bane, of the honey-bees.[4]

The reader will have noted the paradoxical expressions that confer on Pindar's style its peculiar colouring; expressions such as 'harmless bane'.

(Aepytus now returns from Delphi, where he has learned that Euadné's child was begotten of Apollo and is destined to become a great prophet. He 'inquired of all in the house, touching the child'; but they had not seen it—Translator),[5]

---

[1] Trans. cited, p. 57.
[2] *Ibid.*
[3] Aepytus, king of Arcadia, was foster-father of Euadné (Translator).
[4] Trans. cited, p. 59.
[5] I have inserted these details in order to explain what follows (Translator).

though it had been born five days before: and no marvel; for it had been hidden amid the rushes and in the boundless brake, with its dainty form steeped in the golden and the deep purple light of pansies; therefore it was that his mother declared that he should be called for all time by the undying name of Iamus.[1]

These flowers, with their rays of gold and purple were wild pansies, which in Greek are called *ion*, a word that also designates the violet.

From Delphi, Apollo claims his son; and the last scene of the myth shows us what we should call the baptism or consecration of the young boy:

. . . when he had attained the ripe bloom of Hebe of the golden crown, he stepped down into the midst of the Alpheus, and there invoked his grandsire Poseidon that ruleth afar, and the Archer that watcheth over heaven-built Delos, praying that his head might be crowned with honour, and with the care of the people. There, in the night, he stood beneath the open sky; and in accents clear his father's voice replied to him, and sought him out: 'Arise, my son, and follow thou my voice, and hither come to a haunt that welcometh all!' And so they went to the steep rock of the lofty hill of Cronus, where the god gave him a double boon of prophecy. . . .[2]

One realizes the supreme brilliance of such poetry. With its unusual movement it floods us, like the flowers the poet evokes, with rays of gold and purple. It shines like sunlight and again it glitters like a changing rainbow.

The last part of the ode brings us back to the present time, to a eulogy of the victor, which is also a eulogy of Pindar's verse. Taking up a coarse sarcasm of the Athenians regarding Boeotian lack of culture, a sarcasm which must have touched him to the quick, he (calls on Aeneas, the trainer of his Chorus) 'to know whether in very truth we have escaped the old reproach that telleth of "Boeotian swine" '.[3] His poem is a reply to the insult. He declares that he is inspired; in a language enigmatic and full of secret meanings, he says: 'Methinks I have upon my tongue a whetstone shrill, that stealeth over me, nothing loth, with fair streams of inspiration.'[4] And then, addressing the chorus-leader who is to accompany Hagesias to his new home and there direct the presentation of the ode, he cries:

For thou art a faithful messenger, a very scroll-wand of the fair-haired Muses, a sweet wassail-bowl of loudly-sounding songs.[5]

The last verse of the ode is a prayer to the Lord of the Ocean (to grant a safe voyage and) to

give new growth to the gladsome flower of my songs.[6]

[1] Trans. cited, pp. 59, 61.   [2] *Ibid.*, p. 61.   [3] *Ibid.*, p. 65.
[4] *Ibid.*, p. 63.   [5] *Ibid.*, p. 65.   [6] Verse 105. *Ibid.*, p. 67.

15. *Daughter embracing her father. Cup of Douris* (c. 480)

One need scarcely comment or explain the connexion between the three parts of the poem: the eulogy of the victor, the myth, the good wishes for the victor and prayers for the poet. These elements, based on historical reasons, are clear enough but external to the poetry. The connexion is not one of transitions or circumstances, but is internal to the poetry of the ode. I have suggested it in passing.

The golden pillars before the porch of the hymn, the mules speeding along the sunlit track, then the flood of the central images: the woman with the crimson zone who bears the child of a god, the babe's flesh bathed with the light of field-flowers, the night-sky that overlooks the scene of baptism in the Alpheüs, and, at the end, the 'shrill whetstone' on the poet's tongue and the secret language of the fair-haired Muses—all this makes up a unique poem, a sort of half-frenzied vision, a poetry at once familiar and celestial, composed of strange images and dream-shapes, which, in the onrush of a style that animates the whole, confers on the work an indescribable continuity. A style is born and from the first verse to the last, unfolds like a rare and marvellous blossom.

Pindar crossed to Sicily more than once. Living in close touch with Theron of Acragas and Hieron of Syracuse, he vied with the great Simonides, and with Bacchylides, in singing their praise. More than that: he was their counsellor and friend, and in the difficult part he thus had to play, he addressed to them the strongest moral exhortations, based on his own religious faith which girded him with every kind of courage. Thus some notable commissions, which he might have had, went to Bacchylides who was more accommodating.

The Third Pythian shows us the intimacy of his relations with Hieron. It is not, properly speaking, an epinician ode but a personal letter written by the poet; not on the occasion of a sporting victory but of an attack of gravel from which Hieron was suffering. Thus it is a friend's letter of consolation to a sick man.

He begins by regretting that the centaur Cheiron who, according to the old tradition, was the father of medicine and the master of Aesculapius, is no longer alive. Then he relates the birth of the god of medical science, Asklepios (Aesculapius). This was the story of the loves of Apollo and the nymph Coronis. This nymph was of wayward imagination:

. . . she was enamoured of things otherwhere—that passion, which many, ere now, have felt. For, among men, there is a foolish company of those who, putting shame on their home, cast their glances afar, and pursue idle dreams in hopes that shall not be fulfilled.

H

16. *Olive-trees growing in the old gymnasium at Delphi*

She was exposed, in short, to the most hazardous circumstance. She, who 'bare within her the pure seed of the god', had not the patience to await the marriage which, according to custom, Apollo promised to prepare for her, for

she slept in the couch of a stranger who came from Arcadia; but she escaped not the ken of the watchful god; for, although he was then at the sacrificial shrine of Pytho, yet Loxias, the king of the temple, perceived it in his mind that knoweth all things, with his thought convinced by an unerring prompter.[1]

He caused the faithless one to be chastized by his sister Artemis, who pierced her with arrows.

The body of Coronis was already laid on the funeral pyre, surrounded by her kinsmen, and the wild flames of Hephaestus were playing around it when the god, suddenly remembering the child, cried out: 'No longer can I endure in my heart to slay my own child by a death most piteous. . . .'[2] He stepped forward; the flames opened before him and he snatched the child from his mother's body. He confided him to Cheiron who was to make him a physician. Such is the story of the birth of Asklepios.

Apart from the natural link between this myth of the god of medicine and the sick man to whom the story is related, the character of Coronis suggests a discreet but precise lesson for Hieron. The poet insists on the dangers of a chimerical fancy, on the error that consists in pursuing phantoms; and it is in this sense that he develops his exhortations at the end of the ode.

Pindar continues the narrative with a magnificent picture of the career of Asklepios. We see the procession of sick and wounded, some suffering from ulcers, other having been wounded with spear or sling-stone, others wasted away with fevers, from 'summer's heat or winter's cold', but all cured and delivered by operation or remedy.

But Asklepios allowed himself to be tempted by the unrealizable. He wished to force the hand of nature by snatching from death a man whom nature had condemned.[3] Without hesitation the thunderbolt of Zeus struck down both doctor and patient in the death that destiny had willed.

We now return to the train of reflexions inspired by the portrait of Coronis. We should not seek the impossible but consider 'what lieth before our feet'. And what is this? To know 'of what estate we are'. Here the poet utters valiant and splendid words:

---

[1] Trans. cited, p. 187.   [2] *Ibid.*, p. 189.

[3] But also he was 'enthralled by the love of gain; even he was seduced, by a splendid fee of gold laid upon his palm, to bring back from death one who was its lawful prey'. (Trans. cited, p. 191)—Translator.

Seek not, my soul, the life of the immortals; but enjoy to the full the resources that are within thy reach.[1]

Such is the counsel he has the courage to proffer to a sick man. No doubt Asklepios effected many cures. But remember that thou must die, and meanwhile act. But Pindar does not suggest this lesson in the tone of a lesson. He does not say: 'Do this. Hope not for that.' It is to himself that he says: 'Seek not, my soul. . . .' This indirect speech is dictated by tact as much as by friendship.

After establishing these terms of confidence and intimacy between the prince and himself, Pindar completes his words of exhortation. He even speaks of resignation. Thou hast enjoyed the favour of the gods, he says, thou art the prince and leader of the people. It is true that life for thee has not always been cloudless. But thou art not alone: think on the heroes of the past. Which leads to this maxim for the conduct of life:

. . . if any mortal hath in mind the course things take in very truth ('truth' with Pindar often means 'reality'), right it is for one, who hath received favour from the blessed ones, to enjoy his lot. Yet changeful are the breezes of the winds that blow on high.[2]

The language was well suited to Hieron, a man of a very realistic and positive cast of mind; he was not unaware of the law of vicissitude.

In the concluding verses Pindar returns to speak of his own lot, as if he feared that he had sermonized Hieron too directly.

Small shall I be, when small is my estate, and great, when it is great.

Proudly he declares that he too knows greatness. It is the poet's songs that confer glory. He lets it be understood that if great power like Hieron's is rare, a great poet like himself is no less rare. For a moment we seem to hear, as by anticipation, the voice of the French poet:

. . . Direz, chantant mes vers, et vous esmerveillant,
Ronsard me celebroit du temps que j'estois belle.[3]

But the feeling is not exactly the same. There is in Pindar both a deeper humility

[1] *Ibid.*   [2] *Ibid.*, p. 195.
[3] The most famous of Ronsard's sonnets for Hélène de Surgères. The first quatrain goes something like this:

> *When in old age your spinning-wheel you ply*
> *Beside the hearth, by candle-light, and sing*
> *My verses to your beauty, marvelling*
> *That Ronsard hymned your praise in days gone by*—(Translator).

and a greater pride, and these he has received from his knowledge of the law which the gods prescribe for men.

◎

Before we go further into the relations between Pindar and the Syracusan prince, let us indulge the pleasure of reading, simply for its beauty, the myth related in the Tenth Nemean. But not entirely for its beauty. Every poem of Pindar's is full of instruction. In his eyes beauty is the most perfect expression which he can give—which the gods grant him to give—to the correctness of his thought.

The Tenth Nemean was written for an Argive who had been winner in the wrestling-match. In the first third of the ode he sketches out, with broad sweeps of the brush, a mythical background. He rapidly calls up to our imagination the great myths of Argos, a medley of gods and heroes and celebrated beauties. Alcmena and Danaé are visited by Zeus; Perseus is carrying the head of Medusa; Hypermnestra, the only one of the Danaids who, on the night of her marriage, spared her husband, is thrusting the dagger back into its sheath; we see Epaphus founding numerous cities in Egypt with his own hands; and lastly Heracles, the most illustrious son of an Argive lady, appears on Olympus beside his consort Hebe, youngest of the immortal goddesses.

In the angle of this stage-setting, the second third of the poem presents the winner, the Argive Theaeus. Standing in the front of the stage, though somewhat withdrawn, he carries the crowns he has won in various games. We even see the great amphora with its provision of oil which he has brought back from Athens, one of the 'Panathenaic' amphorae that are familiar to us through archaeological research. His parents, also winners in the games, form with him a kind of modern group.

Next—after roughly brushing in the background and rapidly introducing the few contemporary figures—the poet develops his myth in full daylight and with an incredible firmness of touch. This is the story of the two divine athletes who are patrons of athletes, Castor and Pollux: a splendid story from the plastic point of view and for the vigour of the sentiment.

The twin brothers were living at Sparta in their native valley; but they had enemies, also brothers, Idas and Lynceus. One day when Castor was reposing in the hollow of an oak, Lynceus, the lynx-eyed, descried him with his keen sight from the heights of Taÿgetus. He called Idas; the two of them surprised Castor asleep, and Idas smote him with his spear, a mortal blow. Pollux, however, who alone of the two was the son of Zeus and immortal, set off in pursuit of the murderers. He came up with them in a graveyard. Here they turned at bay, and to defend themselves snatched up a headstone which was that of their father's grave. With this they struck Pollux in the breast; but, unflinching, the hero thrust his bronze spear-head into Lynceus' side, while Zeus, glorifying his son, hurled a smoking thunderbolt against Idas;

and in that lonely place they were consumed together.[1]

Pollux hastens back to his brother, whom he finds still breathing but shaken with 'convulsive gasps'. Pollux burst into tears. Could not his father, who is all-powerful, save this beloved brother, his dear companion in toil? He prays to his father. Without Castor, he has no wish to live. Then Zeus appears to his child. Father and son stand face to face. The god offers Pollux only a hard choice; and yet his words have a gentleness that surprises us:

Thou art my son . . . lo! I grant thee thy full choice in this; if thou desirest to escape death and grievous eld, and to dwell thyself in Olympus with me, and with Athene, and with Ares of the darksome spear, thou canst have this lot appointed thee. But, if thou contendest for thy brother, and art minded to have an equal share with him in all things, then mayest thou breathe for half thy time beneath the earth, and for half thy time in the golden homes of heaven.[2]

Pollux does not hesitate for a moment; and so he sees Castor's eyes open and hears his voice once more.

The myth, which is related in less than forty verses, is of a matchless beauty. The vivid colouring and the perfect propriety of the narrative stand out in strong relief from the deliberately vague background of the ode. The beauty is in the feelings as well as the attitudes, and both have a common attribute which is nobility. All the attitudes—father and son facing each other—all the feelings, Pollux's prayer and, dominating everything, the severe choice that Zeus offers his son, and lastly Pollux's reply which is simply a gesture of brotherly love: to have Castor's eyes opened—all this is full of grandeur.

But there is nothing conventional in this nobility; on the contrary, some un-foreseen detail constantly produces an effect of surprise. The young man resting in the hollow tree, the strange battle in the graveyard—such touches invest the ancient myth with freshness and novelty.

Among the most radiant odes written by Pindar in honour of a prince, we must reckon the Second Olympian which was for Theron of Acragas, winner of the four-horse chariot-race. When he composed this epinician ode Pindar had for

[1] Trans. cited, p. 423.   [2] *Ibid.*, p. 425.

many years been acquainted with the family of the Emmenidae, with which
Theron, the master of Acragas, was connected. He knew about their success, their
greatness and the trials over which Theron and his family had hitherto always
ended by triumphing. The Emmenidae, who had encountered ill-fortune and then
glory, might well, like the family of Laius and Oedipus, serve to illustrate the
theme of vicissitude, that faithful companion of man's destiny. Pindar has no real
tragic sense; he is always inclined to reassure and console, to speak of the goodness and holiness of the gods. A whole current in his work leads him to hope for
the immortality of the human soul. Plato, who knew his poems, was to borrow
from him images and arguments to that effect.

The Second Olympian both testifies to Theron's greatness even in his trials,
and clearly holds out to him the supreme hope which charms the heart of man.

The ode belongs to the year 476. For Theron the end of the great adventure is
drawing near. Fifteen years of a glorious dictatorship, seized in a lucky moment;
Acragas girded with the crown of temples which still inspire our admiration. Life
also is drawing to its close. This is the moment for the thoughtful and friendly
poet to speak to the prince of the power of Fortune over our lives. He speaks of
our human lot and of death; it is not too much to say that he seems to be bringing
him the consolations of religion.

In short and striking phrases the ode begins by recalling the splendour, lofty
yet always menaced, of Theron and his ancestors:

*Theron . . . who is the bulwark of Acragas, the choicest flower of an auspicious line
of sires—those sires who, by much labour of mind, got them a hallowed home . . . , and
were the eye of Sicily, while their allotted time drew on. . . .*

*Under the power of noble joys, a cruel trouble is quelled and dieth away, whenever
good fortune is lifted on high by a god-sent fate. . . .*

*But diverse are the currents that at divers times come upon men, either with joys or
with toils.*[1]

The poet gives examples of the glorious triumph of good fortune:

*This saying befitteth the fair-throned daughters of Cadmus, who sorely suffered, but
their heavy sorrow was abated by the presence of greater blessings. Semele of the
streaming hair liveth amid the gods Olympian, when she had been slain by the thunderbolt—Semele, beloved for ever by Pallas and, in very deed, by father Zeus; beloved
by her ivy-crowned son.*[2]

Further on, he praises Theron's virtues, of which the principal is energy:

Now, to win the victory when essaying the contest, giveth us release from hardships.

[1] Trans. cited, pp. 19, 21.   [2] *Ibid.*, p. 21.

Theron is rich:

. . . verily, wealth adorned with virtues bringeth the fitting chance of divers boons, prompting the heart of man to a keen and eager quest.[1]

At the height of this eulogy, in which we see the success of the man of action often thwarting 'necessity', comes the supreme promise, that of the tower of Cronus, which awaits good men after their death:

. . . while the good, having the sun shining for evermore, for equal nights and equal days, receive the boon of a life of lightened toil, not vexing the soil with the strength of their hands, no, nor the water of the sea, to gain a scanty livelihood; but, in the presence of the honoured gods, all who were wont to rejoice in keeping their oaths, share a life that knoweth no tears, while the others endure labour that none can look upon—But, whosoever, while dwelling in either world, have thrice been courageous in keeping their souls pure from all deeds of wrong, pass by the highway of Zeus unto the tower of Cronus, where the ocean-breezes blow around the Islands of the Blest, and flowers of gold are blazing, some on the shore from radiant trees, while others the water fostereth; and with chaplets thereof they entwine their hands, and with crowns, according to the righteous councils of Rhadamanthys, who shareth for evermore the Judgment-seat of the mighty Father, even the Lord of Rhea with her throne exalted beyond all beside.[2]

Pindar then names two or three of the elect who dwell in the tower of Cronus; such as Achilles, whose victories seem to incite the poet to engage in battle with the men who are disputing with him the favour of Theron. Seized with irresistible rancour, he now breaks out in threats:

Full many a swift arrow have I beneath mine arm, within my quiver, many an arrow that is vocal to the wise; but for the crowd they need interpreters. The true poet is he who knoweth much by gift of nature, but they that have only learnt the lore of song, and are turbulent and intemperate of tongue, like a pair of crows, chatter in vain against the god-like bird of Zeus.

Now, bend thy bow toward the mark![3]

Let us interpret. The true poet, the god-like bird of Zeus, is Pindar, and he alone. The rivals who are croaking against him are Simonides and Bacchylides, loquacious crows.

As if this outburst had restored his sense of balance, Pindar now turns to Theron and declares, in concluding, that if self-conceited envy wills to assail the glory of this prince, it will be silenced by his noble actions, provided he devotes himself wholly to them. There is a touch of exaggeration in the concluding verses:

[1] *Ibid.*, p. 23.   [2] *Ibid.*, pp. 23, 25, 27.   [3] *Ibid.*, p. 27.

. . . sand can never be numbered, and who could ever count up all the joys that he hath given to others?[1]

Passages like the one about the 'tower of Cronus' are not rare in those of Pindar's works that have been preserved. I mentioned that Plato remembered one of them—the following:

But, as for those from whom Persephone shall exact the penalty of their pristine woe, in the ninth year she once more restoreth their souls to the upper sunlight; and from these come into being august monarchs, and men who are swift in strength and supreme in wisdom; and, for all future time men call them sainted heroes.[2]

Note also these verses in which the poet describes the happiness of just men:

For them the sun shineth in his strength, in the world below, while here 'tis night; and, in meadows red with roses, the space before their city is shaded by the incense-tree, and is laden with golden fruits.[3]

These beliefs regarding a future life are not the only ones we find in Pindar. He did not remain fixed in a dogmatic fashion, which was not the ancient way of believing: the most pious of the Greeks were indeed always very reserved in what they said about the beyond. Elsewhere in Pindar we see man's survival assuming forms more modest:

The days of mortals are deathless, although the body die. Yet he, whose house is not reft of children nor utterly overthrown . . . liveth free from toilsome labour.[4]

Which means that the children live, while he reposes in eternal sleep. Immortality is here bound up with the survival of the descendants.

In other passages which are still more numerous it is the memory of the living that assures immortality, it is the poet's song that procures the longest survival. To live long in the memory of one's friends and kinsfolk, because one has acted rightly, because one has lived as a man in good conscience—these are the thoughts which, on days when hope of the tower of Cronus grows dimmer, enable Pindar to accept his mortal lot.

---

[1] *Ibid.*, p. 29.

[2] This is Fragment 133 (ed. Sandys, p. 593). Sandys interprets Pindar's belief as follows: After death, the soul is judged in nether world, and if accounted righteous, rests in the Elysium described in Fragment 129. But in the ninth year it is again incarnated, this time in one of the noble personages indicated above; a second death and reincarnation follow; and lastly, having been wholly purified, the soul departs to the Islands of the Blest (ed. cit., pp. 592–3 note)—Translator.

[3] Fragment 129 (ed. Sandys, p. 589). This is the Elysium in Hades: a place of rest and renewal for the souls of just men (Translator).

[4] Fragment 104, p. 567.

Grant me, O Zeus . . . to remain ever true to ways of frankness, that so at death I bequeath to my children no tarnished fame. . . . And as for me, I would yield my body to the earth, without ever ceasing from giving pleasure to my countrymen, and praising what merits praise, and apportioning blame to scoundrels.

It is useless to ask which of these two men is the real Pindar—the one who believes in immortal life or the one who forgets death ('The man who had done what is seemly forgetteth death') or who cries: 'O my soul, aspire not to immortal life.' But there are not two Pindars. There is one poet who believes and who hopes and who forgets, and for whom wisdom and a good conscience are enough—in fact a man full of contradictions and not a theologian. A believer, however, because even in the days when he hopes for nothing, when he does not *know*, he believes that there are gods: they, at least, *know*.

After these personal passages let us take a more official ode, the Second Pythian, which will afford a basis for our conclusion. Whatever the date of this work—which is disputed—its meaning is clear. Pindar is addressing Hieron who had won the four-horse chariot-race at Delphi,[1] a prince then in full possession of his power and at a very high point of fortune. He judges that the moment has come to put him on guard against the temptations of success, against being intoxicated with good fortune. Hence the choice of the myth. At the same time he warns him against the allurements of flattery. Pindar, who knows that people have slandered him in the prince's ears, claims, and exercises, the right of speaking frankly.

The poem opens with a eulogy of Syracuse: 'Mighty city of Syracuse!' In this address to Hieron's city, the poet puts the accent, as he rarely does, on military power. Syracuse is the 'holy ground of Ares . . . nursing-place divine of heroes and steeds that rejoice in steel!'[2] Further on Hieron is called 'prince and lord of many a battlemented street and of a host of men'.[3] Pindar does not, however, in this ode enumerate Hieron's exploits, but is content with citing an unexpected witness in support of his noble acts. This is the maiden of Locri:

after bewildering troubles of war, thanks to thy power, her glance is now steadfast.[4]

The Locrian maiden can indeed, from the threshold of her dwelling in Magna

[1] Probably not at the Pythian games, but at the Theban Iolaia (see Sandys, ed. cit., p. 168)—Translator.
[2] Trans. cited, p. 171.
[3] *Ibid.*, p. 177.
[4] *Ibid.*, p. 173. Hieron had prevented Anaxilas, tyrant of Rhegium, from seizing Locris (Translator).

Graecia, sing the praises of Hieron who had saved her city from the covetous enterprise of a neighbouring state.

The girl who obeys the duty of gratitude to a benefactor may remind the prince himself of this same duty toward the gods. The theme of the grateful maiden in fact opens the way for the myth of Ixion, most ungrateful of princes. Ixion illustrates the essential truth that fortunate kings who do not give the glory to God, the sole author of their felicity, are unworthy men.

Ixion had known the very summit of fortune, he had been the guest of the gods in heaven. But, says the poet, 'he could not be content with his great prosperity'.[1] To endure good fortune is for princes the most difficult of virtues. Ixion dared to raise his eyes to Hera, and a fearful punishment was visited on his crime. With his four limbs bound to the four spokes of a wheel, he was hurled into space by Zeus. After recounting the myth Pindar bursts into a canticle of praise to the glory of God. He has just been speaking of Zeus, suddenly he names God, because this word, more vast, is better fitted to his religious feeling. So he sings his psalm:

God fulfilleth every purpose, even as he desireth, God that not only overtaketh the winged eagle, but also surpasseth the dolphin on the sea, and bendeth many a proud mortal beneath his sway, while to others he giveth glory that knoweth no eld.[2]

Having thus asserted God's sovereign power, the poet does not refuse to eulogize the prince; his praise being mingled with counsel even in poems as official as this one or as the First Pythian. And, truly, Hieron deserves praise:

I shall ascend a prow that is crowned with flowers, while I sound the praise of valour.[3]

Pindar says elsewhere[4] that the first of Hieron's virtues is a steadfast soul, and he compares him to Philoctetes, the hero who, though tormented with a grievous sore, did yet cause his adversaries to give way. In this connexion the old commentators tell us that Hieron, who was suffering from gravel, had himself carried in a litter to the battlefield. But energy is not the prince's only virtue, and Pindar reminds him that justice too is needed:

Steer thy people with the helm of justice, and forge thy tongue on the anvil of truth![5]

Every virtue is a gift of the gods:

From the gods come all the means of mortal exploits.[6]

[1] *Ibid.*, p. 173.
[4] In the First Pythian, 470 B.C.
[2] *Ibid.*, pp. 175, 177.
[5] *Ibid.*, Trans. cited, p. 165.
[3] *Ibid.*, p. 177.
[6] *Ibid.*, p. 159.

The worst fault in a prince, or indeed in any man, is to be untrue to himself, to be an 'ape'. Pindar says this in the most striking manner:

Be true to thyself, now that thou hast learnt what manner of man thou art. It is only in the eyes of children . . . that the ape is 'pretty', ever 'pretty'.[1]

This is a lesson on the Delphic theme: 'Know thyself.' One knows that from Pindar's saying: 'Be true to thyself . . .', Goethe fashioned the splendid '*Werde der du bist*'—'Become what thou art.'

Coming back to himself, Pindar finishes the Second Pythian Ode with proud words that free him from the calumnies of men who were flattering the king and tempting him to play the ape. These calumnies are of small account, since

I, like a cork above the net, float undipped in the brine.[2]

Because he is honest, 'a man of straightforward speech'. The straightforward man always prevails with the prince, and triumphs over flatterers. Pindar has no fear of Simonides and Bacchylides who, according to the ancients, served him ill, and are here referred to. He fears only one thing—that of displeasing the gods.

◎

In every expression he utters of modesty or even humility, Pindar's pride is always incomparable. He knows that poets are the equals of princes and that the latters' glory exists only through the poet's praise. Pindar is never humble in face of the prince, but only in face of God, as the prince himself should be. He was thus able to eulogize princes while remaining wholly independent. Besides he praised those princes who deserved it. Hieron and Theron were men of great capacity, men enamoured of greatness for their cities as well as for themselves. From this greatness moral elevation was not excluded.

If Pindar praised much, he also demanded much. We may suppose that he is aiming, in his eulogies, at fortifying the prince's feeling of his true merit. He encourages him too by saying that divine protection is above him; and at the same time he reminds him that his talents and successes are but gifts of God: as he says to Arcesilas, King of Cyrene:

Forget not to give God the glory.[3]

For in truth the good fortune of princes endures only as long as it is founded on the fear of God and the practise of justice. To act 'with God' is the great principle of government.

The poet is inspired. It is because he is a 'prophet' that he can demand much of

---

[1] Trans. cited, p. 179.   [2] *Ibid.*   [3] Fifth Pythian, p. 237.

the prince. What he demands are all the virtues of the old aristocratic code: justice, uprightness, liberality, and also respect for the people, gentleness toward those he governs, who are not his subjects but his 'fellow-citizens'. What he demands above all are courage to endure ill fortune and that steadfastness, which is no less difficult, in bearing prosperity.

Pindar does not think that the princely form of government is the best, and he says so. He prefers the aristocratic form, which he calls the government of the 'wise'. But the government of the good prince, the prince who would be the best and wisest (and this makes one think of Plato, in spite of the differences in time and temperament), a rule nobly conducted, Pindar does not reject.

What was he really attempting in his dealing with the Sicilian princes? Was it not the same attempt that Plato was to make in regard to later Sicilian rulers? He was trying to develop in them a sense of responsibility. In addressing these 'new men', he, an aristocrat by birth and temperament, was trying to make them real nobles.

This he could do, not because he was a hired poet but because, faithful to the mission of the gods, he revealed to souls enamoured of greatness the meaning of human life, which is to accomplish 'noble deeds'. So he holds out the example of heroes and invites the prince to choose the heroic life. Thus in the Fourth Pythian, written for Arcesilas, we see the young princes thronging round Jason. (Hera kindled in them the love of enterprise):

that none should be left behind . . . , nursing a life that knoweth no peril; but should, even if death were to be the meed, win, with the aid of his comrades, a peerless elixir of prowess.[1]

They choose the noble and difficult way. Again, in the First Olympian, written for Hieron, we see Pelops choosing the heroic life:

But high emprise brooketh no coward wight. Yet, as all men must needs die, why should one, sitting idly in the darkness, nurse without aim an inglorious eld, reft of all share of blessings?[2]

The examples he offers the prince are those of heroic and noble lives. Glory is the prize, and the surest immortality. The poet confers it. 'By the poet's songs,' declares Pindar, 'virtue becomes enduring.' In another place we read: 'The voice of noble verses rings out immortal; thanks to them, over the leagues of fertile soil and the ocean-wastes, the glory of noble deeds shines out for ever.' And lastly this admirable line: 'But for the poet's song, all virtue dieth in silence.'

Why this enthusiasm and certainty? Because the service of the poet and the service of the prince are both divine.

[1] Trans. cited, p. 219.   [2] Pp. 11–13.

CHAPTER SIX

HERODOTUS AS EXPLORER
OF THE OLD CONTINENT

Herodotus has been called the father of history; but he might equally well be called the father of geography. He offered his contemporaries of the mid fifth century a picture of the whole barbarian world, the word 'barbarian' being taken merely in the sense of 'foreign', in the sense in which the Greeks used to say that the swallow 'speaks barbarian'. He presented his readers with the old continent, the known, the unknown and the sometimes imaginary, the three old continents. He does not know why three are counted, because, as he says, the earth is one. 'Besides,' he remarks, 'I cannot understand why three different names have been given to the earth, which is one.' These names are Europe, Asia and Libya, meaning Africa. The observation was to remain accurate until A.D. 1492.

The earth is both single and diverse, peopled with races and nations which, governed by the same elementary needs, satisfy these needs by an infinite variety of different customs. Herodotus' fundamental aim was in the first place to relate the great exploits of the Persian wars. These took place about the time of his birth (he was born towards 480 B.C.) and occupied almost exactly the first half of the fifth century. For young Greece they were a decisive ordeal. It was not only the Medes and Persians but the enormous mass of the peoples of inner Asia, from western India to the Aegean Sea, not forgetting Egypt which was also subject to Persia, that these great kings—the 'Great King', as the Greeks used to say—flung against Hellas. The Greeks overcame the ordeal, fighting the invader as one would struggle against the tide; fighting often one against ten and thus safeguarding that fierce love of independence which, according to Herodotus, distinguished the Greeks from all other peoples and made them, not subjects of Asiatic or Egyptian sovereigns, but free citizens. Herodotus was not mistaken in distinguishing the Greeks from the 'barbarian' world by this feature. They wished to remain free and that is why, under the difficult conditions of a terrifying numerical inferiority and of the chronic internal divisions that set each city in opposition to the others, and, inside each city, aristocrats in opposition to democrats, they won the victory. It was their ineradicable love of liberty that enabled them to prevail. Herodotus says so clearly; and that is why he loved his people.

But if he loved them he was no less curious to ascertain and to make known to the Greeks the other, far more powerful, peoples who, in certain cases, had been civilized far longer. He was curious, too, as regards the diversity and oddity of foreign customs. For this reason he places before his history of the Persian Wars a vast *enquiry* into the nations who had attacked Greece and with whom at this time the Greeks were still very ill acquainted. This leads him step by step to extend his enquiry and to inform his readers about the whole known world of his time.

The title of his work is, precisely, *Enquiries*, in Greek, *Historiai*, a word which then had no meaning other than enquiries. Before Herodotus, historical research did not exist. By giving the name of *Enquiries* to a work that was both historical and geographical, Herodotus founded these two branches of knowledge on scientific research. It is nevertheless true that his temperament drove him at the outset and indeed right through his work, toward geographical or ethnographical research before it incited him to seek historical truth.

Of what then was he curious? Speaking generally and without fear of error, one might answer: 'of everything'. Beliefs, manners, monuments, what we call 'public works', the nature of the soil, climate, fauna and flora (especially fauna), the extent of deserts, voyages of discovery, the ends of the earth, great rivers whose source is unknown—and especially the activity of man, his living conditions, his physical complexion, his pleasures, his gods, the remote antiquity of his past or, on the other hand, the primitive character of his way of life. Man and his work, and his adventure, man in his natural environment and studied in the strangeness of his customs: there lies the main interest of Herodotus' *Enquiries*. By virtue of his eagerness to depict the man of all countries and all peoples, Herodotus stands out as one of the most attractive figures in ancient humanism.

The word 'curiosity' which I used is, all things considered, inadequate to define Herodotus. I will return to this point. But, having used the expression 'historical truth', I am anxious to explain myself regarding a word which, it seems to me, is too readily applied to him. Herodotus, people say, is credulous. It is true that, with all the good will of a conscientious enquirer, he still has the *naïveté* of a child. His credulity appears at first as infinite as his curiosity, and one can scarcely speak of the one without the other. But when everything has been taken up and verified in the light of the most recent knowledge, it must be said that, at least as regards what he saw with his own eyes, he was rarely mistaken. On the other hand he records the innumerable stories that were told him, without discernment and usually without critical judgment. He allows himself to be imposed upon by the often ignorant priests who served as guides in many of the countries he visited; sometimes by the first comer. This is because he is far too fond of the marvellous, of which the stories people told him were full, to be able decisively to reject it. The more wonderful a story, the more it enchants him; and he hastens to relate it, however improbable it seems to him. He would, for that matter, think he was failing in his task as an enquirer, if he did not relate it; while letting us understand, afterwards, that he is not a dupe. Note the reservation he makes when concluding the brilliant Egyptian story of the king and the two thieves: 'If these relations appear credible to some man, he may believe them; as for me, my only aim in this work [the reservation applies therefore to the work as a whole] is to write down what I hear stated by this man or that.'

Herodotus' history constitutes, then, a queer mixture of scientific probity and of credulity. He is honestly seeking truth and gives himself enormous trouble in pursuing it to the ends of the earth; but at the same time he still has that taste for the marvellous which characterizes the young peoples. Paradoxically, he would like the truth he is seeking to have, if one may say so, a marvellous character, he would like his enquiries to supply the marvellous in bushels. For the father of history, the acme of the historical would in short be the marvellous guaranteed by reliable witnesses. He has the air of wishing that history were a sort of fairy tale, with the proof to hand that it had really happened.

Of Herodotus' two passions—his taste for fine stories and strange peoples, and his taste for the truth—it is only too evident that one damages the other. Hence, in his *Enquiries*, so many absurd (and also amusing) narratives which he owes to informers who found it easy to abuse so ingenuous a curiosity. But one kind of error we never find in this author, namely deliberate error. Herodotus never lies. He is deceived, he misunderstands, he becomes confused among his notes, and especially he lets himself be deceived with disconcerting facility, provided he is being amused. But, despite all the learned works that have subjected him to a severe and even distrustful criticism, Herodotus has never been caught in the act of lying. He was a very honest man, imaginative too, but perfectly sincere.

And this was a great merit. To readers who were ignorant of practically everything about the countries he had visited, it was easy to relate anything. '*A beau mentir qui vient de loin!*'[1] people say. Herodotus did not yield to a temptation into which so many travellers have fallen.

He was a great traveller, and went far and wide to collect the information he gives us. He explored the earth with his eyes and feet, and often no doubt on a

[1] 'The traveller may lie with impunity.'

donkey or on horseback, and often by ship. His itinerary in Egypt has been established. He was there during the period of the flooding of the Nile and went up the
Nile valley as far as Elephantine (Assouan) which is at the extreme limit of ancient
Egypt, near the first cataract; and that makes a thousand kilometres. To the east, he
went at least as far as Babylon, which, if you start from the Aegean, makes about
two thousand kilometres. He may perhaps have gone to Susa, though this is uncertain. In the north, he visited the Greek colonies on the shores of the Black Sea,
bordering on the modern Ukraine. It is probable that he sailed up the lower waters
of one of the great rivers of the Ukrainian steppes, perhaps the Dnieper (Borysthenes), as far as the region of Kiev. To the west he took part in founding a Greek
colony in southern Italy. He also visited the modern Cyrenaica and no doubt
Tripolitania.

It was therefore a personal enquiry, conducted on the spot, that our geographer
undertook. We hear him in these pages constantly asking questions and gazing at
novelties. In Egypt he goes into an embalmer's establishment and obtains detailed
information regarding the methods of procedure and the price charged for the
operation. In the temples he gets someone to translate the inscriptions and interro-
gates the priests about the history of the Pharoahs. He attends religious festivals,
where his eyes drink in the bright colours of the robes and the shape of head-
dresses. Under the Pyramids he measures the base by counting his steps, and is
scarcely mistaken in the measurements he gives. When, however, he tries to judge
the height simply by the eye, his error is pretty wide. And so on, in all the countries he visits and in the very many countries for which, as he does not visit them,
he refers to the accounts of the Greek or Barbarian travellers whom he has met in
hostelries.

But enough of generalities: Herodotus is too concrete for me to dwell further
on them. What are the centres of interest which it seems preferable to examine?
One of these might naturally be Egypt, a country about which he writes in-
exhaustibly. But his Egyptian stories are too well known and I prefer to take my
reader further. Without therefore entirely neglecting Egypt, I shall distinguish
three centres of interest, though this will not prevent me from straying a little
beyond, much as he does. Now the three centres in question were the principal
corn-growing countries of the ancient world, a fact which, though its significance
may have escaped Herodotus, points clearly to the human needs that gave birth
to the science of geography. Geography was born of hunger, the atrocious hunger
of the ancient world which drove one of the most wretched and yet active peoples

17. *To return to Delphi in the spring, Apollo travels on a winged tripod*

18

of the time—the Greeks—from a land that was sterile and especially ill-cultivated and badly distributed.

The three corn-growing countries were the land of the Scythians (the Ukraine), Mesopotamia and North Africa. With the help of these examples and by pointing out, in Herodotus' explanations, what is correct and what is erroneous (and why it is erroneous), I shall try to characterize his peculiar genius. For if geography was born of the needs of the Greek people, it was also most commonly, as it seems to me, born of the appearance of a new literary genre or of a new science, of a genius that seems to have come down from heaven. I do not by that mean that this birth of genius is inexplicable or miraculous, but only that, even if the conditions which permit it exist, it is in no way necessary: it might not come into being, and often does not. In that event, science and literature suffer.

Coming now to our tour of the ancient world, let us begin with Babylonia. Herodotus saw the great city of Babylon. The area enclosed by the walls, he tells us, was square. The figure he gives for one side of this square would indicate a perimeter of eighty-five kilometres; which is greatly exaggerated. The perimeter of Babylon scarcely measured twenty kilometres. Herodotus has a child's love of big figures. He makes it clear that in his time the walls had been razed to the ground by Darius; although fragments still subsisted. He wanted to know how the wall had been built. It was explained to him that it was built of bricks and that between every thirty layers of bricks a bed of interwoven rushes had been placed in the asphalt that served to bind the layers. Now the mark of these rushes can be traced in the asphalt which is still visible today in the ruins of the wall.

Herodotus describes Babylon as a very great city. It was the greatest he had seen, and in fact, at that time, the largest in the ancient world. He describes the big straight thoroughfares intersecting at right-angles; he admires the houses, three- or four-stories in height, a kind unknown in Greece; he knows of the existence of the two parallel walls built by Nebuchadnezzar. The total thickness of this double surrounding-wall was about thirty metres. Herodotus, who is here for once on the modest side of the truth, says about twenty-five. He gives the city a hundred gates. This is an error; it was only in epic poems that cities had a hundred gates. In any event, he could not count them—as he admits himself—in a wall that had been partially demolished.

In the sanctuary of Baal, or Bel, he describes fairly accurately the great tower which rose from it in eight successive tiers, and its spiral stairway.[1] We know

---

[1] This stairway was constructed *outside* the 'towers' (as Herodotus correctly describes them). There was a resting place, with seats, half-way up (Translator).

I

about this tower of Bel, which is our tower of Babel, from excavations and from Babylonian documents. Regarding the chamber in the uppermost storey, Herodotus remarks:

These same Chaldeans say (but I do not believe them) that the god himself is wont to visit the shrine and rest upon the couch. . . .[1]

Herodotus then tries to enumerate some of the kings and queens who had reigned in Babylon. He speaks of Semiramis, a princess who lived from the ninth to the eighth century B.C., as attested by an inscription, but who was not the legendary consort of Ninus, the Semiramis of the hanging gardens who figures in tragedies and operas. He also speaks of another queen whom he calls Nitocris, and who built on the Euphrates, upstream from Babylon, fortifications to protect the city against the growing menace of the Medes. Now this queen Nitocris was no other than our king Nebuchadnezzar. The Persian form of the king's name, which has an ending that sounds feminine to the ear of a Greek, accounts for Herodotus' mistake. It is however true that this Nitocris-Nebuchadnezzar did build, to the north of Babylon, various defensive works, including the Sippara reservoir, which our author describes and which served to irrigate the country as much as to defend the capital.

It appears, however, from a cuneiform inscription, that there was no siege of Babylon by Cyrus, although this is related by Herodotus in a well-known passage. On the approach of the Persian armies a rebellion broke out and Cyrus was able to make a triumphal entry. But no doubt when Herodotus was in Babylon he received a version of its fall more flattering to the pride of the great city. He also tried to gather information about the new masters of Babylonia. He doubtless never went to Persia properly so-called, that is, the region of Persepolis and the mountains of Iran. He does not pretend to have done so. But on the roads of the Empire and in the inns at Babylon (or at Susa, if he went as far) he cannot have failed to meet and question many Persians, and he seems to have tried to check their statements one against the other. The information he gives about their education and religion is regarded as correct, apart from a few details, by modern historians. However summary his description of Persian customs, Herodotus appears to have caught a glimpse—and not without surprise—of the moral climate of Persia.

The following passage, on education, is celebrated and strictly accurate:

They educate their boys from five to twenty years old, and teach them three things only, riding and archery and truth-telling.[2]

---

[1] *Herodotus*, with an English translation by A. D. Godley, London and New York, Loeb Classical Library, 1931, Vol. I, p. 227.
[2] Book I, § 136. Trans. cited, I, 177.

Persian religion did in fact inculcate the love of truth; and nothing could be more striking to a Greek who admired the 'faultless lies' of Odysseus. Herodotus also knows about the religion of Ormuzd and Ahriman; he knows that Persian priests are forbidden to kill useful animals like the dog and others he has forgotten—all the animals that Ormuzd had created—while it is meritorious to kill ants and snakes which are creatures of Ahriman.

From these examples, and if we recall the recent invasion of Greece by the Medes and Persians, we shall see that the word 'curiosity' that I used to describe Herodotus is now inadequate. This curiosity has turned into amazement and even admiration, whether as regards the old Babylonian city or the moral climate of Persia, so remote from what were then the customs in Greece. The same feeling arises from Herodotus' long study of Egypt and its wonders.

Before passing on to other peoples, I should like to show how Herodotus pictures the earth. He ridicules those authors of *Voyages round the World* like Hecataeus of Miletus, who gave the world the shape of a flat disk 'perfectly circular, as if drawn with a compass and surrounded by the stream of Ocean'. But in this passage and elsewhere he only protests against the existence of a river called Ocean and against the regularity of a perfect circle which would be the shape of the earth. He too sees the earth as a disk and not a sphere. If the image he forms of it is not perfectly circular, it seems to incline to the symmetry of a circle.

Asia, as Herodotus imagines it, is inhabited as far as India. Beyond this lie deserts. Indo-China and China have been amputated. Africa has been deprived of its southern portion. The periplus of the Phoenicians in the sixth century and the periplus of Scylax in 509 B.C. allow Herodotus to decide that southern Asia and southern Africa are surrounded by water. To the north of these two southern continents, we have Europe which, 'stretching as to its length over the same space as the other two parts of the earth', extends right into Siberia. But Herodotus cannot decide whether to the north, the north-west and the east this Europe is surrounded by water.

Here is the passage that concerns the first of the voyages I mentioned. It was Nechao II, whom Herodotus calls Necos, who dispatched the expedition:

So the Phoenicians set out from the Red Sea and sailed the southern sea;[1] *whenever autumn came they would put in and sow the land, to whatever part of Libya*[2] *they might come, and there await the harvest; then, having gathered in the crop, they sailed on, so that after two years had passed, it was in the third that they rounded the Pillars*

[1] The Indian Ocean.   [2] Africa.

of Heracles and came to Egypt. There they said (what some may believe, though I do not) that in sailing round Libya they had the sun on their right hand.[1]

Herodotus was mistaken for once in being sceptical. In doubling the Cape of Good Hope the sailors would in fact, at noon, see the sun in the north, on their right; because they were in the southern hemisphere. Herodotus did not know enough cosmography to understand; but this circumstance, which could not have been invented and which he refuses to admit, guarantees the truth of the periplus round Africa.

Next in his narrative comes the periplus of Scylax, which showed that southern Asia like Africa is surrounded by water. '*These* [Scylax and his companions] *set out*,' writes Herodotus, '*from the city Castapyrus* [which is a town in the Punjaub, situated on a tributary of the Indus] ... *and sailed down the river towards the east and the sunrise till they came to the sea*; [This river is the Indus. One need scarcely say that it does not flow east and that Herodotus is either confusing it with the Ganges, or simply making a mistake. He continues:] *and voyaging over the sea westwards, they came in the thirtieth month to that place whence the Egyptian king sent the Phoenicians afore-mentioned to sail round Libya.*'[2]

I now come to the Scythians. Established towards the end of the eighth century in the steppes of the Ukraine, from the Carpathians to the loop of the Don (the Tanaïs of Herodotus), the Scythians were still but little known to the Greeks. Our traveller devoted an important section of his work to describing their country and customs. To conduct his enquiry, he visited the Greek cities on the shores of the Black Sea, and stayed at Olbia, the most important of these trading-towns, a place built at the outlet of the Scythian country, by the lower waters of the Dnieper. It is not impossible, as I have said, that he went up this stream with some convoy and so gained the region, not far from Kiev, where were the tombs of the Scythian kings which he describes with great precision. In any event his information about the Scythians appears to be very exact. His description of customs is rarely inter-mingled with legendary elements. The excavation of the mounds, or *kourganes*, in that country—among others, the exploration of the site of Koulaba, near Kertch—have confirmed his testimony where it could be confirmed. As to the bizarre rites and beliefs which he notes with delight, these have been recently rediscovered among tribes of the same level of culture as the Scythians had then reached.

What Herodotus first brings out clearly is the great ingenuity of the Scythians in the matter of resisting invasion. This ingenuity consists in retreating before the

[1] Book IV, § 42. Trans. cited, Vol. II, pp. 239–41.
[2] Book IV, § 44. Trans. cited, Vol. II, p. 243.

aggressor, so as not to let him come up with them when they do not wish him to, and so in drawing him on into their vast plains until they are ready to fight him. In this procedure they are greatly assisted not only by the nature of the country, which is a vast grassy plain, but also by the great rivers that flow through it and constitute excellent lines for resistance. Herodotus enumerates these rivers, with some of their tributaries, from the Danube to the Don. He even names one too many.

Here, since one must select amid such an abundance of information, are a few details regarding the practice of divination among the Scythians:

But whenever the king of the Scythians falls sick, he sends for the three diviners most in repute, who prophesy in the aforesaid manner; and they for the most part tell him that such and such a man (naming whoever it is of the people of the country) has forsworn himself by the king's hearth; for when the Scythians will swear their mightiest oath, it is by the king's hearth that their custom is to swear most solemnly. Forthwith the man whom they allege to be forsworn is seized and brought in, and when he comes the diviners accuse him, saying that their divination shows him to have forsworn himself by the king's hearth, and that this is the cause of the king's sickness; and the man vehemently denies that he is forsworn. So when he denies it the kings sends for twice as many diviners and if they too, looking into their art, prove him guilty of perjury, then straightway he is beheaded and his goods are divided among the first diviners; but if the later diviners acquit him, then other diviners come, and yet again others. If then the greater number of them acquit the man, it is decreed that the first diviners shall themselves be put to death.

It will be observed that the truth of the divination is decided by a majority vote. Herodotus continues:

And this is the manner of their death. Men yoke oxen to a waggon laden with sticks and make the diviners fast amid these, fettering their legs and binding their hands behind them and gagging them; then they set fire to the sticks and drive the oxen away, affrighting them. Often the oxen are burnt to death with the diviners, and often the pole of their waggon is burnt through and the oxen escape with a scorching. They burn their diviners for other reasons, too, in the manner aforesaid, calling them false prophets. When the king puts a man to death, neither does he leave the sons alive, but kills all the males of the family; to the females he does no hurt.[1]

What most strikes one in such narratives is the imperturbable calm with which Herodotus relates the worst cruelties. Here now is what our historian says about the tombs of the Scythian kings:

[1] Book IV, §§ 68, 69. Trans. cited, Vol. II, pp. 265, 267.

The burial-places of the kings are in the land of the Gerrhi,[1] which is the end of the navigation of the Borysthenes.[2] There, whenever their king has died, the Scythians dig a great four-cornered pit in the ground; when this is ready they take up the dead man—his body enclosed in wax, his belly cut open and cleansed and filled with cut marsh-plants and frankincense and parsley and anise seed, and sewn up again—and carry him on a waggon to another tribe. Then those that receive the dead man at his coming do the same as do the Royal Scythians; that is, they cut off a part of their ears, shave their heads, make cuts round their arms, tear their foreheads and noses, and pierce their left hands with arrows. Thence the bearers carry the king's body on the waggon to another of the tribes which they rule, and those to whom they have already come follow them; and having carried the dead man to all in turn, they are in the country of the Gerrhi, the farthest distant of all tribes under their rule, and at the place of burial. Then, having laid the dead in the tomb on a couch, they plant spears all round the body and lay across them wooden planks, which they then roof over with hides; in the open space which is left in the tomb they bury, after strangling, one of the king's concubines, his cup-bearer, his cook, his groom, his squire, and his messenger, besides horses, and first-fruits of all else, and golden cups; for the Scythians make no use of silver or bronze. Having done this they all build a great barrow of earth, vying zealously with one another to make this as great as may be.[3]

In the numerous *kourganes* which have been excavated in southern Russia, many human skeletons together with the bones of horses and a profusion of articles in gold have been discovered. An Arab traveller named Ibn Foszlan, writing about the year A.D. 920, tells us that the funeral rites described by Herodotus were still practised for the chieftains of the Ukrainian peoples. This traveller saw the burning of the chief's body together with one of his concubines who had previously been strangled.

After the completion of a year, the ceremony is renewed, this time by strangling fifty of the king's trustiest servants and the same number of horses. The fifty servants are then empaled and seated upon the fifty horses which have also been empaled, in a circle round the tomb. These trophies have not of course been discovered because they were placed outside the tomb. The obvious pleasure that Herodotus takes in relating such stories without flinching is one of the distinctive features of Greek civilization. It was not only in the noble sides of their nature that the Greeks felt themselves akin to other men, but in every side. The most cruel are not the least important. Their humanism was not one-sided; it did not simply incline to the ideal.

[1] Apparently in the region of Kiev.
[2] I.e., the furthest point upstream at which the Dnieper is navigable (Translator).
[3] Book IV, § 71. Trans. cited, II, 269, 271.

After describing the Scythians Herodotus enumerates the nations which border on the Scythian lands to the north, south, east and west. Of the majority of these except perhaps the Getae, at the mouth of the Danube, or the Tauri in what is now the Crimea, he speaks only by hearsay. Most of his information came from Greek traders who, from the Danube to the Volga, travelled through the Ukrainian lands, buying cereals, furs and slaves, and selling oil and wine in beautiful painted vases, and sometimes cheap goods from Egyptian bazaars. Herodotus makes more than one reservation in this part of his *Enquiries*, but he also at times gives **a** suggestive piece of information. He says about the Neuri:

It may be that they are wizards; for the Scythians, and the Greeks settled in Scythia, say that once a year, every one of the Neuri is turned into a wolf, and after remaining so for a few days returns again to his former shape. For myself, I cannot believe this tale; but they tell it nevertheless, yea, and swear to its truth.[1]

Here is a better-informed passage about the Androphagi or Man-eaters:

The Man-eaters are of all men the most savage in their manner of life; they know no justice and obey no law. They are nomads, wearing a dress like the Scythian, but speaking a language of their own; they are the only people of all these that eat men.[2]

The remark about the language has led to the supposition that these people were of Finnish stock; and it is known, besides, that the Finns practised cannibalism until the Middle Ages.

Herodotus knew that, beyond the country of the Scythians, the Neuri, the Man-eaters and many others, still more to the east and north, the earth was still inhabited and that instead of the sea, which one would expect, high mountains, which we may identify with the Urals, rose from the plain. Our chronicler's information now grows more sparse, or rather, as the distance increases, fabulous elements intermingle with it. He, however, sorts out the material in his usual way, recording everything but indicating to his reader the limits which credulity refuses to overstep.

Apropos of the dwellers in the hill country north-east of Scythia, he writes: '. . . there are men inhabiting the foothills of high mountains, who are said to be all bald from their birth (male and female alike) and snub-nosed and with long beards.' The description of these 'bald' men, by which Herodotus means that their hair is sparse, makes one think of the Kalmuks. He says further on:

The tree wherefrom they live is called 'Pontic'; it is about the size of a fig-tree, and bears a fruit as big as a bean, with a stone in it. When this fruit is ripe, they strain it

[1] Book IV, § 105. Trans. cited, II, 307.   [2] § 106, II, 307.

through cloth, and a thick black liquid flows from it, which they call 'aschu'; they lick this up or mix it with milk for drinking.[1]

'Aschy' is the name of the national drink of the Tartars of Kazan.[2] The Kalmuks still use the wild cherry in the way described by Herodotus; and it is probable that the tree in question is the cherry, which was then unknown in Europe.

Now as far as the land of these bald men we have full knowledge of the country . . . but, for what lies beyond the bald men, no one can speak with exact knowledge.[3]

The land, he says, is mountainous. He had heard that the mountains were inhabited by men with goats' feet, whom he calls 'Goat-feet', a figurative way of describing good climbers. He adds:

. . . but for my part I believe them not [the bald men who tell him about the 'Goat-feet']. These bald men say . . . that beyond these [the land of the Goat-feet] are men who sleep for six months of the twelve. This I cannot at all accept for true.[4]

And yet we no doubt have here a confused knowledge of the long polar nights.

One of the features that Herodotus observes of all the countries he names after Scythia is the cold which, according to him, begins at the Cimmerian Bosporus (the straits between the Sea of Azof and the Black Sea). He says:

All this aforementioned country is exceeding cold; for eight months of every year there is frost unbearable, and in these you shall not make mud by pouring out water but by lighting a fire; the sea freezes, and all the Cimmerian Bosporus; and the Scythians dwelling this side of the fosse lead armies over the ice, and drive their wains across to the land of the Sindi (Kuban). So it is ever winter for eight months, and it is cold in that country for the four that remain [an error: the summers are very hot in Russia]. Here is a winter of a different sort from the winters that come in other lands; for in the season for rain there falls scarce any, but for all the summer there is rain unceasing; and when there are thunderstorms in other lands, here there are none, but in summer there is great plenty of them; if there come a thunderstorm in winter they are wont to marvel at it for a portent.[5]

In Greece thunderstorms occur in spring and autumn, sometimes in winter, but never in summer. Hence Herodotus' remark.

[1] Book IV, § 23. Trans. cited, II, 223.
[2] Mr Godley remarks in a note to 'aschu' that 'the fruit of the "Prunus Padus" is said to be made by the Cossacks into a drink called "atschi" '. It seems likely that certain species of plum and cherry were used widely for this purpose in eastern Europe and western Asia (Translator).
[3] Book IV, § 24. See Godley, II, 225.   [4] § 25. *Ibid.*
[5] Book IV, § 28. Trans. cited, II, 227.

But as touching the feathers whereof the Scythians say that the air is full, insomuch that none can see or traverse the land beyond, I hold this opinion. Northward of that country snow falls continually, though less in summer than in winter, as is to be expected. Whoever has seen snow falling thickly near him knows of himself my meaning; for the snow is like feathers; and by reason of the winter, which is such as I have said, the parts to the north of this continent are uninhabited. I think therefore that in this tale of feathers the Scythians and their neighbours do but speak of snow in a figure.[1]

◎

Leaving the north, Herodotus takes us to the southernmost portions of Asia. Nature's rarest and choicest products are, according to him, found in these far southern countries. The Indies are the land of gold, Arabia of perfumes. Herodotus is less interested here in the customs of the people than in the gathering of the most brilliant signs of riches which had reached Hellas from the fabulous Orient. Things as rare as gold and spices could only be obtained in some marvellous fashion; hence our author makes a perilous use of a sort of primitive and still fantastic natural history, with tales of gigantic ants, legendary birds and flying serpents. I will touch only on one of the ways of collecting gold, leaving aside the others and also the fabulous gathering of aromatics.

Speaking of the country 'northward of the rest of India', Herodotus says:

. . . in these parts all is desert by reason of the sand. There are found in this sandy desert ants not so big as dogs but bigger than foxes.

These 'ants' seem to have been marmots: the Indians may have called marmots ants because they burrow in the earth. The *Mahabharata* ascribes to powdered gold the name of ant-gold; and the ant-hills in that country are said sometimes to contain gold in a powdery form. These facts, jumbled together and misinterpreted, have given rise to the story which Herodotus tells us and which was to be repeated and enriched with new details as time went on, until the end of the Middle Ages.

These ants make their dwelling underground, digging out the sand in the same manner as do the ants in Greece, to which they are very like in shape, and the sand which they carry forth from the holes is full of gold. It is for this sand that the Indians set forth into the desert. They harness three camels apiece, a male led camel on either side to help in draught, and a female in the middle: the man himself rides on the female, careful that when harnessed she has been taken away from as young an offspring as may be. . . .

I do not describe the camel's appearance to Greeks, for they know it; but I will show

[1] Book IV, § 31. Trans. cited, II, 229, 231.

them a thing which they do not know concerning it: the hindlegs of the camel have four thigh-bones and four knee-joints.

What strange anatomy! It is, however, regarded as excusable by friends of Herodotus—and of the camel. They say that the camel's metatarsus is so long that the heel looks like a second knee, which leads one to imagine two thighs; and then, when the camel kneels down he folds up such a length of leg beneath him that one is easily confused.

Thus and with teams so harnessed the Indians ride after the gold. . . .
So when the Indians come to the place with their sacks, they fill these with the sand and ride away back with all speed; for, as the Persians say, the ants forthwith scent them out and give chase, being, it would seem, so much swifter than all other creatures that if the Indians made not haste on their way while the ants are mustering, not one of them would escape. So they loose the male trace-camels that they lead, one at a time (these being slower than the females); the mares never tire, remembering the young that they have left.[1]

We are to understand that the male camels were only brought in order to delay pursuit by the ants; and that they are loosed, one at a time, when the ants have overtaken the convoy. The ants presumably stop in order to eat them. The text, which suggests this explanation, may perhaps present a lacuna at this point.
The pages on Arabia contain curious reflexions on the relative fertility of animals.

The Arabians also say that the whole country would be full of these snakes were it not with them as I have heard that it is with vipers. It would seem that the wisdom of divine Providence (as is but reasonable) has made all creatures prolific that are cowardly and fit to eat, that they be not minished from off the earth by devouring, whereas but few young are born to creatures cruel and baneful.

This argument may have been founded on the part which Anaxagoras and before him Xenophanes had ascribed to Intelligence in the government of the universe. Herodotus is nevertheless, as far as we know, the first who developed this curious view of final causes in respect of the animal world. Herodotus continues as follows:

The hare is so prolific, for that it is the prey of every beast and bird and man; alone of all creatures it conceives in pregnancy; some of the unborn young are hairy, some still naked; while some are still forming in the womb others are already being chased and killed.

---

[1] This passage about the 'ants' is in Book III, §§ 102–5. Trans. cited, II, 129, 131, 133.

Aristotle does not neglect to repeat the story of the triple superfetation of the doe-hare and add further details. But here comes the birth of the lion-cub:

. . . the lioness, a very strong and bold beast, bears offspring but once in her life, and then but one cub; for the uterus comes out with the cub in the act of birth. This is the reason of it: when the cub first begins to stir in the mother, its claws, much sharper than those of any other creature, tear the uterus, and as it grows, much more does it scratch and tear, so that when the hour of birth is near seldom is any of the uterus left whole.

Herodotus forgets to explain what, according to this system, providence has done to perpetuate the race of lions: arithmetic would prevent him. He continues as follows:

It is so too with vipers and the winged serpents of Arabia: were they born in the natural manner of serpents no life were possible for men; but as it is, when they pair, and the male is in the very act of generation, the female seizes him by the neck, nor lets go her grip till she have devoured him. Thus the male dies; but the female is punished for his death; the young avenge their father, and eat their mother while they are yet within her; nor are they dropped from her till they have devoured her womb.[1]

Clytemnestra—that viper as Aeschylus calls her—murdered Agamemnon. Orestes, by murdering his mother, avenged the death of his father. Herodotus, who had read or seen the *Oresteia*, seems here to be writing the *Oresteia* of vipers.

It will be observed that marvels increase as one reaches the distant parts of the earth. But these legendary tales would grow wearisome, and I prefer to recall a few features of the picture Herodotus gives us of one of the north African peoples.

He did not travel through north Africa, but simply made a few excursions from the Greek city of Cyrene into the Libyan desert and into Tripolitania. At Cyrene and even in Egypt he made many enquiries about these unknown lands and tried to extend his knowledge of the world to these vast regions which, from Egypt to Gibraltar, from the Syrtes to Lake Chad and from Carthage to Senegal, were haunted by nomadic tribes and wild beasts or spread far and wide in deserts dotted with miraculous oases. He appears also to have consulted the log-books of sailors from Rhodes, Samos or Phocaea who had sailed along the African coast and described the seaboard populations. And he succeeded in drawing up a description of north Africa which, in spite of frequently absurd details, is fuller and more accurate than one would expect.

Herodotus knew about a great many of the peoples of the north African coastal

[1] Book III, §§ 108, 109. Trans. cited, II, 135, 137.

regions, and he describes their customs which were sometimes those of Berber tribes, sometimes of the Tuaregs. I will recall only what he says of the Nasamones:

Next westward . . . is the populous country of the Nasamones, who in summer leave their flocks by the sea and go up to the land called Augila to gather dates from the palm-trees which grow there in great abundance and all bear fruit.

The oasis of Augila, the modern Aoudjila, is a great centre for gathering dates and is on the caravan-route from Cyrenaica to Fezzan. Herodotus continues:

They hunt locusts, which when taken they dry in the sun, and after grinding sprinkle them into milk and so drink it.

Some of the Tauregs eat dried and powdered grasshopper. Herodotus continues:

It is their custom for every man to have many wives; their intercourse with women is promiscuous . . . ; a staff is planted before the dwelling and then they have intercourse. When a man of the Nasamones first weds, on the first night the bride must by custom lie with each of the whole company in turn; and each man after intercourse gives her whatever gift he has brought from his house.[1]

Polyandry was practised 'en famille' by many ancient peoples, including the Spartans.

After enquiring at Cyrene about the sources of the Nile, Herodotus wrote the following account of the Nasamones which was long regarded as suspect:

But this I heard from certain men of Cyrene, who told me that they had gone to the oracle of Ammon, and there conversed with Etearchus king of the Ammonians, and that from other matters of discourse they came to speak of the Nile, how no one knows the source of it. Then Etearchus told them that once he had been visited by certain Nasamonians. These are a Libyan people, inhabiting the country of the Syrtis and the country a little way to the east of the Syrtis. When these Nasamonians on their coming were questioned if they brought any news concerning the Libyan desert, they told Etearchus that there had been among them certain sons of their chief men, proud and violent youths, who, when they came to man's estate, besides planning other wild adventures, had chosen by lot five of their company to visit the deserts of Libya, and see what they might beyond the utmost range of travellers. . . . When they left their companions, being well supplied with water and provisions, they journeyed first through the inhabited country, and having passed this they came to the region of wild beasts. After this, they travelled over the desert, towards the west, and crossed a wide sandy region, till after many days they saw trees growing in a plain; when they came to these and were plucking the fruit of the trees, they were met by little men of stature smaller than

[1] Book IV, § 172. Trans. cited, II, 375, 377.

common, who took them and led them away. The Nasamonians did not know these men's language nor did the escort know the language of the Nasamonians. The men led them across great marshes, which having crossed they came to a city where all the people were of like stature with the escort, and black. A great river ran past this city, from the west towards the rising sun; crocodiles could be seen in it.[1]

This passage which was for long regarded as an example of Herodotus' credulity, especially on account of the 'little men' who were relegated to the land of fable, was rendered plausible by the explorers of Equatorial Africa during the second half of the nineteenth century. It is now known that there exist in those regions really dwarf peoples, the Negrillos. It is not impossible that natives of Tripolitania crossed the desert from the Fezzan oasis to the loop of the Niger, and that, as a consequence, Herodotus took the Niger for the upper Nile.

◎

This brings us back to Egypt. Of all the countries he visited, Egypt was certainly the one which best realized the existence of a history and a geography which he liked to think of as both true and marvellous. There was nothing here which did not transcend his expectation or which did not respond to the most extravagant appeal of his fancy. And yet this was a country that he saw and touched. The history of Egypt went back for thousands of years, enriched with an amazing collection of stories which he further improved on because he misinterpreted the narratives of his lying guides. But then the visible witnesses to this history were remarkable: colossal statues, monuments of a height which easily beat all the records of the Greeks. 'The greatest in the world' is the most natural form of admiration in Herodotus.

And then a river which was a prodigy. For a Greek who was only familiar with streams swollen by spring storms, torrents half-dry during the summer months, the Nile with the enigma of its regular and fertilizing inundations and the mystery of its sources unknown and so distant that Herodotus could not even imagine them—the Nile not only exercised a singular fascination but offered a challenge to his eagerness for knowledge. He took up the challenge. He strove desperately to penetrate the double enigma of the sources and the inundations of the Nile. It is true that the facts he disposed of were insufficient as clues to a strictly logical solution. When criticizing the conjectures of his predecessors he has the air of reasoning at times like a child. But what an intelligent child! As to the result of his researches, it matters little whether he guesses right or wrong. It is his tenacity in questioning the mystery and deciphering the enigma that offers the brightest promise.

[1] Book II, § 32. Trans. cited, I, 311, 313.

Egypt harbours a multitude of strange and sacred animals which excite Herodotus' curiosity. He adores composing bestiaries. What interests him in this exotic fauna is partly the strangeness of its appearance and behaviour and even more the nature of the association which man has formed with animals; a much closer association in Egypt than in Greece and one which imposed peculiar obligations on man. He enquires into the pact concluded by the Egyptian with the cat, the ibis or the crocodile, and this enquiry throws astonishing light not upon the animal but upon man. His Egyptian bestiary is not merely a page of what one may call pre-Natural History, partly recopied, including the mistakes, by Aristotle. It is first of all a page of ethnography, of the human geography of the Egyptians.

There is a final category of facts which struck the traveller's attention. We know that Herodotus likes nothing so much as strange customs. He finds intense pleasure in collecting and describing a multitude of singular rites; and in this overflowing abundance of the unusual, nothing shocks or arouses his indignation. He even at one moment draws a picture of Egypt which is that of a country where everything is upside-down, as in certain popular tales or in Samuel Butler's *Erewhon*.

However absurd and incomplete his picture of Egypt may be, it has nevertheless in most of its details been confirmed by modern historians, or at least held as likely. Here are some examples. Taking up what another traveller, Hecataeus of Miletus, had said, Herodotus declares:

For even though a man has not before been told it, he can at once see, if he have sense, that that Egypt to which the Greeks sail is land acquired by the Egyptians, given them by the river—not only the lower country but even all the land to three days' voyage above the aforesaid lake,[1] which is of the same nature as the other, though the priests added not this to what they said. For this is the nature of the land of Egypt: firstly, when you approach to it from the sea and are yet a day's run from land, if you then let down a sounding line you will bring up mud and find a depth of eleven fathoms. This shows that the deposit from the land reaches thus far.[2]

Herodotus explains himself more precisely further on:

Now in Arabia, not far from Egypt, there is a gulf of the sea entering in from the sea called Red, of which the length and narrowness is such as I shall show: for length, it is a forty days' voyage for a ship rowed by oars from its inner end out to the wide sea; and for breadth, it is half a day's voyage at the widest. Every day the tide ebbs and flows therein. I hold that where now is Egypt there was once another such gulf; one entered from the northern sea towards Aethiopia, and the other, the Arabian gulf of which I will speak, bore from the south towards Syria; the ends of these gulfs pierced

---

[1] Lake Moeris.   [2] Book II, § 5. Trans. cited, I, 279, 281.

into the country near to each other, and but a little space of land divided them. Now if the Nile choose to turn his waters into this Arabian gulf, what hinders that it be not silted up by his stream in twenty thousand years? Nay, I think that ten thousand would suffice for it. Is it then to be believed that in the ages before my birth a gulf even much greater than this could not be made into land by a river so great and so busy?[1]

He continues:

Therefore, as to Egypt, I believe those who so speak (to the effect that the Nile valley is a silted-up gulf), and I am myself fully so persuaded; for I have seen that Egypt projects into the sea beyond the neighbouring land, and shells are plain to view on the mountains and the ground is coated with salt (insomuch that the very pyramids are wasted thereby), and the only sandy mountain in Egypt is that which is above Memphis; moreover, Egypt is like neither to the neighbouring land of Arabia, nor to Libya, no, nor to Syria (for the seaboard of Arabia is inhabited by Syrians); it is a land of black and crumbling earth, as if it were alluvial deposit carried down the river from Aethiopia; but we know that the soil of Libya is redder and somewhat sandy, and Arabia and Syria are lands rather of clay and stones.[2]

This conjecture concerning the geological formation of Egypt is correct, except as regards the number of years which the Nile took to operate the change. Herodotus' remarks, about the seaboard, the shells and the saline deposits are also correct. The sand, however, is much more abundant than he indicates.

Let us pass on to the famous description of the crocodile:

I will now show what kind of creature is the crocodile. For the four winter months it eats nothing. It has four feet, and lives both on land and in the water, for it lays eggs and hatches them out on land, and it passes the greater part of the day on dry ground, and the night in the river, the water being warmer than the air and dew. No mortal creature known to us grows from so small a beginning to such greatness; for its eggs are not much bigger than goose eggs, and the young crocodile is of a bigness answering thereto, but it grows to a length of seventeen cubits and more. It has eyes like pigs' eyes, and great teeth and tusks answering to the bigness of its body. It is the only animal that has no tongue. Nor does it move the lower jaw. It is the only creature that brings the upper jaw down upon the lower. It has also strong claws, and a scaly impenetrable hide on its back. It is blind in the water, but very keen of sight in the air. Since it lives in the water, its mouth is all full within of leeches. All birds and beasts flee from it, except only the sandpiper, with which it is at peace, because this bird does the crocodile a service; for whenever the crocodile comes ashore out of the water and then opens its mouth (and this it does for the most part to catch the west wind), the

[1] Book II, § 11. Trans. cited, I, 285, 287.   [2] § 12. Trans. cited, I, 287, 289.

sandpiper goes into its mouth and eats the leeches; the crocodile is pleased by this
service and does the sandpiper no harm.[1]

This description contains two principal errors, apart from the figure of seventeen cubits, which is exaggerated; although there still exist, further south than Egypt, species which reach a length of six metres. But seventeen cubits make eight metres: a crocodile so long is improbable. Here are the two mistakes. The crocodile is not without a tongue; this is indeed very small and so closely attached that the crocodile cannot project it. Again: it is the lower and not the upper jaw that is articulated. If Herodotus was mistaken, it is because, by letting its lower jaw rest on the ground and raising its head to snap at something, the animal does in fact seem to move the upper jaw. Herodotus did not feel obliged to go very near in order to verify his remarks about the tongue and the jaw. As to the sandpiper it is a sort of plover.[2] According to eyewitnesses, this bird rids the crocodile, if not of leeches, at least of small creatures that have got into its mouth.

To cite an example from ornithology:

Another bird also is sacred: it is called the phoenix. I myself have never seen it, but
only pictures of it; for the bird comes but seldom into Egypt, once in five hundred years,
as the people of Heliopolis say. It is said that the phoenix comes when his father dies.
If the picture truly shows his size and appearance—.[3]

Let us admire the prudence and honesty of Herodotus. He has only seen 'pictures' of the phoenix, and for a good reason. In describing this fabulous bird he has not been guilty of lying.

We may, in conclusion, quote a popular story about a legendary king:

When Sesostris died, he was succeeded in the kingship (so said the priests) by his son
Pheros. This king made no wars; and it happened that he became blind, for the follow-
ing reason: the Nile came down in a flood such as never was before, rising to a height
of eighteen cubits, and the water which overflowed the fields was roughened by a strong
wind; then, it is said, the king was so infatuated that he took a spear and hurled it into
the midst of the river eddies. Straightway after this he suffered from a disease of the
eyes, and became blind. When he had been blind for ten years, an oracle from the city
of Buto declared to him that the time of his punishment was drawing to an end, and
that he should regain his sight by washing his eyes with the issue of a woman who had
never had intercourse with any man but her own husband. Pheros made trial with his
own wife first, and as he still remained blind, with all women, one after another. When

[1] Book II, § 68. Trans. cited, I, 355, 357.
[2] Mr Godley, in a note to this passage (Vol. I, p. 357), says that it is the Egyptian spur-winged lapwing (*Hoplopterus armatus*)—Translator.
[3] Book II, § 73. Trans. cited, I, 359, 361.

19. *The nymph Arethusa. Syracusan coin, struck in 413, after the defeat of the Athenians*
    in Sicily

he at last recovered sight, he took all the women of whom he had made trial, save only her who had made him to see again, and gathered them into one town, that which is now called 'Red Clay'; where having collected them together he burnt them and the town; but the woman by whose means he had recovered sight he took to wife.[1]

Larcher, the French translator of Herodotus, annotates this passage as follows:

One may conclude (from this story) that the corruption of morals had gone very far indeed in Egypt. One has no difficulty in understanding the wise precaution that Abraham took when visiting this country, and also the excessive impudence with which Potiphar's wife behaved towards Joseph.

Abraham's wise precaution, to which Larcher alludes, was to present his wife as his sister. In this way he assured his marital honour, and the fair Sarah could pass into the arms of Pharoah, while her 'brother' drew a notable profit from it. Which was the naïve, and which the more moral, Herodotus or his translator?

I should like finally to quote a page of Herodotus which seems to me to serve as a conclusion to so many passages. This is a page on the diversity of customs, a theme familiar to the historian. It justifies Herodotus' long enquiry. A knowledge of the diversity of customs astonishes the mind, attracts and amuses it. But it does far more. While custom weighs like a yoke on the thoughts of each people, attached as it is to the customs it practises, the knowledge of customs as a whole, in their infinite and contradictory variety, is in the hands of the historian an instrument for the liberation of the mind. Here are Herodotus' reflexions:

For if it were proposed to all nations to choose which seemed best of all customs, each, after examination made, would place its own first; so well is each persuaded that its own are by far the best. It is not therefore to be supposed that any, save a madman, would turn such things to ridicule. I will give this one proof among many from which it may be inferred that all men hold this belief about their customs: When Darius was king, he summoned the Greeks who were with him and asked them what price would persuade them to eat their fathers' dead bodies. They answered that there was no price for which they would do it. Then he summoned those Indians who are called Callatiae, who eat their parents, and asked them (the Greeks being present and understanding by interpretation what was said) what would make them willing to burn their fathers at death. The Indians cried aloud, that he should not speak of so horrid an act. So firmly rooted are these beliefs; and it is, I think, rightly said in Pindar's poem that use and wont is lord of all.[2]

One might think one was reading a page of Montaigne.

[1] Book II, § 111. Trans. cited, I, 399, 401.   [2] Book II, § 38. Trans. cited, Vol. II, p. 51.

K

20. *Four-horse chariot-race. Coin of Acragas* (c. 410)

CHAPTER SEVEN

THE POSITION OF MEDICAL SCIENCE
IN THE FIFTH CENTURY: HIPPOCRATES

When, in Aeschylus' tragedy, Prometheus is enumerating the benefits that primitive men owed him, he gives the first place to medicine.

> *Of all the greatest [arts], if a man fell sick,*
> *There was no remedy, nor shredded herb*
> *Nor draught to drink nor ointment, and in default*
> *Of physic their flesh withered, until I*
> *Revealed the blends of gentle medicines*
> *Wherewith they arm themselves against disease....*[1]

In the fifth century B.C. Hippocrates, with a long tradition to rely upon, was the Prometheus of medicine.

The tradition was a body of medical knowledge, entirely lay and practical in character, which had been handed down through certain corporations of doctors, and, as far we are concerned, went back to the *Iliad*. In that poem where death is always present we meet more than one doctor, sometimes mere amateurs who were, however, capable of opening and disinfecting wounds, of binding them up, of applying compresses and sometimes powder made from pounded roots. It even happens that these doctors in the *Iliad* carry out genuine operations. Homer knows and describes one hundred and forty-one wounds, often precisely; he is also familiar with a great number of the bodily organs. The medical profession is, in this epic, exercised by free men whom everyone respects. 'A physician,' he writes, 'is alone worth many men.'

Magical medicine occupies virtually no place in the *Iliad*. In the *Odyssey*, however, which is a fairy tale, the enchantresses encountered in exotic lands carry

---

[1] Aeschylus: *The Prometheus Bound*, edited with Introduction, Commentary and Translation by George Thomson, Cambridge University Press, 1932, p. 87.

out exorcisms. And in the centuries that followed, including the fifth, a mystical current of eastern origin gathered force and seems to have invaded the popular mind and, even in the eyes of philosophers, to have obscured scientific research. To the sanctuaries of Aesculapius, at Tricca in Thessaly and especially at Epidaurus, pilgrims flocked in numbers and miracles abounded. At Epidaurus, inscriptions made by the priests in the form of votive-tablets bring us an echo of these miraculous cures which always took place in sleep, as a consequence of the god's intervention in a dream (cures by faith, as certain believers still say). Here is one, and not the strangest of them:

Ambrosia of Athens, the one-eyed. This woman came to the god's temple and mocked at certain of his cures. She declared it incredible that the lame and the blind should recover, merely in consequence of a dream. Then she went to sleep in the temple and had a dream. It seemed to her that the god approached her and said he would cure her, but that she would have to offer him, in his temple, a pig wrought in silver, in witness of her folly. When he had thus spoken, he pierced the unsound eye and poured in a remedy. The next day she departed, cured.

Empedocles in the *Purifications* and Plato in more than one place attest the fact that belief in the virtue of incantations and of magical medicine was not foreign to the thought of classical Greece.

Now the inscriptions at Epidaurus date from the same years as the works attributed to Hippocrates. It would be a great mistake to admit, as certain writers still do, that Greek medicine originated in the sanctuaries. In the era of rationalism in Greece there were two medical traditions, parallel but entirely distinct. Whereas, in the orbit of the sanctuaries, exorcisms, dreams, signs and miracles, all docile to the voice of the priests, were numerous, it is remarkable to observe the existence at the same time of a medical art entirely lay and independent, the tendencies of which were indeed very diverse but which never inclined to superstition and in which the outline of the priest who heals, or who interprets the healing god, never appears even as an object of criticism or raillery.

On the one side, there is never a question of methodical scientific research which aims at establishing the material causes of maladies, or rules transcending the particular case of each patient, but only of miracles arbitrarily accomplished by virtue of the good pleasure of the god. On the other side, without the doctor's mind being in any way atheistic, we see him resolutely set aside any explanation that would refer simply to the god. Characteristic and remarkably bold in this respect is the opening of the treatise entitled *The Sacred Disease*. The author declares:

I do not believe that the 'Sacred Disease'[1] is any more divine or sacred than any other disease but, on the contrary, has specific characteristics and a definite cause. Nevertheless, because it is completely different from other diseases, it has been regarded as a divine visitation by those who, being only human, view it with ignorance and astonishment. This theory of divine origin, though supported by the difficulty of understanding the malady, is weakened by the simplicity of the cure. . . .

It is my opinion that those who first called this disease 'sacred' were the sort of people we now call witch-doctors, faith-healers, quacks and charlatans. These are exactly the people who pretend to be very pious and to be particularly wise. By invoking a divine element they were able to screen their own failure to give suitable treatment and so called this a 'sacred' malady to conceal their ignorance of its nature.[2]

This treatise on the 'Sacred Disease' forms part of what, since the time of the Alexandrines, has been called the *Hippocratic Collection*, that is, a group of about seventy treatises attributed by the ancients to the great physician of Cos. Most of these works were in fact written during the lifetime of Hippocrates, in the second half of the fifth century or at the beginning of the fourth. Some, though they are difficult to distinguish, are the work of the master of Cos himself or of his immediate disciples; others on the contrary are by physicians of schools or tendencies in rivalry with the school of Cos.

In the *Hippocratic Collection* one may roughly distinguish three principal groups of writers. There are the medical theorists, philosophers fond of adventurous speculation. At the opposite pole are the physicians of the school of Cnidus whose respect for facts is such that they are incapable of transcending them. Finally—and this third group comprises Hippocrates and his disciples of the school of Cos—there are the physicians who, relying upon observation and taking observation as their only starting-point, are constantly concerned with interpreting and understanding it. They are men of a positive temper; they reject arbitrary suppositions and always appeal to reason. These three groups of writers are all opposed to the medical practice of the sanctuaries; but only the last group were the founders of medicine as a science.[3]

[1] Epilepsy (Translator's note).

[2] *The Medical Works of Hippocrates*: a new translation from the original Greek made . . . by the collaboration of John Chadwick and W. N. Mann. Oxford, Blackwell Scientific Publications, Ltd, 1950, pp. 179-80.

[3] In the whole of the present study I shall closely follow M. Louis Bourgey's work, *Observation et Expérience chez les Médecins de la Collection hippocratique* (1953). This book has guided me in the discovery of material that has been for me very new. I ought to refer to it on almost every line of this chapter; but the practice is not one I could adopt in this work on *Greek Civilization* written for the general reader. I am, however, anxious to pay special homage to M. Bourgey's knowledge and to beg him to allow me to regard this knowledge as a common treasure which he has placed at the disposal of all who are desirous of widening their culture (Author's note).

◎

The medical theorists will not occupy us for very long. They were brilliant jugglers with words, men who were taking part in the vast movement that touched, often accurately, on every branch of human activity and that was called sophistry. Their method in this instance proceeded in a manner contrary to that of the sane scientific method. Instead of starting with an examination of the facts, the writers of this group usually started from general ideas borrowed from the philosophy or the beliefs of the time; they were satisfied with applying in a very arbitrary way one or other of these ideas to the medical facts they had to explain. These ideas were often merely preconceived notions, as for example the predominant place accorded to the number seven in human activities.

The treatises on *The Flesh*, *The Seven-Months' Foetus* and *The Eight-Months' Foetus* show or pretend to show that, if the foetus can come to birth at the end of seven months, or of nine months and ten days, this is because in both cases it counts an exact number of weeks, namely thirty or forty respectively. These treatises also point out, as proofs, that a normal man's resistance to hunger is for seven days, that children's final teeth come at the age of seven, that in severe maladies the crises occur at the end of half a week, of a week, of a week and a half, and of two weeks.

The treatise on *Winds*, which some persist in regarding as containing the key to Hippocrates' doctrine, is less a medical treatise than a prettily written dissertation on the part played by the air and the breeze, both as the principle by which the universe advances, the principle of the change of the seasons, and as the cause of all maladies: epidemic fevers and plagues, catarrhs, inflammations, haemoptysis (spitting of blood), dropsy, apoplexy, colic, and even yawning. Some ten treatises in the *Collection* belong to this sophistical medicine, brilliant but vain, and far removed from Hippocrates' practice. And yet in the least bad of them one encounters judicious remarks which appear to be the result of genuine experience.

For example: in the treatise *On Regimen*, which begins by holding forth at large on the nature of man, and of the soul which is a mixture of water and fire; and oddly groups discussions on the sexes, twins and the arts, one is surprised to come upon a very well composed catalogue of pot-herbs and their properties, a list of the virtues of cereals, for example barley, according as it is absorbed with its husk or freed from its husk and boiled or roasted, or barley-bread, according as it is eaten when it has been kneaded or some time after, or again wheat-bread, whether it is white, brown or leavened. There are pages and pages on vegetables, others on the properties of meat, beginning with beef and not forgetting hedgehog. The discursive and pseudo-philosophical tone of the opening part of the treatise gives

place to incredible menus with marginal information on all the risks of flatulence
and on the diuretic or nourishing effects of each kind of food. The hazy theories
in the introduction—a kind of medicine which Aristophanes ridicules in *The
Clouds*—are replaced by a flood of advice on the usefulness of repeated vomiting
and the value of walking as an exercise. It should be noted that the author says he
has drawn up these regimens for 'ordinary men, those who, living from day to
day, have not the means of abandoning all their work and simply looking after
their health'. After this, he sets out another regimen, a 'fine discovery' he has made
for the use of the well-to-do. No one, he says, had previously thought of this;
whereupon he plunges into a rigmarole of subtle distinctions which minister to
his vanity. Here he has certainly departed from that down-to-earth science which
he had patiently followed for a time.

One must also do justice to the treatises on *The Seven-Months' Foetus* and the
Eight-Months', which, apart from the dissertations about weeks and months,
contains at least one accurate and even moving page on the dangers run by the
new-born child:

> *A danger now arises from the conditions of food and breathing which have been
> modified by birth. If new-born children absorb any unwholesome germ, it is by the
> mouth and nose. Whereas previously only what was exactly sufficient and nothing else
> could enter the organism, many more things will now enter it. And owing to this super-
> abundance of supplies from outside, owing also to the constitution of the child's body,
> eliminations become necessary. These are effected partly through the mouth and nose,
> partly through the intestine and the bladder. Now, previously, nothing of all this took
> place.*
>
> *Therefore, instead of breaths and humours which were congenerous to him and to
> which he was adapted and with which he was familiar in the womb, the child now, as
> soon as he is born, uses things which to him are foreign, rough, harsh and not so to
> speak humanized: hence there necessarily result a good deal of suffering and many
> deaths. Instead of being enveloped in flesh and in humours mild and moist, adapted to
> his nature, the child finds himself clothed in materials like an adult. The navel-string
> is at first the only way by which the mother communicates with the child; it is by this
> means that the child shares in what she receives. Other means are closed to him and
> open only after he is born; at that moment, indeed, everything opens, while the navel-
> string shrinks, closes and dries up.*

At the opposite pole to these theoretical physicians or 'iatrosophists', we find in
the *Hippocratic Collection* the medicine of the school of Cnidus, the rival or emu-
lator of the school of Cos. The treatises that best represent the Cnidian practice in

this collection are the *Internal Affections* and the *Maladies* (Section II). To these one should add about a dozen treatises which, without being strictly Cnidian, are more or less related to the conceptions of that school. These include several works on gynaecology.

The Cnidian practitioners are marked by the taste for precise and even minute-observation, by a concern for giving concrete and detailed descriptions of maladies, and by avoiding any excessive generalizations or 'philosophical' evasions. In this school the physician is directed to what has always been the centre of his art: clinical observation. These Cnidians are therefore primarily practitioners. They scarcely go beyond direct observation and are afraid of straining, or over-interpreting, the statements of the patient. Their fidelity to facts is slightly limited and this limits their horizon. They are content with classifying maladies and, when it comes to treating them, they rely on a therapeutic that has been tested by tradition. They engage in no medical debates and they do not seek out the causes of maladies, reduced to the behaviour of two 'humours', bile and phlegm. They avoid any difficult problem, which they regard as insoluble. In short, they do not try to understand.

In classifying, they multiply divisions and seem to multiply maladies. The *Internal Affections* and the *Maladies*, II, enumerate and describe three kinds of hepatitis, five maladies of the spleen, five kinds of typhus, four maladies of the kidneys, three sorts of angina, four of polypus, four of jaundice, five of dropsy, seven of consumption and a great number of diseases of the brain.

Of course, some of these distinctions were justified, as well as being new, as, for example, those of acute articular rheumatism, and also of gout, which was called 'podagra'. But most of them are imaginary or not well established.

Here, for example, is a description of one of the kinds of consumption mentioned:

This is produced by excess of fatigue. The incidence of the malady is much the same as in the last case, but abatements are more frequent and there is relaxation in summer. The patient expectorates, but the spit is thicker. The cough is more severe in old men. The pain in the chest is greater, as though a stone is weighing on it. There is also pain in the back. The skin is damp. The least effort causes the patient to pant and be short of breath. One generally dies of this malady in three years' time.

Elsewhere, another kind of consumption is described:

As the malady develops, the patient grows thin, except for the legs, which swell. The nails retract. The shoulders become thin and feeble. The patient feels as though his throat were full of down; the breath whistles as through a tube. He is tormented with thirst, and the whole body is enfeebled. In this state one does not last out the year.

The description is often very expressive. Certain features compel one's attention: thus, the patient who is trying to breathe 'opens his nostrils like a running horse: his tongue hangs out like that of a dog who feels scorched by the heat in summer'. These are accurate and striking images. The physicians of Cnidus are none the less subject to a sort of frenzy for nomenclature, and it is remarkable how this profusion of descriptions is matched with a considerable poverty in therapeutics: the watchwords are always: purge, cause to vomit (vomiting being regarded as a purgation), give milk, cauterize. There was, however, one singular kind of treatment which they advocated. The administration of 'errhins' was a strange practice, which consisted in placing substances of varied composition in the nose, in order to cure maladies which the physician believed to be situated in the head, such as apoplexy, jaundice and consumption. These 'errhins' were head-purgatives, and their use supposed a communication between the nose and the brain. But do not we still speak of a cold in the head?

One may also note a method of exploring the lung which was used by the physician who, before attempting any remedial measure, needed to ascertain the exact position of an overflow of which he suspected the existence in the pleural cavity. The text indicates in this connexion that after 'placing the patient on a solid chair and while an assistant holds his hands', the physician 'takes him by the shoulders and shakes him, applying his ear to one side and to the other in order to ascertain whether the seat of the malady is on the right side or the left'. This method which is known as 'Hippocratic succussion'—although it is really Cnidian —was forgotten or disregarded by the medical tradition of later ages, but it illustrates the inventive ingenuity of the Cnidian doctors as regards the observation of facts. Laënnec, however, says that he used it, in accordance with the old treatises, and found it helpful.

'Hippocratic succussion' reminds us that the Cnidian medical practice, the empirical nature of which tended to become purely pragmatic, not to say a matter of routine, was none the less led to make several discoveries of which the principal was auscultation. Thus the habit of faithfully observing symptoms brought its rewards. A passage, other than that already quoted, attests the practice of 'sounding' the patient. The physician, writes the author of *Maladies*, II, 'when applying his ear for some time to the patient's side, hears what sounds like boiling vinegar'. And other passages confirm the view that the auscultation practised by fifth-century doctors was no doubt a Cnidian invention.

Again in the Cnidian treatises or those related to them we find mention of numerous surgical operations and a description of the instruments that made them possible. The treatment of a polypus in the nose was simple and brutal: sometimes it was cauterized by means of a red-hot iron; sometimes it was pulled out with the help of a rod to which was attached 'a cord made of sinew'. The surgeon adjusted it and gave a sharp pull. An incision in the loins is advised in three out of the four renal maladies. The incision, the author specifies, should be made 'at the place where the organ is most swollen', and it should be 'deep'. Incisions in the thorax are numerous: they are made between the ribs and the surgeon first uses a 'convex scalpel' and then continues with a 'slender scalpel'. The most daring operation practised by the Cnidians was trepanning the skull in order to release a liquid overflow which was threatening the sight, and this without damaging the eye. The cures that were effected are mentioned and also the two kinds of trepanning that were employed.

Little more need be said. The medical practice of Cnidus undoubtedly represents an immense effort on the part of professionals with a view to establishing their system on the rigorous observation of facts. One must recognize, however, that this effort did not come to much. The great merit of these doctors lay in their refusal to yield to the attraction of philosophical conjectures which could not be verified. They wished to know and transmit only those facts which had been observed in medical tradition; to this tradition they added the cases they had themselves collected. They paid attention only to patients, whom it was their business to care for according to the methods they judged as having been best put to the proof.

It will no doubt be noticed, and not without reason, that their distrust of speculation and hypothesis led, in the daily practice of their profession, to a more general, unconscious distrust of intelligence itself. To reflect on medicine was not their business. Very rarely indeed do their writings offer the smallest general notion, the smallest formula that sounds like a thought. But one may cite at least one reflexion, that was perhaps unique. It relates to the method which permits medical science to make progress, and is found in the treatise on the location of the organs in the body. The author of this work was, if not a Cnidian doctor, at least a doctor closely related to the school; and his is by far the most interesting treatise we have hitherto encountered. He writes: 'The nature of the body is the starting-point of medical reasoning'—a sentence which far transcends the ordinary empiricism of the Cnidians. He understood that all the parts of the body are jointly answerable to each other; and this is why, by taking as his foundation the reflexion I have quoted, he places, before the pathological exposition he has undertaken, a statement on general anatomy that serves to focus it. Thus, in his eyes, medical practice has no more solid foundation than the study of the human organism.

Certain modern writers have associated the sentence quoted above with Claude Bernard: a very great honour, and well deserved, for the modest, anonymous practitioner who wrote the treatise. No other work of the Cnidian school or its associates would call for such a comparison. As regards this author's statements on anatomy, they are far from being exact. However, this doctor, who wrote *The Places of the Organs in Man*, was aware that the sensory organs are connected with the brain; he accurately observed the membranes of the eye and the encephalon; he knew that the upper *vena cava* takes back the blood to the heart; on the other hand he seems to have confused the lower *vena cava* with the *aorta*.

For the rest, it is less a question of noting the accuracy of the results of his enquiry than of observing the soundness of a method which was attempting to found pathology on a knowledge of anatomy.

Before leaving the honest practitioners of Cnidus and considering the authors in the *Collection* who belong to the school of Hippocrates, we should say a few words about the remarkable treatise *Of the Heart*. The influence of the Cnidian school can be traced in this work, here and there. It has recently been attributed, with some likelihood, to the learned Philistion, a doctor of the Sicilian school. This master professed in Syracuse at the beginning of the fourth century, and Plato knew him. There is no doubt that, scalpel in hand, Philistion manipulated a human heart. He not only states that he did, referring to an ancient Egyptian practice, but the exactness of his anatomical description confirms the statement that he had 'extracted the heart from a dead man'. He not only practised dissection but also vivisection of animals; how otherwise could he have discovered that the auricles continue to contract when the ventricles have already ceased beating? This is the fact; and it is why the right auricle is called *ultimum moriens*.

What then was his anatomical knowledge of the heart? He knew that the heart was 'a muscle very powerful, not because of its tendinous (or sinewy) parts, but through the felting of the flesh'. He knew that the heart possesses two ventricles and two auricles; he distinguished between the right side and the left side of the heart and was aware that there is no direct communication between them. He observes: 'The two ventricles are the source of human life. From them issue the [*two*] streams [*the pulmonary artery and the aorta*] which supply all the inside of the body; by them the habitat of the soul is irrigated. When these sources of life are dried up, a man is dead.'

But Philistion made even more delicate observations. He distinguished between the veins and the arteries according to the different nature of their tissue. He noted, very correctly, that the heart is inclined to the left, that its point is formed solely by the left ventricle and that the tissue of the latter is thicker and more resistant than that of the right ventricle. Lastly—and this was the masterpiece of his observation—he briefly but with great precision described the valves which establish communication between the ventricles and auricles and those which are placed on the pulmonary artery and on the aorta. The latter, which are the sigmoid or half-moon valves and are composed of three membranous folds, are able absolutely to close the arterial orifice. He observed too that the valves of the pulmonary artery offer a weaker resistance to pressure than those of the aorta.

It may cause surprise that so sagacious an observer, a scientist who attempted a real experiment—badly conducted, it is true—on a pig in order to discover the origin of the liquid which is in the pericardium and which bathes the heart—it may cause surprise that such a scientist could be satisfied with extravagant conjectures in order to explain the physiological function of the heart. But that is the fact, and it indicates that the author of the treatise *Of the Heart* did not go far beyond the level of scientific exigency which obtained among the Cnidian doctors. But one's astonishment would itself be very 'unscientific'. Science is built up slowly upon a strange amalgam of truths, 'sound intuitions' and errors. For centuries the history of science has been only like the history of the Tower of Babel. The errors of scientists are, in the last resort, as profitable to science as the sound intuitions because they are the first to solicit rectification.

The aim of this brief analysis of the *Hippocratic Collection* is to show that in its early days science advances in zigzags.

◎

But now, in the heart of the *Collection*, we find seven or eight treatises the nature of which can be recognized at once: they are the product of genius. If it is not possible to prove that Hippocrates was personally their author, we can at least affirm that these treatises were written by his closest disciples. It is extremely probable that one or other of them was by the Coan master himself. But which? We must not lose ourselves amid fictitious problems. We know that Hippocrates wrote treatises. Eight works are today ascribed to him now by one critic now by another, and the scholars who recognize this authorship are of the most circumspect kind.

These are the treatises on *Airs Waters Places, Prognosis, Regimen in Acute Diseases, Epidemics,* Books I and III, the first four sections of the *Aphorisms,* lastly the works on *The Joints* and *Fractures,* treatises on surgery which are the masterpiece of the *Collection.* Worthy of the master but certainly by another hand is the work on *Tradition in Medicine* which was composed when Hippocrates was a young man (440 or 430 B.C.) This contains a very masterly definition of positive or rational medicine, the kind which Hippocrates was to practise in his maturity. To this list of major works we must add a few treatises of ethical complexion— *The Oath, The Law, The Doctor, The Canon, The Precepts,* etc.—works which, towards the end of the fifth century and the beginning of the fourth, expanded the medical science of Hippocrates into a medical humanism.[1]

'*Un nuage est jeté sur la vie d'Hippocrate*', wrote Littré. In this situation we can only record the circumstances of which we are most sure.

Hippocrates was born on Cos. Although this island had been colonized by Dorians, its civilization and dialect were Ionian. The date of his birth can be fixed with more certainty than is usual with ancient writers. Born in 460, he was an exact contemporary of Democritus and Thucydides. He belonged to the family of the Asclepiadae, a corporation of doctors who claimed descent from Asclepios, the great physician of Homeric times. It had been only after Homer that the latter was regarded as a god. In this family, an entirely human knowledge of medicine was transmitted from father to son, from master to disciple. Hippocrates had sons and a son-in-law who were doctors, and numerous pupils.

In the fifth century the Asclepiadae, who were also called the school of Cos, maintained like all cultural guilds a registered membership and a set of customs that were entirely religious: for example, the practice of the oath which closely bound the pupil to his master, his colleagues and the duties of the profession. But if the religious character of the guild implied a certain moral attitude, it in no way impaired the search for truth which remained strictly scientific in purpose.

The medical science which was founded in fifth-century Greece, and notably that of the Coan school, was opposed to anything in the nature of the super-natural. If one wished to find an ancestor for the Hippocratic physician, it would not be the priest or the philosopher of nature. The author of *Tradition in Medicine* understood this when he composed a polemical work with the object of defending medicine as an *art*. Actually the word he uses has a sense intermediate between that of technique and science. He blames in particular Empedocles who was both physician and philosopher, whose philosophy was full of intuitions of genius but also of pitfalls for the reason, and who was mistaken when he declared 'that it is impossible to have a knowledge of medicine when one does not know what man is and that this is precisely the knowledge which must have been acquired by him who wishes properly to care for the sick'. No, says the author of *Tradition in Medicine*, the art of healing derives neither from the knowledge of nature nor from any philosophy of a mystical kind. He rejects any connexion between the philosopher (or the priest) and the doctor. The ancestor of the doctor he holds to

[1] In what I imagine to be the latest English translation of *The Medical Works of Hippocrates* (Oxford, Blackwell, 1950), the translators, Mr John Chadwick and Mr W. N. Mann, M.D., F.R.C.P., include the following works: *The Oath, The Canon, Tradition in Medicine, Epidemics*, I and III, *The Science of Medicine, Airs Waters Places, Prognosis, Regimen in Acute Diseases, Aphorisms, The Sacred Disease, Dreams (Regimen, IV), The Nature of Man, A Regimen for Health* and the *Coan Prognosis* (Translator).

have been humble and busied with humble, necessary and positive tasks; he was, he says, the cook.

With great perspicacity he explains that in primitive times men ate their food raw, like wild beasts. This 'indigestible and animal-like diet' resulted in a high rate of mortality. A long period of time was needed for men to discover a more 'diluted' kind of food. Gradually they learned how to husk barley and wheat, how to grind the corn and knead the flour, cook it in the oven and make bread.

They boiled and baked and mixed and diluted the strong raw foods with the weaker ones . . . always with a view to man's nature and his capabilities . . . (because) the body draws nourishment and thus grows and is healthy from food it is able to digest. . . . What fairer or more fitting name can be given to such research and discovery than that of medicine . . . ?[1]

It was this kind of diet planned for the human being, this medical science of health as much as of sickness, a diet for the athletic as much as for the most ailing, that Hippocrates worked for with passionate ardour through the course of a long life. He travelled a good deal in Greece and abroad, continuing the tradition of the itinerant physicians or 'periodeutes'. In reading the pages of Hippocrates we see those travelling doctors of Homeric times as they settle down for long sojourns in some new country and practise medicine while observing the manners and habits of the people.

Hippocrates enjoyed the greatest celebrity in his lifetime. Plato, who belonged to the younger generation but was his contemporary in the wider sense of the term, when comparing medicine with other arts in one of the dialogues, places him in parallel with the greatest sculptors of the time, Polycleitus of Argos and Pheidias of 'Athens. He died at an advanced age, not before 375 B.C., when he would have been eighty-five; it is thought he might have reached the age of a hundred and thirty. Ancient tradition was unanimous in acribing to him great longevity.

Such are the well attested circumstances of a life entirely devoted to the service of the human body. Side by side with them an abundance of legend circulated while the master was still living. The natural practice of medicine seemed an astonishing prodigy, and it gave rise to legends, as it were accompanying too pure a melody. We should ignore these embroideries if one or other of them did not find credit even today. Thus the story of Hippocrates' being in Athens at the time of the famous plague (which was not really a plague) and of what he did to disinfect the city, rests on no serious testimony. Thucydides who records many details of this epidemic and speaks about the doctors who struggled with it, says

[1] Trans. cited, p. 14.

not a word about Hippocrates. This is no doubt an argument *a silentio*, but in the circumstances it is decisive. The story of his refusal to accept Artaxerxes' presents is a pure legend. So too is the story of his conversation with Democritus, to which I have alluded above, when quoting La Fontaine.

What for us counts infinitely more than these 'stories' is the thought, the practice of medicine which fills the authentic writings of the master with absolutely convincing actions and reflexions.

In reading these texts we are, in the first place, struck with his insatiable appetite for information. The physician begins by looking, and his glance is keen: he asks questions and takes notes. The great collection of the seven books of the *Epidemics* is simply a series of notes taken at the patient's bedside, amid the disorder of a round of medical visits: they present cases that have been met with but not yet classified. The text is often interrupted by a general reflexion, unrelated to the other cases but apparently noted by the doctor at the chance dictation of his ever restless mind.

Occasionally one of these reflexions related to the method of examining the patient and the decisive and revealing words often appear on the record with a precision which transcends any simple concern with observation and reveals the scientist's turn of mind. 'The examination of the body is a serious business, requiring good sight, good hearing, and sense of smell and touch and taste, and power of reasoning.' This last word is a surprise and it delights us.

The treatise called *Aphorisms* which is the most famous and which Rabelais used to explain, from the Greek text, to his students at Montpellier—an unparalleled achievement in 1531—and of which he published the first modern edition—this treatise is simply a collection of reflexions which had come into the doctor's mind like shafts of light and been noted down in the midst of a busy day.

Everyone knows the first of the aphorisms, as compact as the compendium of a method tested over a long period: 'Life is short, science is long; opportunity is elusive, experiment is dangerous, judgment is difficult.'[1] In these words we see summarized the whole of a doctor's career, with its failures, its risks, its successes over maladies that have been achieved by science founded on practice, by a diagnostic boldly formulated in the midst of difficulty. Experience here is not separated from reason and reason is rooted, with some difficulty, in 'dangerous' ground.

Here are some reflexions on the examination of the patient, in *Epidemics*, Book I:

The factors which enable us to distinguish between diseases are as follows: First we must consider the nature of man in general and of each individual and the character-

[1] Trans. cited, p. 148.

istics of each disease. Then we must consider the patient, what food is given to him and who gives it—for this may make it easier for him to take or more difficult—the conditions of climate and locality both in general and in particular, the patient's customs, mode of life, pursuits and age. Then we must consider his speech, his mannerisms, his silences, his thoughts, his habits of sleep or wakefulness and his dreams, their nature and time. Next, we must note whether he plucks his hair, scratches or weeps. We must observe his paroxysms, his stools, urine, sputum and vomit. We look for any change in the state of the malady, how often such changes occur and their nature, and the particular change which induces death or a crisis. Observe, too, sweating, shivering, chill, cough, sneezing, hiccough, the kind of breathing, belching, wind, whether silent or noisy, haemorrhages and haemorrhoids. We must determine the significance of all these signs.[1]

The amplitude of these demands will have been noted. The medical examination takes account not only of the present bodily state of the patient, but also of his previous maladies and the traces they may have left. It takes account of his way of life, and the climate in which he lives; it does not forget that this patient is a man like others and that, to know him, one must know other men. It even sounds his thoughts; his very silences are informative. Under so heavy a task, any mind but one of the greatest breadth and scope would find itself lost.

This medical science is definitely psychosomatic. One might express the thought more simply by saying that it is the medicine of the whole man, body and soul, connected with his environment and also with his past. The consequences of this thorough examination will be seen in the treatment, which will require that the patient shall in his turn, under the doctor's guidance, participate body and soul in his recovery.

Along with the scope of the investigation goes that rapid glance in which the doctor judges the gravity of the case; for 'the opportunity' to change the course of a malady for the better is 'elusive'. The famous description of the 'Hippocratic facies'—the 'facies' which reveals the approach of death—bears witness to the sureness and acumen of the master's eye. The author of *Prognosis* writes:

The signs to watch for in acute diseases are as follows. First study the patient's facies; whether it has a healthy look and in particular whether it be exactly as it normally is. If the patient's normal appearance is preserved, this is best; just as the more abnormal it is, the worse it is. The latter appearance may be described thus: the nose sharp, the eyes sunken, the temples fallen in, the ears cold and drawn in and their lobes distorted, the skin of the face hard, stretched and dry, and the colour of the face pale or dusky . . .

[1] Trans. cited, p. 42.

Should the illness have passed the third day before the face assumes this appearance [the doctor should ask certain questions already specified, examine the whole body, and pay] *particular attention to the eyes. For if they avoid the glare of light, or lacrimate without due cause, or squint, or the one becomes smaller than the other* ... *or if the eyes wander, or project, or are deeply sunken, or if the whole complexion of the face be altered; then all these things must be considered bad signs.* ... *It is also a fatal sign if the lips are parted and hang loose and become cold and white.*[1]

The great attention which is given in this passage to the sick person's condition and appearance, as also in the innumerable cases studied in the *Epidemics* where one feels that the doctor, under whatever pressure of work, is anxious to note nothing but that which is exact and of which he has received the 'sensation'—this abundance of immediate observation—does not present Hippocrates from paying similar attention to the conditions of environment in which men live. The treatise on *Airs, Waters, Places* is a study of the highest interest on the relations between environment and the health of the population.

M. Bourgey observes in this connexion: 'The [ancient] doctor takes an interest not only in the sick but, in a larger measure than is done today, in the healthy man by prescribing a whole hygiene of living, with health in view.' As we saw above, *Tradition in Medicine* declared that the medical art, encumbered with philosophy or puffed up with sophistry, could be rediscovered by starting from research into the kind of diet suitable for a healthy man and for a sick man. Hippocrates follows this line of research. He does not wish simply to be a healer, but to enlighten men on the conditions of health, that most precious of gifts. He is the physician of health even more than of disease.

In *Airs, Waters, Places* he studies the mode of life among a great number of peoples and gives descriptions which are precise and stand out in a striking manner. Hippocrates knows that it is useful for the physician as for the specialist in hygiene to know each man's mode of living.

The physician must not fail to know whether his patient is fond of wine, inclined to good cheer, or to sensuality, or whether he prefers gymnastics and physical effort to these more facile pleasures. Only the nature of the social environment and, in the first place, the physical environment will inform him. He devotes an unequalled conscientiousness and perspicacity to determining the exact relationships, those of cause and effect, which in all countries unite man with his natural *milieu*. Facts for his enquiry are provided by very many European and Asiatic countries. In each one, he considers the climate and from this draws conclusions concerning certain local maladies such as fevers

[1] Trans. cited, pp. 112–13.

21. *The Nile at Assouan, the ancient Syene. This was the southern limit of Herodotus' travels in Egypt*

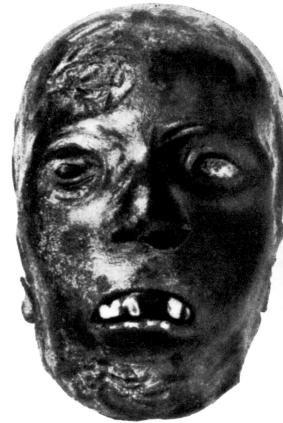

which, when he has discovered their origin, he strives to treat more effectively.

Attentively he studies the seasons. He seeks to discover their influence, and the influence of their changes, at the equinoxes and the solstices, on various maladies. Some seasons have a 'disorderly' and, so to speak, abnormal character. On this question he touches in another treatise. These seasons are, as it were, the sicknesses of the year, and they in their turn give rise to maladies. The doctor is aware of the recrudescence, in the course of the summer, of intermittent fevers.

He studies the water-supply, and treats of the effects which certain waters may have on the human body, particularly brackish water from ponds, and excessively cold water. Stagnant water gives rise to quartan fever. The doctor orders some kinds of water to be boiled.

This treatise is not made up of commonplace statements, repetitions of the axioms that man is dependent on his physical environment, that the nature of the soil contributes to form the nature of the body, and so on. For Hippocrates it is a question of knowing whether such and such a man, living on such and such a spot of the earth's crust, subject to such and such influences, eating this and drinking that, is not liable to contract a specific malady. It is by visiting the countries of Europe and Asia and devoting himself to those concrete enquiries that Hippocrates is led to make serious studies of manners, to show that the soil and the sky exercise a definite influence on the character of peoples. He studies what was formerly called 'ethnopsychy'. Man thinks and acts in accordance with the environment in which he lives. In all this, however, the author does not forget to invoke the influence of social conditions on the development and even the constitution of the organism. In this matter he introduces the distinction, familiar to the sophists, between nature (phusis) and custom (nomos).

All these considerations and many others explain why *Airs, Waters, Places* is an attempt, solidly documented and perhaps the only attempt of its kind in two thousand years, to study attentively and at one and the same time medical and geographical, not to speak of meteorological, facts. This is what makes this modest treatise one of the most original that the ancient world has bequeathed to us. Accustomed as we are to the partitioning of the sciences, our modern minds are rather disconcerted by the multiplicity of facts which Hippocrates has assembled and directed to a single aim—that of health.

◎

But Hippocrates does not stop short at observation. In the strictly Hippocratic treatises of the *Collection,* which at first glance seem to be only an assemblage of observations, we feel the domination of a powerful will—the will to understand

L

22. *Heads of a Scythian king (on the left) and his concubine, discovered in a tomb in the region of the Altai Mountains, where a branch of the Scythian people once flourished*

the facts that have been collected and find in them a meaning that will be useful to men.

'I believe,' writes the author of *Regimen in Acute Diseases*, 'that attention should be paid to all the details of the science (of healing).'[1] Similar formulae recur in most of the treatises ascribed to Hippocrates. Thought is always present, if only on the watch, in the midst of observation. Therein lies the fundamental attitude that distinguishes a doctor of Cos from a doctor of Cnidus.

Here is *Prognosis*. The doctor is considering a case of otitis (acute ear-ache). He notes many symptoms of it, and adds immediately: 'In view of the dangerous nature of this condition, special attention [the mind, the intelligence] must be paid from the first day to any other signs.'[2]

Let us turn now to the *Epidemics*, the clinical doctor's collection of reference-notes. Here we see the physician who we think should be submerged by the observations he is making, free himself from them or rather rest upon them in order to try and generalize from the individual case to the rule, or to elaborate a piece of reasoning. Faced with a sickness subject to relapse, he notes: 'Attention should be paid to the signs of relapse and one should remember that at these moments in the malady, crises will be decisive, either for recovery or for death, or at least that the sickness will incline for better or worse.' Thus the intelligence is always ready for action.

Or again in the treatise on *Head-wounds:*

If the bone has been laid bare, attention must be paid in order to try and discern what is not visible to the eye, and to discover whether the bone is fractured or bruised, or simply bruised, and whether the instrument that inflicted the wound, having produced a hedra (*an oblique lesion*), *there is bruising or fracture, or both bruising and fracture together.*

Here mind remains alert, ready to interpret the results of observation. Very many other examples could be cited.

Thus, abundant observations do not exempt the scientist from the effort to understand. The Greek verbs which mean 'to think', 'to reflect', are numerous. Hippocrates in most cases chooses the one which presents reflexion as a permanent attitude of the mind, and he puts it in the tense that indicates the duration involved: so that 'to reflect' means 'always to put one's heart into it'. He kept always in mind, and as objects for reflexion, the cases which observation supplied, the data of the senses, of the sight, of auscultation and palpation. He possessed that mental patience which can alone confront difficulties and solve problems.

Here is an obvious example, selected among many, and one which clearly

[1] Trans. cited, p. 129.   [2] Trans. cited, p. 125.

brings out the novelty of the method of Cos by comparison with that of Cnidus. The treatise on *The Joints*—a surgical treatise—enumerates the different accidents to which the parts of the body are subject: fractures of the arm, the nose, the leg, dislocation of the humerus, of the femur, etc. It indicates with an abundance of detail the very many methods which permit of mending fractures and dislocations; after which it chooses among these methods and gives exact reasons for the choice. The doctors who do not know how to make and justify this intelligent choice, namely the Cnidian doctors, are severely judged. The author writes: 'Among doctors, there are some who have skilful hands but who lack intelligence.' Cnidus is indicated here.

The establishment of the prognostic is one of the essential objects of Hippocratic medicine, and it furnishes a good example of the union of observation with thought. The doctor proposes, as we know, to reconstitute the malady in its entirety, with its causes, its complications, its name and its consequences. According to the *Epidemics* and the treatise on *Prognosis* he wishes 'to say what has been, to know what is, and to predict what will be'. Later on, the medical school of Alexandria was to give separate names to these three operations: *anamnesis* is reconstruction of the past; *diagnostic* is determination of the malady by its present symptoms; *prognostic* is the forecast of what will happen.

Most histories of medicine do not render full justice to the Hippocratic prognosis, of which it is said that this is a means of establishing the doctor's authority over the patient and those about him. No doubt, and the *Hippocratic Collection* says so, incidentally. This judgment on prognosis reminds one of an amusing remark made by a Lausanne professor to his students: 'A sound diagnosis astonishes you yourselves. A successful treatment astonishes your colleague. But what astonishes the patient is an exact prognosis.' A humorous judgment; but the humour is beside the point. In any case prognosis is not dust thrown into the patient's eyes by a charlatan. If on the one hand it is a means of inspiring confidence in the patient, it is above all for the doctor the solution he proposes for an extremely complex problem.

A sick man in bed is like a terrible knot to be untied. Obscure causes, old and recent, have brought him to this pass; but what causes? And what is going to happen to him, death or recovery? The prognosis, which if unfavourable will not be communicated to the patient, is the setting in order by the doctor's mind of the extraordinary tangle of facts which observation offers him. Hippocrates is very sensible of the great complexity of the facts which every malady offers the doctor. On the other hand he is aware of the relative value of these facts. For example, he is not ignorant of the fact that the surest signs of a fatal issue may, in certain maladies that he names, be contradicted by favourable signs which the doctor will do well not to forget. It is on the basis of innumerable signs taken all together that the doctor must establish his prognosis; and yet this prognosis is still of a hypothetical and, if one may so put it, a shifting character. An excellent formula occurs more than once in the Hippocratic writings, under varied forms: for example: 'One must still take the other signs into consideration.' These are words of intellectual honesty, but also of hope. Life is too complex a phenomenon for one not always to be able, by some unexpected shift or expedient, to undertake to save it and often succeed in doing so.

Modern scientists, it is true, do not fail to emphasize the weaknesses of the Hippocratic prognosis. These weaknesses derive from a fact one must always remember, namely the doctor's almost complete ignorance of anatomy and especially of physiology. How, being persuaded for example that the arteries are conductors of air—how could the doctor be in a position to form a prognosis which should be founded, as he would wish it to be, on the causes of the malady? There are cases, however, in which the slight knowledge he has of these matters allows him to do so. As soon as he learns more, his prognosis will improve.

Apart from this, prognosis is not for Hippocrates an end in itself. What he establishes is treatment, and in this sense treatment is equivalent to modern diagnosis. Now in the matter of treatment the doctors who did not belong to the school of Cos were the playthings of their imagination and of chance. Either they relied on arbitrary and theoretical considerations, or they accepted without verification those treatments which had supposedly been tested by tradition. The author of *Regimen in Acute Diseases* speaks ironically of the contradictory kinds of treatment which these ignorant doctors were led into:

Physicians (he says) are quite unaccustomed to propound such questions, and perhaps they do not appreciate them when they are propounded. The science of medicine has fallen so low in popular estimation as not to seem the science of healing at all. As a result, if, in the acute cases at least, practitioners differ so widely that the diet prescribed by one is regarded as bad by another, the science could almost be compared to divination. Seers think the same bird to be of good omen if it appears on the left and bad if it appears on the right, while other seers hold exactly the opposite view. . . .

I assert that this study of regimen is much to be recommended, and it is something closely allied to the most numerous and most vital studies which compose the science of medicine. To the sick it is a powerful aid to recovery, to the healthy a means of preserving health, to athletes a means of reaching their best form and, in short, the means by which every man may realize his desire.[1]

The good sense of this passage makes one think of Molière, and not without

_____
[1] Trans. cited, p. 130.

reason. The author's indignation on the one hand, and, on the other, his enthusiasm for a kind of medicine that requires a study 'much to be recommended'—these feelings come out strongly through his irony.

Other passages clearly indicate the good method that is to be followed in giving prescriptions. Without going into detail, we may indicate one of the directions which can be definitely traced in the *Hippocratic Collection*, and which is one of the highest directions followed by Hippocrates himself.

He knows the limits of the science he is engaged in founding, limits fixed by the nature of man and the nature of the universe. The microcosm-man and the macrocosm-world are each the mirror of the other. No mythical conception of the natural world enters into this mode of thought and expression; nothing but a fundamental realism. Hippocrates recognizes that there are barriers to the achievements of medicine over sickness and death. He admits, on the other hand, that these two worlds, microcosm and macrocosm, each resting on the other, are at once frontiers of knowledge and means to cures. Healing takes place in man thanks to the cooperation of nature and, in the first place, by the work of the human organism itself. Hippocrates' object, which at first sight appears modest, is to assist the curative action of nature. Thus we read in *Epidemics*, Book V:

Nature is the physician of diseases. It is nature herself who opens the way for her own action. She has no need to reflect. . . . The tongue alone does its own work. And many other things are done in the same way. Nature which has received no instruction and has learned nothing, nevertheless does what is suitable.

And we read elsewhere that 'Nature acts without masters'.

The doctor, whose business it is to maintain man in a state of health, seeks and finds in the natural world and in the human body allies whom he knows to be beneficial. The normal treatment of the patient consists in opening the right way for the work of 'curative nature', a way that will be appropriate to the specific case. For the organized body possesses as it were an active vitality proper to it: it tends of itself to maintain itself alive by deploying very many resources. Thus the cooperation afforded by the professional, thanks to his knowledge of these curative activities of the body, is not at all negligible: there are cases where it is decisive.

This notion of the curative power of nature is not, as some historians have supposed, the confession of an indolence which would end up in leaving nature to act alone. On the contrary it is a knowledge, founded on observed facts and according to which every human organism is a reservoir of biological forces which defend themselves spontaneously against their own destruction. The physician aids man to the extent to which he knows the play of these forces that animate and constitute life. Knowledge associated with action is one of the classical themes of Greek civilization.

Certain processes in the self-defence of the body act by themselves; but we are not excluded from supposing that this self-defensive action may also be assisted by the doctor who has discovered its mode of working. Nature needs sometimes to be supported. Hippocrates asks the doctor to be always ready to answer the appeals and the possibilities of the organism and to remedy any insufficiencies which may occur in it. The standard example in this matter is the practice of artificial respiration. The lungs, deprived of oxygen, have already tried to increase the rhythm of breathing; the blood has multiplied the red globules; and all this is a natural and spontaneous act of defence. Now the doctor who practises artificial respiration is simply making up for the deficiencies of nature; he is manoeuvring the last resources of a body which was not far from giving in.

Is not this doctor who collaborates with nature fulfilling a higher and more intelligent office than the ignorant wonder-worker who prides himself on 'creating health' out of nothing? The doctor who remains on the watch for 'elusive opportunity' on the very ground of 'dangerous experiment' is modestly but effectively maintaining life. As the poet does not make images out of nothing but by starting from what exists, so the doctor makes a man healthy by starting from what he finds in the patient's body, from human nature observed and utilized. It was not from nothing but from the sun that Prometheus wrested the gift of fire.

Such are the strict procedures of Hippocratic medicine, such is the philosophy of the medical profession that Hippocrates drew from his study of nature and the human body. I have insisted on the methods of the science he founded rather than on the results he achieved. This is because science advances rather by the soundness of its methods than the accumulation of results. So much intellectual elevation united with such modesty finds its splendid crown and accomplishment in the moral behaviour that Hippocrates demanded of his disciples and practised himself.

I have indicated above the moral writings in the *Collection*—*The Oath, The Law, The Doctor*, etc. I recall that they were no doubt composed in the time of Hippocrates' old age or soon after his death but in conformity with his principles and practice. *The Oath*, which gives a written form to an ancient and no doubt primitive usage of the school, is for this reason both the most ancient text in the *Collection* and yet, in its present form, rather more recent than the great Hippocratic treatises of the fifth century. It is also the most important of the moral texts. Here is a complete translation of this oath which was pronounced by doctors at the moment of entering on their profession:

I swear by Apollo the healer, by Aesculapius, by Health and all the powers of healing, and call to witness all the gods and goddesses that I may keep this Oath and Promise to the best of my ability and judgment.

I will pay the same respect to my master in the Science as to my parents and share my life with him and pay all my debts to him. I will regard his sons as my brothers and teach them the Science, if they desire to learn it, without fee or contract. I will hand on precepts, lectures and all other learning to my sons, to those of my master and to those pupils duly apprenticed and sworn, and to none other.

I will use my power to help the sick to the best of my ability and judgment; I will abstain from harming or wronging any man by it.

I will not give a fatal draught to anyone if I am asked, nor will I suggest any such thing. Neither will I give a woman means to procure an abortion.

I will be chaste and religious in my life and in my practice.

I will not cut, even for the stone, but I will leave such procedures to the practitioners of that craft.

Whenever I go into a house, I will go to help the sick and never with the intention of doing harm or injury. I will not abuse my position to indulge in sexual contacts with the bodies of women or of men, whether they be freemen or slaves.

Whatever I see or hear, professionally or privately, which ought not to be divulged, I will keep secret and tell no one.

If, therefore, I observe this Oath and do not violate it, may I prosper both in my life and in my profession earning good repute among all men for all time. If I transgress and forswear this Oath, may my lot be otherwise.[1]

Most modern states require doctors to take an oath. But the very use of the word has most frequently become subject to misuse. The doctor usually only pledges his honour or makes a promise. The old text of Hippocrates seems to have been nearly emptied of its content by the evolution of beliefs and the progress of science. In my country, Canton Vaud, the doctor pledges himself before the prefect of the district representing the Council of State, which exercises executive power.

After taking cognizance of the fundamental principles of deontology[2] *and of the legal provisions that regulate my profession, I pledge myself on my honour to respect them faithfully, I promise on my honour to exercise this profession with the conscience, dignity and humanity that its helpful object demands.*

There is nothing now about the prohibition against giving poison; the doctor of today who understands the toxic elements that a remedy may contain, prescribes

[1] Trans. cited, p. 9.
[2] This word means the 'science' or ethics of moral obligation (Translator).

'poison'-remedies all day long. There is no prohibition against procuring abortion if requested: in more than one case abortion has become legal. There remains deference towards one's colleagues which is prescribed in the provisions of deontology. There also remains the rule of professional secret which is safeguarded, at least in theory, by the *Loi sanitaire vaudoise* of December 9, 1952 and equally by the *Code pénal suisse* of which article 321 provides that those 'who shall have revealed a medical secret, confided to them by virtue of their profession, may be punished by imprisonment and fine'. Above all, in the Vaudois promise which may be taken as an example, there remain the fine words of *conscience*, *dignity* and *humanity*, and the pursuit simply of a *helpful object* which are like a distant but authentic echo of the love Hippocrates had for his patients and which he demanded by his disciples.

The promise made by the Genevese doctor, which is entitled *Serment de Genève*, has remained nearer to the Hippocratic Oath. It is taken before the General Assembly of the Medical Association, and not before a political authority.

> *At the moment of being admitted to membership of the medical profession:*
>
> *I solemnly pledge myself to devote my life to the service of humanity.*
>
> *I will maintain toward my masters the respect and gratitude which are due to them.*
>
> *I will exercise my art conscientiously and with dignity.*
>
> *I will consider my patient's health as my first concern.*
>
> *I will respect the secrets of those who confide in me.*
>
> *I will, to the best of my power, maintain the honour and noble traditions of the medical profession.*
>
> *My colleagues shall be my brothers.*
>
> *I will not allow considerations of nation, race, party or social class to intervene between my duty and my patient.*
>
> *I will maintain absolute respect for human life, from the moment of conception.*
>
> *I will not, even in the face of threats, allow my medical knowledge to be used contrary to the laws of humanity.*
>
> *I make these promises solemnly, freely and on my honour.*

This *Geneva Oath* was adopted by the General Assembly of the International Medical Association meeting in Geneva in September 1948.

◎

The Oath, The Law, and the other moral treatises of Hippocrates call for a few further remarks.

The first, which is not unimportant, is that the instructions given to the doctor for the practice of his profession, if they are collected in these writings and enforced by an oath, are never contradicted but on the other hand confirmed by the other treatises in the *Collection* and notably by those which we may attribute to Hippocrates. We are therefore, here, in presence of a simple codifying of ancient usages, and this codification is in conformity with the master's inspiration and wholly faithful to his memory. Thus, none of the practices forbidden in *The Oath* is met with in the seven books of the *Epidemics*, which, as we have seen, consist of notes roughly jotted down, without thought for publicity and part of which is undoubtedly from the hand of Hippocrates himself. The whole of them are a stainless mirror of the practice of the Coan school.

The other moral treatises pay the greatest attention to the doctor's deportment, to his physical and moral behaviour. He goes into houses only 'to help the sick'. The sick person, whoever he may be and whatever his social standing, whether it be a question of a woman, a man or a child, whether free or bond—this sick person is for the doctor only a suffering creature, a 'patient' in the strong, etymological sense of the word. He has a right to the doctor's consideration and respect, and the doctor respects him as he should respect himself. The author of the treatise on *Decorum* writes:

The doctor, like the good philosopher whom he resembles, practises disinterestedness, reserve and modesty; he dresses decently; he is serious and tranquil in his judgment, serene and pure in his life. . . . He possesses knowledge of all that is useful and necessary; he is exempt from superstition.

The author of the book entitled *Of the Physician* in his turn declares that the physician should practise continence and 'keep his hands pure. . . . His morals will be honourable and without reproach and, together with this, he will be grave and human as regards all men.'

His attitude, in a word, is that of a gentleman, and he is 'agreeable to gentlemen'. In respect to his patient he is neither impulsive nor hasty. He is never ill-humoured, and 'at the same time not excessively gay'. 'The doctor's relations with his patients are not minor relations,' says the same author. They require the 'justice' both of judgment (meaning, in this case, exactitude) and also of conduct. One of the most necessary virtues of this doctor who is also a gentleman is modesty, which is an intellectual as well as a moral quality. He may make a mistake: this he will recognize as soon as he takes notes of it, and, at least in the case of 'small errors', in front of the patient. His education, which has been long and conducted under the guidance of enlightened masters, will generally preserve him from serious errors. If he commits any, which may involve death, he must not recognize them in the patient's presence, as this would risk compromising the latter's calm. He will prefer to consign them to writing so as to enlighten doctors in generations to come.

Modesty, besides, imposes on the doctor the duty of appealing to his colleagues if he is in difficulties. We read in the *Precepts*:

The doctor who, by reason of inexperience, does not understand a case, will seek the assistance of other doctors, with whom he will consult regarding the patient and who will associate with him in finding a solution. . . . Doctors who conjointly see a patient will not wrangle or ridicule each other. I assert under oath that a doctor who advances an argument [as to the right treatment] ought never to envy a colleague's argument: if he does so, he is only displaying the weakness of his own.

Lastly, and still out of concern for modesty, the doctor will refrain from using methods of an ostentatious kind, by which he might seek to impose on the sick man; for 'it would be shameful if, after so much noise and exhibition and so many words, he in the end achieved nothing useful'. In all circumstances the doctor should choose the mode of treatment that entails the minimum of display. This attitude is the only one worthy of a 'man of feeling' who is also 'a man of his craft'. Each term involves the other, because the craft of medicine is for the service of men. The *Precepts* remind us of this in an unforgettable formula: 'Where there is love of men there is also love of the craft.'

The physician's modesty is a result, first, of the love he bears his craft. He in fact knows the immense exigencies of this craft; he becomes daily aware of this in exercising his profession, as he also becomes aware of the limits of his capacity. But, in the second place, because he loves the men he cares for, and because he has a keen feeling for the precious and complex character of the life he desires to protect, modesty is imposed on the doctor who bears the responsibility for this life. The love of men and the love of his craft are the two poles of his humanism.

One must insist on a last feature, scarcely indicated hitherto. In none of the many treatises contained in the *Hippocratic Collection* is the least distinction ever made between slaves and free men. Both have the same rights to the physician's care, attention and respect; and not only the slaves but the poor who towards the end of the fifth century were everywhere becoming numerous in the Greek world and whose life was often no less hard than that of the slaves.

In those books of the *Epidemics* which were not written by Hippocrates, who in his notes rarely records the profession of his patients, here are a few of the trades or professions indicated by the doctor: carpenters, cobblers, curriers, fullers, vine-growers, gardeners, miners, stone-masons, elementary schoolmasters, tavern-keepers, cooks, ostlers, professional sporting-men, various officials, who may have been state slaves, and so on. In very many cases, the trade is not indicated. There are also many women, both free and bond. These trades, it will be seen, are modest and even humble. It is probable that many of the workmen were slaves. More than once this is indicated.

What is certain is that it made no difference to the doctor whether his patient was a slave, a stranger or a citizen. The author of the *Precepts* even asks that 'particular care should be taken of the sick man who is a stranger and poor'. Now it so happens that this precept was followed and more than followed. If we read the reference-notes to patients contained in a single book of the *Epidemics*, selected at hazard—Book V—we shall observe that out of an hundred patients, nineteen and perhaps more—it is often hard to decide—were certainly slaves. Of these, twelve were men or boys, seven were women. Many of them were treated at Larissa in Thessaly during the fairly long stay which the travelling doctor who wrote Book V made there. All seem to have benefited from vigilant and often prolonged attention. One of the female slaves died towards the fortieth day of an encephalic disease, after she had long been unconscious. Here is the case of a young ostler, one of the nineteen slaves mentioned above. He was eleven years old and had been wounded on the forehead, above the right eye, by a kick from a horse's hoof:

The bone did not appear healthy [writes the doctor], *and a little blood came out. The invalid was trepanned, widely, as far as the diploa* [the seam or suture of two bony plates that form the inner and outer surfaces of the skull]. *Then he was treated by keeping the bone uncovered, and the treatment dried up the portion of the bone which had been sawn through at the outset. Towards the twentieth day tumefaction set in near the ear, with fever and shivering; in the daytime, the swelling was greater and more painful. The fever began with shivering. The eyes, the forehead and the whole face became tumified. The right side of the head was the more affected but the tumefaction also set in on the left side. However, nothing untoward came of it; the fever was less continuous towards the end. This phase lasted eight days. The invalid recovered. He was cauterized, took a purgative, and was given medicinal applications on the swelling. The wound had nothing to do with the complications.*

The diseases affecting the patients in Book V were of the most varied. Here are some examples: angina, deafness, gangrene or sphacelus, pleurisy, pneumonia, consumption, diarrhoea and other troubles of the intestine or the stomach, stomach-tumour, bladder and bile trouble, stone, feverish anorexia, erysipelas, and many others. Often, too, there are sores resulting from accidents or again from pregnancy. Generally speaking, the doctor appears to have attended or noted in his book only serious maladies; he was not interested in slight ailments.

The mortality was very high. Of the nineteen slaves attended in Book V twelve died. But the proportion of those who died was scarcely higher for the invalids as a whole than for the slaves. Of forty-two cases recorded in Books I and II of the *Epidemics*, twenty-five proved fatal. A doctor who lived towards the end of the pre-Christian era said that one should read the *Epidemics* because they are 'a meditation on death'. The men of that age were still dying like flies. How could it have been otherwise? Medical science, as we have described it, being ignorant of the essentials of anatomy, because dissection was forbidden by the manners of the time, was not yet in a position to lower the 'natural' death-rate. By 'natural', I mean the rate which the natural environment and the human body had fixed for the human species. But a day was to come when doctors would be able to say, elsewhere than in Molière: 'We have changed all that.'

Medical science at least did not then distinguish among beings so mortal; in its eyes slaves too were human beings. This is a fact so surprising that it deserves to be brought out. The owner of the slave may certainly be interested in preserving his capital. But what was this boy of eleven worth, the boy whose story I related? Less than nothing, less than the practitioner's expenses, no doubt.

The tone, moreover, in which the doctor's notes are written, the same tone whatever the patient's social status might be, appears to reveal that mixture of scientific interest and human sympathy which characterized Hippocrates' humanism. One thinks of the two great philosophers of the following centuries and of their scorn for slaves, those 'animated tools'. By its astonishing appetite for knowledge, by the rigour of its researches ever animated by reasoning, by its devotion to the suffering creature, by the friendship it offers all men without distinction, the medical science of Hippocrates reaches the highest level of fifth-century humanism and, on the last point, boldly transcends the ways of life and thought in that age. By offering all men the bodily salvation which it is with difficulty seeking on their behalf, this science represents, even amid the shadows of ignorance, the fairest of promises. For the rest, we must not forget Lord Bacon's saying that the art of medicine can do more than it knows.

CHAPTER EIGHT

ARISTOPHANES' LAUGHTER

Was Aristophanes' laughter the least attic, the most 'gaulois', the grossest in the world? Or else the most graceful and nimble? Neither, or perhaps truly both. It was every kind of laughter, that of satire at one extreme and of joy at the other, with everything that lies between.

It includes, then, two principal kinds. The first participates in anger, it is the laughter that rends in pieces the absurd imbecilities which were springing up like weeds from the soil of that 'social order' of late fifth-century Athens. The golden age was wearied with producing masterpieces in marble that no one would ever complete. The great empire which was paying for them with its toil and money was disintegrating. The metropolis was in vain striving to sew the pieces together in the midst of bloody repressions. And then during all the last quarter of the century, in the theatre of Dionysus, the laughter of Aristophanes could be heard rolling like thunder. His satire denounced the contradictions by which imperialistic democracy was damaging itself; it emphasized the disasters of the war, the haggard misery of the people; it pilloried the lying, thieving and profiteering demagogues, the imbecile and conceited generals, the stupidity of the Sovereign People deceived by sophistry and flattery; it brought fully to light the evil results of the new education; it charged with infamy the rule of oratory over the multitude who listened with folded arms—and all this without ever ceasing to laugh and to fill stage and sky with its acrobatic somersaults. This satiric laughter was the laughter *against*.

But we must not forget the laughter *with*, the laughter that restores us to the love of things, of the country and the simple blessings of life—bread, wine and peace. It revives in our hearts a sense of the beauty of trees and flowers, of the shy grace of the beasts of farm and woodland, it speaks the ineffable language of birds. It flowers in our natural gestures, in the movements of love; it is the physiological and lyrical laughter of joy.

This laughter, which is the simple jubilation of a creature happy to be living in the sunshine, restores us to a sense of reality and, in a last somersault which appears to defy the laws of gravitation, plants our feet once again on solid earth. All satire now forgotten, it expresses the sheer pleasure of living in the bright world of colours and forms, and of possessing reality; it expresses a man's joy in finding himself in the midst of the world's beauty, and in laughing because one is a man. Aristotle says: 'Man is the only living creature who can laugh'; and Rabelais translates this very correctly in the epigraph to *Gargantua*: '*Pour ce que rire est le propre de l'homme.*'

What these two kinds of laughter, the satiric and the lyric, which are really inseparable, have in common is their curative virtue. Aristophanes regards himself as the 'schoolmaster' of Athenian society, the educator of its youth. Laughter is part of his therapeutic. Man reaches plenitude, society gains balance in joy recovered. There exists a 'catharsis' or purification by laughter. In restoring us to good sense it restores us to our true nature; when we are sick, it restores us to health.

Indissolubly united as they are, these two kinds of laughter separate none of the things which, in reality and in man's heart, are united or at odds. They do not separate words from the things they describe or the actions they invite. They do not separate hatred of war from love of peace. They do not separate bodies from souls, as if, separated from the body, the soul could live any but an amputated life, as if body and soul were not, in their conjunction, each the means by which the other breathes.

◎

Let us now examine the twin sources of these two kinds of laughter.

The satirical kind had its roots in a folklore common to all times and all countries. Before the time of Aristophanes there existed, particularly in Dorian states like Sparta and Megara, popular and improvised farces that were born of the mere pleasure man takes in imitating and caricaturing what is ridiculous. Despite the poverty of our information, we know that the Spartan mimes, wearing terrifying or comical masks, represented toothless old women, or stealers of fruit and meat, or learned foreign doctors. Fairly recent excavations have unearthed some of these masks. At Megara, the farces disposed of a collection of masks of which the best known was that of the ogre-cook.

Associated with these masks in Greece, there arose comic types; and these typical personages were, as a matter of fact, the same as those we find in all popular comedies ancient and modern. There is nothing more curious than to find on the boards of the *Commedia dell'arte*, or in the court of the Valois kings, or in

English villages, even in Molière and Shakespeare, characters who are as like as brothers to those of the Latin *Atellanae*[1] or of the plays of Aristophanes and Menander. Across centuries of time, the same moral or physical sources of ridicule, the hump on Punch's back or the jargon of a foreign doctor, amuse publics who have nothing in common but the faculty of that laughter which is the property of man. To recall a few of these types may throw light on Aristophanes.

First, the mask of the pedant, the learned foreign doctor. This type figures in the Latin *Atellanae* under the name of Dosennus, the hump-backed pedant. On the Italian stage he is *il dottore*, sometimes jurist, sometimes physician. His knowledge is inborn and he expresses himself learnedly. In the German *Puppenspiel* he is a wonder-worker and charlatan named Dr Faust. In Molière we have the company of Diafoirus, Desfonandrès and their fellows; in Shakesperian comedy, the extraordinary Dr Caius in *The Merry Wives*, whose jargon is supposed to be that of a French physician.

Another type is the lascivious, jealous and miserly old man: he is represented by Pappus in the *Atellanae*, Euclion in Plautus, Pantalone at Venice, Volpone in Ben Jonson, and later, on the French classical stage, Harpagon and Bartholo. One must not forget that Harpagon is not simply a miser, although in him this feature is pushed to the extreme; we may see in his grotesque love, in his rivalry with his son, traces of the old debauched Pantaloon.

I have already mentioned the ogre-cook with the big mouth and long teeth, now gluttonous and again ferocious. At Megara, years before Aristophanes' time, he was called Meson. Later he appears as Manducus in the *Atellanae*, and in the *Puppenspiel* as the gluttonous and obscene drunkard, Hans Wurst, a sort of doddering bogy-man. In Italian comedy he is Harlequin, wearing a negro's mask and sometimes carrying a cutlass in his teeth.

Next come the great company of braggarts: Aristotle speaks of them as essential to Greek comedy. These boasters are often impostors and always intruders. They encumber Aristophanes' later comedies with their various pretensions, and they are everywhere deflated and beaten. The Neapolitan Pulcinella and the French Polichinelle belong to the family of braggarts who get a drubbing. Much the same happens to the importune bores in the *Kasperlspiel*, a curious popular drama which was still being played a few years ago in north Germany. Kasperl is a good fellow who, like Dicaeopolis or Trygaeus in Aristophanes, only asks to live in peace with everyone. He is frustrated by a procession of killjoys: a tax-collector, a Polish

[1] The *Atellanae fabulae*, so-called apparently because the scene was usually placed at Atella, an old town in Campania, whether because these farces originated there or because, as the town long lay in ruins, no actual community would take exception to the ridiculous persons who were caricatured (Translator).

hawker, his own wife, his mother-in-law, the Devil, Death and other persons, all of whom he drives out with his cudgel and a torrent of jibes. The scenario of this play approximates closely to the cudgelling of bores which runs through *The Acharnians*, *The Peace* and *The Birds* of Aristophanes.

One type deserves special mention—that of the braggart soldier. This mask is as widespread in the history of comedy as the face of war has been in human history. He is the *Miles gloriosus*, 'the man who storms citadels' (Purgopolineikes)[1] in Plautus, the 'Capitan' in the *Commedia dell'arte*, the 'Matamore' of Spanish comedy. A character named Matamore reappears in Corneille's *Illusion comique*, in which he delights the audience with his fantastic imaginings. Nor must we forget 'le capitaine Fracasse', a Franco-Italian invention. I pass by other masks, such as those of valets, for example.

Aristophanes' plays are full of these masks, or at least of the imprint they left on the character of his personages. He no doubt inherited from the earlier popular comedies a collection of comic types, of whom I have mentioned the principal: the pedant, the dissolute old skinflint, the ogre-cook, and boasters of every stamp. He rejuvenated these traditional types by applying the masks that mark them to historical persons in the Athens of his day, to one or other of his contemporaries who might be sitting in the theatre; or, if he did not exactly apply the appropriate mask, he drew inspiration, when inventing a character, from the images it suggested.

Two characters in Aristophanes appear to have worn the mask of Matamore. The first was Lamachus in *The Acharnians*, the comedy written when the poet was twenty[2]—a play directed against Athenian imperialism and the war that was the result of it. This Lamachus was an honest general who was later to be killed when fighting bravely on the Sicilian Expedition. Unfortunately he had a name which in Greek meant 'the Battle'. Aristophanes dresses this Lamachus-the-Battler as a 'Capitaine Fracasse', sends him to guard the frontier-passes deep in winter snow and makes him the hero of a grotesque adventure from which he returns with a dislocated ankle, supported by two soldiers. In the grandiloquent style of epic poetry he tells the story of his ridiculous exploit, and then says farewell to the plume on his helmet with the kind of emotion with which Iphigenia says farewell

---

[1] This type was probably taken by Plautus from one of the Tarentine farces attributed to Rhinthon. It will be remembered that Tarentum was a colony of Sparta, a circumstance which again points to a Dorian origin for some of these masks (Translator).

[2] Or, more probably, at least 25—unless he was born much after 452 B.C. He had already written two plays, *The Banqueters*, produced in February 427, and *The Babylonians*, March 426, and had been acquitted after a lawsuit brought against him by Cleon. He retorted on Cleon with *The Acharnians*, produced in February 425, still under the name of Callistratus, who had obliged him by 'fathering' the first two comedies (Translator).

23. Achilles dressing the wound of Patroclus. Cup by Sosias (c. 500)

24

to the light of day—and all this under the ironical gaze of Dicaeopolis-good-citizen who, after making a separate peace for himself and his people, returns victoriously from a drinking-party, supported by two scantily-dressed courtesans.

A more notable personage who might have worn the mask of the boastful soldier was the Aeschylus of *The Frogs*. For the satirist Aristophanes, who greatly admired him and rallied him in a friendly way, Aeschylus was the poet of soldiers and swashbucklers. His heroes talk only of pikes and spears, of white-plumed helmets and greaves; their spirits are clad in seven thicknesses of ox-hide. And he boasts of it. His style is described in military terms, and instead of the poet's mask, he wears the matamore's:

> *So when he had humbugged thus awhile, and now his wretched play*
> *Was half-way through, a dozen words, great wild-bull words, he'd say,*
> *Fierce Bugaboos, with bristling crests, and shaggy eyebrows too.*[1]

Aristophanes seems to have applied the mask of the learned doctor to one of the most illustrious of his contemporaries, that enigmatic sage Socrates; as he does also to the subtle and argumentative Euripides, the tragedian. Socrates, with his pretensions to having encompassed the mystery of man and nature, with the dialectic of his endless conversations which left his interlocutor baffled and disconcerted, with the knowledge which he said he did not possess and which he was really concealing under the cloak of a percussive irony—Socrates for the ordinary Athenian was only an amusing word-juggler: he was not a real sage, but the most sophistical of sophists. As for Euripides, the 'intellectual', the poet with the clever tongue, the word-dissecter whose argumentative subtleties are the ruin of high inspiration and every effort of genius—he was simply another impostor to be shown up. Both Euripides and Socrates recall the mask of 'the learned foreign doctor' and both have a right to it.

Here, again, recognizable in the comedy of *The Knights*,[2] is the mask of the ogre-cook: the mask of the gluttonous ogre and that of the gormandizing parasite that derives from it. The mask of the ogre contributes to the invention of the principal character in the play, the redoubtable Agoracritus, pork-butcher[3] by trade and demagogue by good fortune. Many features point to this illiterate and loud-mouthed orator as being derived from a bogy-man cook. He was, he tells us, a scullion in his childhood.

[1] *The Frogs of Aristophanes*: the Greek text revised, with a Translation, Introduction and Commentary by B. B. Rogers. London, G. Bell & Sons, Ltd, 1902, p. 141.

[2] Or more strictly, the 'Cavaliers' or 'Horsemen'. They were the Athenian gentry who supplied the cavalry-brigades: conservatives for the most part and opposed to Cleon. As they formed the Chorus in the play, their hostility to the idol of the multitude was in accordance with the current situation (Translator).

[3] In English versions of the play he is traditionally known as the Sausage Seller (Translator).

M

24. *Hippocrates (or Aesculapius), marble bas-relief inspired by a chryselephantine statue of the beginning of the 4th Century: the work of Thrasymedes*

Sausage-Seller. *Now by the knuckles which in youth would discipline my head,*
And those hard-handled butchers' knives they often used instead,
I think in Shamelessness I'll win. . . .
O how I used to chouse the cooks by shrieking out Ahoy!
Look lads, a swallow! Spring is here. Look up, look up, I pray.
So up they looked whilst I purloined a piece of meat away.[1]

The most savoury images he uses are images from the kitchen:

And I, if I love you not, Demus, am game to be slaughtered by chopping and mincing,
And boiled in a sausage-meat pie; and if THAT is, you think, not entirely convincing,
Let me here, if you please, with a morsel of cheese, upon this to a salad be grated. . . .[2]

In moving from the pork-shop into politics, Agoracritus will still be exercising the same trade:

Sausage-Seller. *. . . but how can I, I wonder,*
Contrive to manage Demus' affairs.
Demosthenes. *Why nothing's easier. Do what now you do:*
Mince, hash, and mash up everything together.
Win over Demus with the savoury sauce
Of little cookery phrases. . . .[3]

He has the ogre's appetite:

I'll eat the paunch of cow and swine, and quaff thereon their stew,
And rising from the board with hands which water never knew,
I'll throttle all the orators, and flutter Nicias too.[4]

Notice also that if he manages to supplant his rival in the good graces of Demos, it is in a cooking-competition; and it is by a culinary operation that, at the end of the play, he rejuvenates the Sovereign People; as he cries

Old Demus I've stewed till his youth is renewed, and his aspect most charming and
nice is.[5]

The invention of the character of the Sausage-Seller in *The Knights* can, then, be traced to the mask of Meson, the ogre-cook of Megara. Aristophanes has obviously repainted the mask with entirely fresh colours, taken from current politics; but that is another matter, an aspect of his genius with which I am not dealing at the moment. I must, however, mention another character in the play,

[1] *The Knights of Aristophanes* . . . the Greek text revised with a Translation, Introduction and Commentary by B. B. Rogers, London, 1910, p. 61.
[2] *Ibid.,* p. 109.   [3] *Ibid.,* pp. 30–1.   [4] *Ibid.,* p. 53.   [5] *Ibid.,* p. 185.

the adversary of the Sausage-Seller, namely the Paphlagonian slave Cleon. Some light is thrown on this character by a type which we know existed prior to Aristophanes' time and which also derives from the cook, though with marked differences. This was the no less frightening glutton, the profiteer, the flattering parasite.

The Cleon[1] of *The Knights* is a slave who has wormed himself into the house of a wealthy burgher named Demos, an allegorical figure easily recognizable in Athens. He governs his master by flattery and by little services such as slipping a cushion under him at the right moment or offering his own hair for Demos to wipe his fingers on, when he has been blowing his nose. The clever parasite has ended by becoming steward of the household and, as this household is the Athenian community, the sponger of the middle-class household has become, through allegory and metaphor, the exploiter of the democracy. I do not insist on the marvellous way in which the poet utilizes this transposition of the parasite from the private plane to the public. It is enough to indicate the probable origin of the invention. The mask of the parasite becomes the figure of the profiteer.

So much for the sources of satiric laughter. This laughter, as I have said, derives from old popular traditions which were then supplying, and were to supply for centuries to come, material for comedy. But something more is needed to explain the brilliant flowering of Aristophanic farce, and that was the passionate wrath that burned in the poet's heart, his generous anger against the approaching degradation of democratic institutions, and the already threatening decay of private and public morals. The presence of this anger which rejected the Athenian world as it then was, a world which was ruining itself, was the spirit which gave life to the revival of masks and types inherited from the past.

Side by side with the laughter of wrath, and closely mingled with it, was the laughter of joy. Where did it come from?

From the village festivals of the Attic countryside. It was the laughter of girls

---

[1] It is important to remember that he is not presented as Cleon, but as 'Paphlagonian'. A recent law had apparently forbidden comic dramatists to present living persons as such; but everyone knew who was meant, just as they recognized Demosthenes and Nicias from their dress and manner. On the other hand the *Chorus*, whose rights were of sacred origin and could not be abrogated by law, openly attacked Cleon and named him. In the *dialogue* he is never addressed by name. Even so, the audacity of Aristophanes was unparalleled. Cleon thought he had established his reputation by the success of the expedition to Pylos and Sphacteria, for which he took the credit. Aristophanes undeceived him by a satire more virulent than ever. None of the actors dared impersonate Cleon on the stage, nor did the costumiers and mask-makers dare produce a mask for the purpose—all of them rightly dreading the vengeance of the unscrupulous politician. In this conjuncture Aristophanes himself daubed his face and acted the part. It was doubtless the most courageous act of his life (Translator).

running with their hair loose in the wind, catching each other up, as they carry pitchers of wine to the field-workers. It was the laughter that accompanied the light wine you drank on feast-days, or on rainy days by the fire with you friends.

Chorus. *What a pleasure, what a treasure,*
     What a great delight to me,
     From the cheese and from the onions
     And the helmet to be free.
     For I can't enjoy a battle,
     But I love to pass my days
     With my wine and boon companions
     Round the merry merry blaze,
     When the logs are dry and seasoned,
     And the fire is burning bright,
     And I roast the pease and chestnuts
     In the embers all alight,
     —Flirting too with Thratta
     When my wife is out of sight.

Epirrhema. *Ah, there's nothing half so sweet as when the seed is in the ground,*
     God a gracious rain is sending, and a neighbour saunters round.
     'O Comarchides!' he hails me: 'how shall we enjoy the hours?'
     'Drinking seems to suit my fancy, what with these benignant showers.
     Therefore let three quarts, my mistress, of your kidney-beans be fried,
     Mix them nicely up with barley, and your choicest figs provide.
     Syra run and shout to Manes, call him in without delay,
     'Tis no time to stand and dawdle pruning out the vines today,
     Nor to break the clods about them, now the ground is soaking through.
     Bring me out from home the fieldfare, bring me out the siskins two,
     Then there ought to be some beestings, four good plates of hare beside
     (Hah! unless the cat purloined them yesterday at eventide;
     Something scuffled in the pantry, something made a noise and fuss):
     If you find them, one's for father, bring the other three to us.
     Ask Aeschinades to send us myrtle branches green and strong;
     Bid Charinades attend us, shouting as you pass along.
      Then we'll sit and drink together,
      God the while refreshing, bless
       All the labour of our hands.'

(Antistrophe). *O to watch the grape of Lemnos*
     Swelling out its purple skin,

When the merry little warblings
Of the Chirruper[1] begin;
For the Lemnian ripens early.
And I watch the juicy fig
Till at last I pick and eat it
When it hangeth soft and big;
And I bless the friendly seasons
Which have made a fruit so prime,
And I mix a pleasant mixture,
Grating in a lot of thyme,
—Growing fat and hearty
In the genial summer clime.[2]

Aristophanes was a country boy. He was born, if we may believe *The Achar-nians,* on the isle of Aegina a few years after the building of that temple, dedicated to a local goddess, whose ruins among the olive- and pine-groves still beckon to the traveller. No doubt his father owned a small property there. It was there that he grew so closely acquainted with the rustic life that he defends throughout his plays, there that he learned to know the flowers of the field and the garden, and all the names and songs of the birds. He heard in their chirping the call of the rural Muse. He handled the spade and hoe, of which the well-polished metal shines in the sun and fills the peasant's heart with joy. He took part in those festivals, at once serious and joyful, at which the landowner and his family, to increase the harvest, promenaded round the fields and vineyards the emblem of generation, an enormous painted phallus. So, on his return home from the war, we hear him sing a phallic hymn, one of the those songs in which Aristotle was not mistaken in seeing one of the sources of comedy. Such songs, even when enlivened with pleasantries, are full of a healthy comic vein and of the joy of life in the Eden-like serenity of the gods of *The Iliad,* full too of their Homeric laughter which is a laughter antecedent to sin and to the law.

Aristophanes came to the city when still young, and promptly won fame, at the same time that, as he himself tells us, he became bald; but he never forgot his country childhood. It is with the peasant's laughter that he jeers at the townsfolk and lampoons their stupidity and malice. Bad citizens, conceited posers and imbeciles can make him angry but will not take away his joy.

[1] This was the cicada—'tettix' in Attic. Aristophanes here and in *The Birds* uses the Doric name, 'achetas'—the 'chirruper' (Translator).

[2] *The Peace* (421 B.C.), ed. and translated Rogers, London, 1913, pp. 143–7.

The reader will already have grasped some notion of the great variety of tones in Aristophanes. It is not enough to say that his comedies are both satiric and lyrical. Harsh with anger, overflowing with sarcasm and invective, full of instruction too, capable of speaking home truths to the great ones and the small ones of the earth, smeared with the grossest ribaldry—there are times when these comedies wallow in the obscene, yet emerge crowned with poetry. The coarse laughter of the wine shop can be heard side by side with the most delicate irony, the subtlest parody and the rarest humour. But in this medley of tones everything bears the mark of its inventor, a mark which is his alone.

The first mark of his inventiveness lies in the creation of hybrid characters, a weird poetical tribe, wasps and judges in one for example. Caricatured as they are, they impose their truth on us, the truth that they are wasps and judges at the same time, the wasp which buzzes and stings throwing light on the spiteful, crotchety judge who condemns. Aristophanes grafts the wasp on to the judge, as he grafts the matamore on to Aeschylus, the ogre on to the demagogue or again Euripides on to the fair Helen or the romantic Andromeda. Thus characters at once true and grotesque swarm in the drama of Aristophanes, and the monsters sprung from his imagination turn out to be truth itself, and this because of the action in which the poet involves them.

For Aristophanes is not simply a wonderful inventor of character; he is above all a prodigious inventor of comic action. There are few of his comedies which do not start off from an extravagant situation, one which offends against logic, braves the rules of social or moral equilibrium and yet restores to order and simple common sense the lives of men and cities, torn as they are by incoherent dissensions.

The action operates, with respect to the real world, a slight displacement which transports us into a world at once like and unlike our own. Aristophanes invents a series of worlds in which the natural laws and the principles of reasoning do not work exactly as in ours. It is as if he were amusing himself by taking us to a planet in which, the laws of gravitation being different, we could easily make enormous jumps and raise prodigious weights. It is only in this world which has been invented for them that Aristophanes' characters appear authentic: here the unusual nature of their behaviour suddenly becomes the most natural thing there could be.

During the last quarter of the fifth century, when war was ruining Athens and devastating her countryside, the poet three times devises a new invention to restore a fresh peace to his compatriots. All he needs is to mix with the most authentic realities of the time a grain of hellebore that will purge them of the miasmas of war and cure them of its folly. With the same stroke of his wand he introduces his public—which is no other than the citizens as a whole, reeling along in a mood of mild gaiety—into an imaginary but seemingly real world, in which dwells another kind of folly, the folly of peace. This other world, which bears so fair a name, will attract men by the magic of poetry, and they will end by believing in this other kind of reality that enchants them. They will collaborate with the poet who is giving life to the most cherished of their dreams. Aristophanes wishes that one day men should walk in peace, as on feast-days one goes for a country walk, *en famille*.

Let us review these inventions.

In *The Acharnians* (we are in the Spring of 425, the sixth years of the war), the honest peasant Dicaeopolis, who has observed that any proposals for peace brought up in the Assembly are flouted by the magistrates and booed by the people, who have been duped—Dicaeopolis conceives the following very simple notion, absurd in its common sense: 'Supposing I made peace just for myself!' He makes peace and returns to his village. Immediately every kind of commodity flows into his market: sucking-pigs from Megara, eels from Boeotia, and so on, all copiously enumerated; but not before Dicaeopolis has publicly denounced before the assembled people those who have been responsible for the war and, first of all, Pericles, who in that Olympian skull of his, shaped like a squill, had conceived the sinister decree that closed the ports of Attica to the Megarians, reduced the food-supply in Athens, ruined Megara and threw the whole of Greece into confusion. And all this mixed up with a story of public women abducted from a house of which Aspasia, Pericles' favourite, is represented as the keeper:

> From these three *Wantons* o'er the *Hellenic* race
> Burst forth the first beginnings of the *War*.[1]

Dicaeopolis cares nothing for that. Secure in the peace he has made, he triumphs over his enemies who are inflamed with the war-fever, sour-tempered wine-growers who want to stone him because their vineyards have been ravaged, towns-men too whom the lies of war-propaganda have blinded with pride and vengeful rage. But the man 'who has made peace by himself' wins the game that Aristophanes is playing against the city. He wins it by dint of buffoonery and also of reason; and his jubilation bursts out like a storm of joy. His fellow-citizens have only to imitate him.

In this way Aristophanes' inventive talent remains close to the daily, historical realities of the time. Thucydides records the decree against Megara as the key to the diplomatic situation which gave rise to the war. But the poet recomposes the real events on the plane of caricature and then of imagination, and he proposes all this for the amusement of his public and also for them to reflect on. The extrava-

[1] *The Acharnians of Aristophanes*: the Greek text revised, with a Translation, Introduction and Commentary by B. B. Rogers, London, 1910, p. 81.

gance and at times the poetry of the action blow into fragments the grossness and absurdity of the political situation as the stupidity of the people was maintaining and consolidating it.

Another anti-war comedy, performed in 411 in a particularly dark period of those internecine massacres, is the one entitled *Lysistrata*. Aristophanes was not unaware of the suffering of the masses who had been dragged into the conflict which we now call the Peloponnesian war and which was simply the first 'world-war' of ancient times. In face of the bloodshed, famine and misery which reigned throughout the Greek world and which had been increasing over the twenty years since the outbreak of war, the poet replies courageously by imagining the most risky and buffoonish comedy one could imagine. In order to brand, curse and stigmatize war which, one must not forget, is a man's invention, and also because, freeing himself from any narrow nationalism, he wishes all the Greeks, all the men of the known world from Sicily to Persia, to hear the urgent appeal of human brotherhood demanded by the peoples—it is for these reasons that Aristophanes places in the centre of his play a woman speaking to women. This is the resolute and warm-hearted Athenian Lysistrata. The poet supposes that, under the inspiration of this capable person, all the women of the countries at war unite against the sinister folly of the men and take a very simple decision, confirmed by an oath solemnly grotesque. Against their husbands and lovers they will declare a love-strike. He here imagines a suspension of the laws of physiology. What would happen if, out of love of peace, all the women forced the men to continence? This is the question answered by the world that Aristophanes has invented. A world of hallucination. What torture for the soldiers on leave, what torture for the honourable magistrates sent to negotiate with the women who have occupied the Acropolis! A torture which is described and shown very crudely on the stage. Waves of laughter and anger break over the tiers of benches. The situation invented in a simplicity which is that of genius, gives rises to scenes which may be considered very risky and even perhaps obscene, but so joyous and healthy that there is no man or woman who could not be greatly amused. The consequences of this suspension of a great natural law are rigorously developed. One consequence, unforeseen by Lysistrata but not by the poet, is that the women are caught in their own trap; and we see some of them who, on various absurd pretexts, try to leave the women's camp in order to go and do, each with her husband, what a moment before they had sworn not to do and what they now regret as much as he.

First Woman.   *I must just run home.*
                        I left some fine Milesian wools about,
                        I'm sure the moths are at them.

Lysistrata.   *Moths indeed!*
                    Get back.
First Woman.   *I only want to spread them on the couch.*
Lysistrata.   *No spreadings out, no running home today.*
Third Woman.   *O holy Eileithyia, stay my labour*
                    Till I can reach some lawful travail-place.
Lysistrata.   *Why yesterday*
                    You were not pregnant.
Third Woman.   *But today I am....*
Lysistrata.   *What's this hard lump?*
Third Woman.   *That's a male child.*
Lysistrata.   *Not it.*
                    It's something made of brass, and hollow too....
                    What! cuddling up the sacred helmet there....[1]

She brings them all back into the fold. Other women, meanwhile, take a diabolical pleasure in keeping on tenterhooks the husbands who have come to seek them, obviously 'a prey to all the frenzies of Aphrodite'. Myrrhina provokingly a score of times is on the point of giving herself to her husband Cinesias, who can bear it no longer. But she needs a couch. False exit. Then a mat. Another exit. Then some scent which she goes to find. Finally she undresses, but immediately disappears, with the words: 'My dear, don't forget to vote for peace.'

Peace triumphs in the end and there is a reconciliation between the sexes and between the various peoples who have been at war.

The play is perhaps the most obscene that has ever appeared on the stage, but it is in no way licentious. There is nothing in *Lysistrata* to pervert, or to promote disorderly morals. In an atmosphere of laughter it displays feelings deeply rooted in all human beings, namely love of peace and, more simply, the love of life which is only perpetuated by physical love and the pleasure taken in it. So, the laughter of this play expressed the vital health of the Greeks and, even more, of the human species.

One of the best of the anti-war plays is a peasant-comedy which had been already gladdened by the approaching conclusion of the armistice of 421, an armistice which however was illusory. This comedy, which was earlier than the *Lysistrata*, was simply called *The Peace*.

It is the story of a vine-grower named Trygaeus (which means that he likes new wine) who, wearied of the palavers of the politicians about a peace which they say they are always ready to conclude but never do, decides to go himself to look for

[1] *The Revolt of the Women*: a free translation of the *Lysistrata* by B. B. Rogers, London, 1911, pp. 191–2.

Peace in Heaven—on Olympus. She has in fact retreated there because men are continually outraging her. But misfortune has befallen her. A frightful giant named Polemos, the bugaboo of war, has imprisoned her in the depths of a cave. As to the gods, they no longer trouble themselves about men's affairs: men, with their wars, are decidely too stupid. So the gods have deserted Olympus and emigrated to the outer canopy of the heavens. Hermes alone has remained behind to look after the plates and dishes, and act as *concierge*.

Once again the poet's inventions are strikingly simple and extravagant. Since Peace is in Heaven, Trygaeus will go and seek her, and bring her back to the Earth. In order to reach the palace of Zeus, he recalls a fable of his childhood—a fable which La Fontaine was later to rehandle—and he mounts on to an enormous flying-beetle which will transport him through space. This insect is called a dung-beetle because it feeds on dung. Trygaeus has captured one and had it fed in this manner by two slaves, one of whom, being half-suffocated, begs the audience to give him a nose without openings.

Let us now picture the stage-scenery. The platform is divided into two sections: on the right is Trygaeus' farm, and on the left Olympus with the palace of the gods. Between the two is the opening of a cavern, blocked up with huge stones. A piece of stage-machinery hoists Trygaeus on his beetle and makes him describe a semicircle in the air, while his little girls, amazed at seeing him fly off into the sky, wish him *bon voyage* and await his return for the fruit-pie and the friendly smacks that he has promised them. Finally the machine deposits Trygaeus in front of Zeus' mansion. He now sets to work by trying to rescue Peace from her cavern. He is aided in this task by the Chorus, which is composed of people from all the countries then at war; which shows that Aristophanes knew that all the peoples then fighting really desired peace. Trygaeus explains that they are, above all, peasants, artisans, workmen and merchants. These good people manage, though not without difficulty, to clear the opening of the cavern. But there is still the problem of pulling Peace, by means of a great rope, up from the bottom of a well in which she seems to have been imprisoned. All the contingents do not haul on the rope as cheerfully as they might. Trygaeus berates the slackers, addressing each with jokes appropriate to his political connexions. Finally, after repeated cries of 'Haul, ho!' the goddess of peace emerges from the gloom. She is a statue, but she is accompanied by two fine young women, big-boned and plump, and wearing the simple costume of Mother Nature. One is Opora, the goddess of fruits and harvests, of the ripening gifts of autumn; the other is Theoria, goddess of festivals and junketing. During the past ten years of war the Athenians had been sorely stinted of bread, fruit and festivals.

Trygaeus salutes this apparition with a lyrical enthusiasm in which poetry, pleasantry and satire make up a charming medley, full of grace and the promise of better days:

Trygaeus. *Giver of grapes, O how shall I address you?*
O for a word ten thousand buckets big
Wherewith to accost you: for I've none at hand.
Good morning, Harvesthome: good morn, Mayfair!
O what a breath! how fragrant to my heart,
How sweet, how soft, with perfume and inaction.

Hermes, a popular god, the friend of simple folk, asks:

Not quite the odour of a knapsack, eh?
Trygaeus. *Faugh! that odious pouch of odious men, I hate it.*
It has a smell of rancid-onion-whiffs;
But SHE of harvests, banquets, festivals,
Flutes, thrushes, plays, the odes of Sophocles,
Euripidean wordlets. . . .
The bleating lambs, the ivy-leaf, the vat,
Full-bosomed matrons hurrying to the farm,
The tipsy maid, the drained and emptied flask,
And many another blessing.
Hermes. *And look there,*
See how the reconciled cities greet and blend
In peaceful intercourse, and laugh for joy. . . .[1]

Peace has returned, and everyone now can go and work in the fields. Trygaeus is already frolicking at the thought.

In the second part of the comedy we attend the marriage of Trygaeus and Harvesthome: a marriage full of merry-making, but hampered by a number of bores from the pleasure of dancing in a ring. There are the arms-manufacturers who come to complain with long faces. The armourer, the breastplate-maker, the spear-maker, and trumpet-maker—a shoal of them come on the stage each with his special product. Trygaeus humorously but energetically sends them about their business, while pretending to buy weapons for domestic purposes. But there is nothing to be done. The weapon is useless as a tool. Only the spears find grace in the eyes of our vine-grower: he buys a hundred for a drachma: 'Sawn in two, they will make vine-props,' he says. Then, too, it is desired that the school-children shall sing at the wedding; but they only know military songs, which makes Trygaeus furious. The comedy ends in a great scene of junketing.

[1] *The Peace*, trans. cited, pp. 65, 67.

Such are the comic actions invented in the service of peace by Aristophanes. Extremely fantastic and imaginative, they are yet far from turning their back on reality. On the contrary, they enable us better to understand it in its deepest exigency, in the demand for peace which the Greek people were then making. Aristophanes himself is an impenitent realist. He is not satisfied with depicting the reality of his own time, but has to explore and make known the reality his people are calling for, that of the most distant future. He discovers it by means of imagination. His imaginary plots make his comedies a sort of machine for exploring time, and this is true not only of the plays he wrote on peace, but of many others.

One of his plays indeed seems to detach itself even more from reality than those we have treated, to take wing and soar even higher in poetry, and that is *The Birds*. At the moment when Athens, prostrated by the Sicilian disaster, torn more than ever with internal strife and pinched with hunger, was getting ready to face the final assault which her enemies new and old and the cities of her own empire were preparing against her—at this moment Aristophanes was able to show his fellow-citizens a marvellous new world of joy and laughter. He did not offer it as a means of escape or a few moments of forgetfulness, but in order to give them a 'paradise' (the word means a beautiful garden), the only one that men can enter in all ages, the only one that provides toil and the fruits of toil, and food and rest, the only one in which the Greeks found once more the primitive fraternity of living things, the friendship of animals and birds, and familiar intercourse with the gods. This paradise was nature. Here the poet rediscovered the delights of his childhood and offered the Athenians a golden age regained.

The invention in itself was amusing. But in this catastrophe of their history was there anything more important or more serious for the Athenians than the laughter of *The Birds?*

One day two good citizens decide that they have had enough of Athens. As Euelpides says:

> *Not that we hate our city, as not being*
> *A prosperous mighty city, free for all*
> *To spend their wealth in, paying fines and fees.*
> *Aye, the cicalas chirp upon the boughs*
> *One month, or two, but our Athenians chirp*
> *Over their lawsuits all their whole life long.*[1]

[1] *The Birds of Aristophanes*: the Greek text . . . with a Translation, Introduction and Commentary by B. B. Rogers, London, 1930, pp. 7, 9.

These were political lawsuits which, in the critical days which Athens was passing through, professional accusers were bringing against those citizens who were suspect. Well, Euelpides and Peisthetaerus have had more than enough of them; they have had enough of the political chicaneries, calumnies and wranglings in this Athens which, as Aristophanes realizes, is beginning to go to pieces. We see the two friends out in the country, at the edge of a wood, looking for

> *some city, soft*
> *As a thick rug, to lay us down within.*[1]

They would like to find or, failing that, to found a city without factions or roguery or lawsuits, or debts, and especially without money—a city where one would enjoy life as on a feast-day. And why should not they go to the kingdom of the birds? The birds among the bushes stuff themselves with myrtle, poppy and mint; they lead a kind of honeymoon existence. Why, thinks Euelpides, why not found among the birds and with the birds an entirely new city between heaven and earth, a city in the clouds?

They come to an agreement with the Hoopoe who had once lived as a man before he became a bird, and they ask him to convoke all the birds in the world.

First of all the Hoopoe calls the Nightingale, Philomela herself, who is his wife:

> *Awake, my mate!*
> *Shake off thy slumbers, and clear and strong,*
> *Let loose the floods of thy glorious song,*
> *The sacred dirge of thy mouth divine*
> *For sore-wept Itys, thy child and mine;*
> *Thy tender trillings his name prolong*
> *With the liquid note of thy tawny throat;*
> *Through the leafy curls of the woodbine sweet*
> *The pure sound mounts to the heavenly seat,*
> *And Phoebus, lord of the golden hair,*
> *As he lists to thy wild plaint echoing there,*
> *Draws answering strains from his ivoried lyre,*
> *Till he stirs the dance of the heavenly choir,*
> *And calls from the blessed lips on high*
> *Of immortal gods, a divine reply*
> *To the tones of thy witching melody.*

(The sound of a flute is heard within, imitating the nightingale's song.)

Euelpides cries out in enchantment:

[1] *Ibid.*, p. 17.

O Zeus and King, the little birdie's voice!
O how its sweetness honeyed all the copse![1]

As the Hoopoe says, the Nightingale's song is so lovely that it awakens to song the choir of the gods themselves. There is nothing more Greek than this poetry, which expresses the deep unity of Nature: from the gods to the birds the same harmony prevails.

Responsive, meanwhile to the Hoopoe's summons, all the birds of earth and sky and sea appear on the stage and form the many-coloured Chorus of the play.

Aristophanes was well acquainted with the birds, he knew about their nests, their food and their way of life. The Hoopoe, in summoning them, classifies them according to their domains or, as we should say, their habitats, mingling warblings and trills with the melody of his verses, successions of resonant syllables in which the bird-songs are transcribed:

Hoopoe. *Whoop-ho! Whoop-ho! Whoop-hoop-hoop-hoop-hoop-ho!*
        Hoi! Hoi! Hoi! Come, come, come, come, come!

Come hither any bird with plumage like my own;
Come hither ye that batten on the acres newly sown,
    On the acres by the farmer neatly sown;
And the myriad tribes that feed on the barley and the seed,
The tribes that lightly fly, giving out a gentle cry;
And ye who round the clod, in the furrow-riven sod,
With voices sweet and low, twitter flitter to and fro,
    Singing tío, tio, tío, tiotinx;
And ye who in the gardens a pleasant harvest glean,
Lurking in the branches of the ivy ever green;
And ye who top the mountains with gay and airy flight,
And ye who in the olive and the arbutus delight;
Come hither one and all, come flying to our call,
    Triotó, triotó, totobrinx.

Ye that snap up the gnats, shrilly voiced,
    Mid the deep water-glens of the fens,
Or on Marathon's expanse haunt the lea, fair to see,
    Or career o'er the swamps, dewy-moist,
And the bird with the gay mottled plumes, come away,
    Francolín! Francolín! Come away!
Ye with the halcyons flitting delightedly

[1] *Ibid.,* pp. 27, 29.

Over the surge of the infinite Sea,
Come to the great Revolution awaiting us,
Hither, come hither, come hither to me.
Hither, to listen to wonderful words,
Hither we summon the taper-necked birds.

For hither has come a shrewd old file,
Such a deep old file, such a sharp old file,
His thoughts are new, new deeds he'll do,
Come here and confer with this shrewd old file.
Come hither! Come hither! Come hither!
Toro-toro-toro-torotinx!
Kikkabau, Kikkabau!
Toro-toro-toro-toro-lililinx![1]

Soon, a vast fluttering of wings invades the wide semicircle reserved for the Chorus. As the birds arrive the two men reel off their names breathlessly:

Here you see a partridge coming. . . .
Here a widgeon onward hurries, there's a halcyon. . . .
Here's an owl. . . .
Jay . . . , lark and turtle, thyme-finch, ring-dove. . . .
. . . cuckoo, falcon, . . .
Lammergeyer, prophyrion, kestrel . . . water-hen. . . .[2]

And others whom we cannot identify.

They now all begin to twitter and dance to the melody of the lyric song—dances and songs at first full of defiance and hostility toward man, the hereditary foe. Then comes a comic battle in which the two men just escape the vengeful anger of the birds who, with pointed beaks, outspread wings and sharp talons threaten to put out their eyes. But finally, on the Hoopoe's intervening, Peisthetaerus is allowed to explain his marvellous projects.

In a series of admirable speeches, of staggering virtuosity, at once logical and fantastic, and supported by numerous examples, he demonstrates that the Olympian gods are usurpers and that the government of the world formerly belonged to the birds. And here we see an outline of that religion old as well as new, that bird-cult which Aristophanes invented for the comic stage, for a day, and which in the distant memory of the Greeks was connected with a primitive religion traces of which in certain country districts can be vouched for in the time of Aristophanes.

[1] *Ibid.*, pp. 31, 33.   [2] *Ibid.*, pp. 39, 41.

Peisthetaerus. *In times prehistoric 'tis easily proved, by evidence weighty and*
            ample,
            That Birds, and not Gods, were Rulers of men, and the Lords of the
            world; for example,
            Time was that the Persians were ruled by the Cock, a King autocratic,
            alone;
            The sceptre he wielded or ever the names 'Megabazus', 'Darius' were
            known;
            And the 'Persian' he still by the people is called from the Empire that
            once was his own. . . .
            So mighty and great was his former estate, so ample he waxed and so
            strong,
            That still the tradition is potent, and still, when he sings in the morning
            his song,
            At once from their sleep all mortals upleap, the cobblers, the tanners,
            the bakers,
            The potters, the bathmen, the smiths, and the shield- and the musical-
            instrument makers;
            And some will at eve take their sandals and leave. . . .[1]

After citing many other examples of the antique supremacy of the birds, Peisthetaerus describes their present abasement.

        Now they treat you as knaves, and as fools, and as slaves;
           Yea they pelt you as though ye were mad.
        No safety for you can the Temples ensure,
        For the bird-catcher sets his nooses and nets,
        And his traps, and his toils, and his bat, and his lure,
        And his lime-covered rods in the shrine of the Gods!
        Then he takes you and sets you for sale in the lump
        And the customers, buying, come poking and prying,
           And twitching and trying,
        To feel if your bodies are tender and plump.
        And if they decide on your flesh to sup
        They don't just roast you and serve you up.
        But over your bodies, as prone ye lie,
        They grate their cheese and their silphium too,
           And oil and vinegar add,

[1] *Ibid.*, pp. 61, 63.

25. *Aristophanes. A bronze head. Replica of a famous original of c. 200 B.C.*

Then a gravy, luscious and rich, they brew,
And pour it in soft warm streams o'er you,
As though ye were carrion. . . .[1]

After stirring up the birds to a state of indignation, Peisthetaerus invites them to recover their lost kingdom. He suggests that they build a city in the sky, which will cut off communication between gods and men, deprive the dwellers on Olympus of the scent of the sacrifices by which they live and by famine reduce them to surrender. As to men, the winged tribes will reign over them as over so many grasshoppers.

Peisthetaerus' motion is voted on and carried with enthusiasm. The worship of birds is re-established. Let mortal men take heed, and each time they sacrifice to an ancient god let them add at least one offering to a bird:

If a sheep to Poseidon ye slay, to the duck let wheat as a victim be brought;
And a big honey-cake for the cormorant make, if he offer to Heracles aught.
Bring a ram for King Zeus! But ye first must produce for our Kinglet, the gold-
crested wren,
A masculine midge, full formed and entire, to be sacrificed duly by men.[2]

Then the poet becomes lyrical. Fitter by far to reign than the gods are the birds:

Peisthetaerus. *Ay fitter by far!*
No need for their sakes to erect and adorn
Great temples of marble with portals of gold.
Enough for the birds on the brake and the thorn
And the evergreen oak their receptions to hold.
Or if any are noble, and courtly, and fine,
The tree of the olive will serve for their shrine.
No need, when a blessing we seek, to repair
To Delphi or Ammon, and sacrifice there;
We will under an olive or arbutus stand
With a present of barley and wheat,
And piously lifting our heart and our hand
The birds for a boon we'll entreat,
And the boon shall be ours, and our suit we shall gain
At the cost of a few little handfuls of grain.[3]

Won over by Peisthetaerus, the birds soon reach a height of lyric rapture equal to his; and they now prepare, under his direction, to build the new city. They give

[1] *Ibid.,* pp. 67, 69.   [2] *Ibid.,* p. 73.   [3] *Ibid.,* p. 81.

N

26. *A comic figure in the Latin Atellanae—perhaps Dosennus*

it the magnificent name of Nephelococcygia, which can be translated by 'Cloud-cuckoo-borough'.

In the construction of the city or the organization of the republic, each bird has a duty related to his way of life or physical appearance. The swallow is a mason's apprentice. Aristophanes had seen him with a little mortar in his beak and noted that his tail was shaped like a trowel. The woodpecker is a carpenter who squares off the beams with great blows from his beak. The duck with his white apron is in the building-trade; he carries the bricks. The storks who fly across frontiers are obviously destined to deliver passports to travellers by air. The sparrow-hawks, as the policemen of space, are sent on patrol to guard against the perils to Cloud-cuckoo-borough which are now beginning to take shape.

This is because, being built between heaven and earth, the city of the birds is threatened both by men and gods.

The men would like to infiltrate the city on pretext of performing services for the new republic. And now appear the very people whom Euelpides and his friend had tried to flee from: priests who perform interminable ceremonies; poetasters who come to sell their wretched verses composed to the glory of the birds; inspectors of public works; lawmakers; professional informers and black-mailers; not forgetting Meton, a famous surveyor of the time[1] who was very conceited of his up-to-date knowledge. Peisthetaerus and his friend thrash all these tiresome intruders.

But the gods are not pleased, either; because, as Peisthetaerus had foreseen, the birds by founding Cloud-cuckoo-borough have cut off the only means by which they receive their daily nourishment, namely the smoke of the sacrifices. The gods are now dying of hunger in the empyrean. The birds have become men's gods, for they are simply the most ethereal children of that Nature in which man finds food and happiness. The choral songs of the *Birds*, outdoing Peisthetaerus in enthusiasm, declare and repeat the charms and advantages of the new religion:

> *Then take us for Gods, as is proper and fit,*
> *And Muses Prophetic you'll have at your call*
> *Spring, winter, and summer, and autumn and all*
> *And we won't run away from your worship, and sit*
> *Up above in the clouds, very stately and grand,*
> *Like Zeus in his tempers: but always at hand*
> *Health and wealth we'll bestow . . .*

[1] Dr Rogers achieved a good pun in translating this passage:
> Meton. *I come to land-survey this Air of yours,*
> *And mete it out by acres* (p. 137)—Translator.

> *And happiness, plenty, and peace shall belong*
> *To you all; and the revel, the dance, and the song,*
> *And laughter, and youth, and the milk of the birds*
> *We'll supply....*[1]

As there is no such thing as 'birds' milk', it is the Greek for 'perfect happiness'. It is in the nature of Aristophanes never to say anything that he has really at heart without a touch of raillery at his own expense.

The gods being hungry and annoyed send three of their number as an embassy to the insolent republic. One is the great Poseidon, a god very dignified, the second is Heracles, a glutton who thinks only of eating, the third is the god of a barbarian people who does not understand a word of Greek and speaks a pidgin dialect.

Peisthetaerus receives the embassy and lays down his conditions for restoring the worship and sacrifices of the gods. He requests that Zeus should give him his daughter, whose name is Sovereignty, in marriage. He then invites the ambassadors to lunch. Poseidon nobly refuses the conditions and the meal. Heracles—and Peisthetaerus, while negotiating, has held under his nose a savoury-smelling dish which he is preparing—Heracles accepts everything. The final decision will therefore remain with the barbarian god who understands nothing and whose own speech is incomprehensible. But what he says is interpreted to signify a general reconciliation.

Thus the satiric poet who was so severe on some of his contemporaries and who, in the quarrels between the cities and the fearful war that was dividing the Greek world, saw a premonition of something that threatened the whole of ancient civilization—the satirist Aristophanes was also the poet of gaiety, of the pagan love of life and nature and all of nature's children.

Throughout the action of this play, which is more like a fairy-comedy than a satirical, Aristophanes displays the greatest affection for birds. He amusedly makes them set forth a theogony which claims to prove that the birds are the oldest creatures in the world.

Chorus. *There was Chaos at first, and Darkness, and Night, and Tartarus vasty and*
> *dismal;*
> *But the Earth was not there, nor the Sky, nor the Air, till at length in the*
> *bosom abysmal*
> *Of Darkness an egg, from the whirlwind conceived, was laid by the sable-*
> *plumed Night.*
> *And out of that egg, as the Seasons revolved, sprang love, the entrancing, the*
> *bright,*

[1] *Ibid.*, pp. 99, 101.

> *Love brilliant and bold, with his pinions of gold, like a whirlwind, refulgent and sparkling!*
> *Love hatched us, commingling in Tartarus wide, with Chaos, the murky, the darkling,*
> *And brought us above, as the firstlings of love, and first to the light we ascended.*
> *There was never a race of Immortals at all till Love had the universe blended;*
> *Then all things commingling together in love, there arose the fair Earth, and the Sky,*
> *And the limitless Sea; and the race of the Gods, the Blessed, who never shall die.*[1]

In such terms do the birds express themselves to men:

> *Yet men who are dimly existing below, who perish and fade as the leaf,*
> *Pale, woebegone, shadowlike, spiritless folk, life feeble and wingless and brief, ...*
> *Come listen with care to the Birds of the air, the ageless, the deathless, who flying*
> *In the joy and the freshness of Ether, are wont to muse upon wisdom undying.*
> *We will tell you of things transcendental....*[2]

Further on, the birds remind the spectator of the services they render mankind. They are the peasant's calendar, and the seaman's; they give the surest auguries and deliver the most reliable oracles:

> *And the chiefest of blessings ye mortals enjoy, by the help of the Birds ye obtain them.*
> *'Tis from us that the signs of the Seasons in turn, Spring, Winter, and Autumn are known.*
> *When to Libya the crane flies clanging again, it is time for the seed to be sown,*
> *And the skipper may hang up his rudder awhile, and sleep after all his exertions....*
> *Then cometh the kite, with its hovering flight, of the advent of Spring to tell*
> *And the Spring sheep-shearing begins; and next, your woollen attire you sell,*
> *And buy you a lighter and daintier garb, when you note the return of the swallow,*
> *Thus your Ammon, Dodona, and Delphi are we; we are also your Phoebus Apollo.*[3]

Elsewhere—and this is another mark of Aristophanes' love of the birds—we hear the assembly of the feathered folk promulgate a severe decree against a famous bird-dealer who had been martyring their kin and outraging the bodies of dead birds:

> *We, the Birds, will give a notice, we proclaim with right good will,*
> *Sirs, Philocrates, Sparrovian, whosoever of you kill,*
> *Shall receive, reward, one talent, if alive you bring him, four;*

---

[1] *Ibid.*, p. 93.   [2] *Ibid.*, p. 91.   [3] *Ibid.*, pp. 95, 97.

Him who strings and sells the finches, seven an obol, at his store,
Blows the thrushes out and, rudely, to the public gaze exposes,
Shamefully entreats the blackbirds, thrusting feathers up their noses.
Pigeons too the rascal catches, keeps and mews them up with care,
Makes them labour as decoy-birds, tethered underneath a snare.[1]

Is there not in such passages a humorous protest? There is certainly pity and also a restrained but indubitable sympathy for the winged kindreds among whom, as compared with human life, everything speaks of youth and joy and laughter and singing.

Aristophanes should never be taken literally. In spite of what many passages have suggested, he is not thinking seriously of founding a bird-cult. But, at certain points in the comedy, where does laughter stop and reverie begin? The poet takes pleasure in dreaming of a cult which, we must not forget, was one form of his ancestors' religion. In Greek lands as among most primitive peoples, animals and notably birds were the objects of worship, before gods of human form. Aristophanes did not realize he was so near the mark when he makes Peisthetaerus declare that the eagle was worshipped before Zeus and the owl before Athena. We know, although Aristophanes did not, that the cult of the owl on the Acropolis preceded the cult of Athena—Athena the 'owl-faced' as Homer says, using an epithet of which he no longer understood the meaning. The Greeks worshipped the kite and the dove, the cuckoo and the swan, and the swallow and the nightingale, as attested by the myths and in more than one case by archaeology. The myths reversed the order of the metamorphoses: it was the swan who, after a time, turned into Zeus; not Zeus into the swan. The dim memory of a bird-cult may well have survived in the popular mind and in the memory of the peasants. When Aristophanes, whether guided by some old ritual or simply by intuition, played on the theme of birds, he was perhaps stirring sacred memories and half-raising a buried piety in the hearts of the country-folk.

No doubt, as I have said, the poet was dreaming and amusing himself. But one's dreams and games are not entirely at one's choice. These arise from our deeper nature, they come out of our ancestors' past. In a sense they express us, they express ourselves. One does not, for the purpose of fun, invent the cult of birds among the trees without having greatly loved them. Aristophanes was more serious in this comedy than he thought.

Let me cite a passage in which the comic and humorous touches are no more than a sort of modest shield to cover the hold which nature exercises on his sensibility:

[1] *Ibid.*, p. 147.

Chorus.   *O the happy clan of birds*
        Clad in feather;
    Needing not a woollen vest in
        Wintry weather;
    Heeding not the warm far-flashing
        Summer ray,
    For within the leafy bosoms
    Of the flowery meads I stay,
When the Chirruper in ecstasy is shrilling forth his tune,
Maddened with the sunshine, and the rapture of the noon.
    And I winter in the cavern's
        Hollow spaces,
    With the happy Oreads playing; and in Spring
I crop the virgin flowers of the myrtles white and tender
Dainties that are fashioned in the gardens of the Graces.[1]

There is another passage in which Aristophanes, while ceasing to make use of the beings and things he finds in nature or to dispose of them for comic purposes, seems suddenly to have been caught up by this natural beauty, 'possessed by frenzy' as Plato puts it. He is then for a moment, like the cicada of 'divine voice', or like the nightingale, no more than one of the voices which, out of the silence in which she commonly wraps herself, Nature has chosen to communicate with us. So it is, I think, without laughter that Aristophanes invents a 'woodland muse' who inspires him. The flow of bird-trills, which separate some of the verses and are untranslateable, may be omitted.

    O woodland Muse,

    .   .   .   .   .

    Of varied plume, with whose dear aid
    On the mountain top and the sylvan glade,

    .   .   .   .   .

    I, sitting up aloft on a leafy ash, full oft,

    .   .   .   .   .

    Pour forth a warbling note from my little tawny throat,
    Pour festive choral dances to the mountain mother's praise,
    And to Pan the holy music of his own immortal lays;

    .   .   .   .   .

[1] *Ibid.*, p. 149.

Whence Phrynichus of old,
Sipping the fruit of our ambrosial lay,
Bore, like a bee, the honeyed store away,
His own sweet songs to mould.[1]

In such a passage, laughter turns to gravity. Aristophanes pauses while he listens, in his heart, to the 'warbling note' that the bird raises in honour of the wild nature that is symbolized by Pan, and to the 'festive choral dances' he offers to the greatest of goddesses, the mountain mother. It seems as though, in listening to the bird, the poet lends ear to the sacred silence of the great presences in nature. The bird's voice expresses for him the ineffable.

His own voice has grown grave; for was not the Phrynichus he evokes the father of tragic drama?

From end to end of his comedy, and by many other means, the poet enables us to hear that harmony which prevails at the heart of the world: in that solemn concert participate gods and birds and every living thing.

Even thus the Swans,

.   .   .   .   .

Their clamorous cry were erst up-raising,
With clatter of wings Apollo praising,

.   .   .   .   .

As they sat in serried ranks on the river Hebrus' banks.

.   .   .   .   .

Right upward went the cry through the cloud and through the sky.
Quailed the wild-beast in his covert, and the bird within her nest,
And the still and windless Ether lulled the ocean-waves to rest.

.   .   .   .   .

Loudly Olympus rang!
Amazement seized the kings; and every Grace
And every Muse within that heavenly place
Took up the strain, and sang.[2]

[1] *Ibid.*, pp. 101, 103.   [2] *Ibid.*, pp. 107, 109.

CHAPTER NINE

THE DECLINING DAY

Up to this point the present volume has been presenting a few of the masterpieces of the golden age of Greek civilization. This period extends over fifty years but not more—the second half of the fifth century. Fifty years in the history of mankind is scarcely as long as a fine summer's day. '. . . in the warm far-flashing summer ray . . . when the Chirruper in ecstasy is shrilling forth his tune, maddened with the sunshine and the rapture of the noon,'[1] as Aristophanes sings. Greek civilization at its zenith is like this cry of joy which is drawn from mankind when giving birth to works of genius.

Not just one fine day, but summer in its full maturity, yielding fruit in abundance, the season that rewards the peasant's toil and that the Greeks called *opora*. In the orchards they are gathering apples and pears in hampers and filling the baskets with golden plums. The harvest has been gathered in, and in the vineyards the translucent grapes announce the approach of grape-gathering. Earth, oldest of the gods, most tangible and most nourishing, has once again kept her promise. *Opora* is the glory of declining summer, but also the beginning of autumn. The sun is nearer the horizon.

Not that at the beginning of the fourth century Greek civilization is preparing to die. It is still very vigorous and in the centuries that follow and even into the early centuries of the Christian era, it will still, in the few fields of man's activity which it is going to explore, produce a few masterpieces and also a great number of very interesting works. But still, once the golden age was passed, the question begins to arise of the value of this civilization, or, to speak more crudely, of its success or failure.

A civilization is not a kind of game at which history amuses itself, a mass of mingled habits and achievements which future scholars may classify. It is rather a chance, a series of chances or opportunities which a people creates for its use and for the use of others, chances and circumstances which, if firmly moulded by men's

[1] Trans. cited, p. 149.

hands, may for a long period assure a community's equilibrium and allow the greatest possible number of men to enjoy a more human world, a world in which every man can develop his humanity more fully.

Now if we observe the slow decline and especially the sudden change of direction which Greek civilization took from the fourth century onwards, we shall suspect that as early as the fifth century the classical age must have given some forewarning of these phenomena. It appears necessary to point the reader to the principal signs of this, at a moment when we are about to enter on what I have called the new direction taken by Greek civilization.

First, there was a permanent state of war. A war lasting twenty-seven years had exhausted the vital strength of the Greek cities and especially of Athens during the last third of the fifth century. This was what has been improperly called the Peloponnesian war; it was, as I have already said, the first world war of ancient times. It ended by involving all or almost all the Greek states as well as a few barbarian kingdoms. But this so-called Peloponnesian war was not the only one that corroded the golden age or monopolized the energies of Athens and Greece in the very period when the Hellenic peoples were creating the civilization I have described. Another war, lasting twelve years, which had been waged by Athens in order to extend and consolidate her empire, had preceded the Peloponnesian War. Thus nearly forty years of war coexisted with the golden age, and not without peril, not without slackening in the next century the creative impulse of the Greeks.

These wars were imperialistic. They had not been fought in defence of the homeland, like the Persian Wars at the beginning of the fifth century, nor were they just wars. They were wars of conquest and domination. And this was not only true of Athens, who desired and directed these wars for the increase of her prestige and greatness, but also true of her adversaries who, while pretending to defend their independence and to be fighting for the freedom of the cities, hastened as soon as victory was won, to place these liberated cities under their own yoke.

There were also nearly everywhere domestic wars between the citizens of each city. In the Peloponnesian war both of the opposing camps, and especially that of democratic Athens and her allies, were internally divided into two hostile parties, aristocrats and democrats, of which the weaker compounded with the leaders of the enemy and often committed treachery in their favour. Treachery was in fact the ordinary concomitant of conquest and enslavement. Athens had only recently established and was still only maintaining her empire over the cities she euphemistically called her allies, by effecting in each city a revolution which placed the democratic party in power and banished the aristocrats. And this democratic and warlike Athens only succeeded in maintaining her long imperialistic war by constantly increasing in the popular Assembly the membership of the old Eupatridae and their clients, who favoured an agreement with the Spartan and Boeotian aristocrats. Once indeed, in the year 411, an oligarchical *coup d'état* in Athens swept away democratic institutions for a few months, with the intention of obtaining a favourable peace from the nobles who dominated the other camp. The attempt met with no success but it had consequences. When Athens capitulated in 404, a dictatorial régime, known as the tyranny of the Thirty, was imposed by the conqueror. These Thirty were Athenian citizens of the aristocratic party, and Sparta was in this way rewarding their services.

Thus the war between the Greek cities was also a civil war that extended to most of them, and especially to those with democratic institutions.

These internal divisions appear to have been so extreme that one would be tempted to go further and to see in the Peloponnesian war a class-war as well as an imperialist. But such an expression is not appropriate to the conflict that raged between the Greek states in the late fifth century. Times had changed since the beginning of the century. The meaning of the class-war had been distorted. For the democrats in Athens and elsewhere it was no longer a question of winning or enlarging democracy, but of preventing the rich from having a share in it and also of excluding newcomers from the civic register so as to increase the share of profits for each citizen in the event of there being any to distribute. In a word, it was a question of preserving power and privilege for the democrats who were in possession. The struggle that was going on inside each city had ceased to possess the broad meaning it had had in the times of Solon and Cleisthenes: its meaning was now sterile and negative.

But there was another feature of the Peloponnesian war that must be stressed: its inexpiable atrocity. For wars between Greeks this was an entirely new phenomenon.

Massacre was everywhere a response to massacre. Men frenziedly exterminated each other without the least respect for the law of nations or for the treaties which were rarely invoked except when they were challenged and violated. It seemed as though there were no laws of war, even among Greeks. When a city was taken by assault the population capable of bearing arms was put to the sword; the women and children were sold in the slave-market. Here there was a burning like that of Oradour-sur-Glane; elsewhere mercenaries whose pay had not been settled murdered the children in a school either for revenge or distraction. If the allied cities, even those with which Athens had 'contracted friendship', made a movement of insubordination when Athens was squeezing them for money, they were without more ado condemned to death by a nervous Assembly rendered half-mad by the fanatics for reprisals. This was what happened in 428 at Mitylene in Lesbos, and it was only by chance that a reversal in the voting at Athens just afterwards spared this city, so long a friendly one, from the most frightful brutalities. The fate of Plataea, which was taken and razed to the ground by the Spartans, answered to that of the city on Lesbos. A mock tribunal of Spartan judges appealed to the law in order more impudently to violate it. Elsewhere again the dread inspired by the rigours of Athens and Sparta led to mass-suicide by the terrified populations. This showed, as Thucydides points out when dwelling again and again on these horrors, that 'war teaches violence and puts the passions of the multitude in agreement with the brutality of the facts'.

In this way, and right through the Peloponnesian war, might everywhere brazenly asserted its primacy, and denied rights.

One event especially sums up the character of this horrible war, which coincided with the golden age. This was the affair of Melos. It illustrates the frantic imperialism of Athens; it also makes allowance for factional treachery. It concluded in massacre.

In the spring of 416, during the period of an uneasy cession of hostilities, Athens decided to send an expedition against the isle of Melos. She declared cynically to the Melians that she had not the slightest reproach to bring against them, except that during the hostilities that had preceded the truce Melos had remained neutral. Now a state which like Athens was mistress of the sea felt that the neutrality of an island was like a personal affront. It was an insult to her strength, and in the eyes of other nations a sign of her weakness. Athens therefore required the Melians to submit to her empire, and alleged no other reason than the necessity of making herself feared by all the maritime states. In vain the Melians pleaded the justice of their cause: Athens remained unshakeable. Finally they refused to submit to the Athenians' orders. A fleet then blockaded the port and troops were landed on the island. After a desperate resistance lasting nearly a year, the besieged surrendered unconditionally 'treachery having had something to do with it'. All the adult males were massacred, and the women and children reduced to slavery. Later on the Athenians repopulated the island with their own colonists, among whom the lands of the former owners were distributed. Melos was taken and destroyed in the winter of 416–415. In that winter Sophocles was writing the *Electra*, a kind of sister-play to the *Antigone*; and Aristophanes was meditating the *Birds*.

But, what was more serious than war, was another revealing evil which, in these closing years of the fifth century, gave forewarning of the approaching decline and ultimate disappearance of Greek civilization. This was the presence in Athens, in the midst of the golden age, of a democracy that was at once incomplete and on the way to disintegration.

Athenian democracy in the first instance had been an achievement of the small peasants, artisans, merchants and sailors, the achievement of a great creative impulse. The political and cultural achievements which were the fruit of it multiplied in number from the sixth century to the end of the fifth and in the last part of this period, during the golden age, 450–400 B.C., they were born successively of each other, at least in the cultural field, with an abundance apparently inexhaustible. Even if great numbers of aristocrats collaborated in them, they were the result of the democratic advance because they were all designed for the needs and pleasures of the citizens, who were now masters of their destiny.

But with Pericles and in part owing to Pericles the democratic achievement was stabilized: it was already beginning to crumble. The reader will recall, if he refers to the first volume of this work, that as soon as Pericles came into power, in 451–450 B.C., he refused the status of citizen to anyone who was not the son of a citizen and of the daughter of a citizen. Such a decree, which was voted on his motion by the Assembly, not only closed the civil register but limited Athenian democracy. By this measure the citizen-body became the privilege of a cast of about 20,000 men (the figure is given in Aristophanes' *Wasps*, in 422) who governed a city of 400,000 people, not to speak of a vast empire.

One of Pericles' principal cares was to assure this privileged body of citizens of the possibility of access to the magisterial and other public offices, and of sitting in the Court of the Heliasts (the People's Tribunal composed of 6000 judges). For this purpose, it was necessary for these offices to be paid. Pericles therefore granted a salary to these innumerable officials, a modest salary, it is true, but which was increased by Cleon, one of his successors.

One object of Pericles' imperial policy—whether a primary or secondary object, I do not know—was to provide a means of livelihood for the mass of the people. His policy succeeded in this partly by the grant of pay to the armies, partly by the construction of great public buildings which provided work for numerous classes of craftsmen, work which, when it came to the point, was paid for by the tribute of the allies and the subject-states.

But an imperialist policy led to an imperialist war. The empire quickly became, for Athens herself, a terrible 'tyranny' (Thucydides puts the word into the mouth of Pericles). It became something like a system of cog-wheels or gears in which Athens herself was caught and finally crushed. Rebellion succeeded rebellion. Sparta was watching for her opportunity. Meanwhile the tribute of the allies remained indispensable for feeding and amusing the sovereign people. To escape from the cogs one would have had first to win the war. Athens lost it and was ruined.

The peasantry were the first to be stricken. Against the hostile coalition which her policy had raised against her, Athens was powerful only through her navy.

Pericles therefore decided only to fight on sea and to confine the whole population of Attica behind the walls of the city. Athens and the Piraeus became insular. The peasants had to abandon their fields and villages. The Spartans returned every springtime to ravage the countryside. The peasants meanwhile had to live in horrible conditions in the town. They camped between the two 'Long Walls' which linked Athens with the Piraeus and Phalerum. The plague that broke out in 430 found easy prey in this overcrowded population already weakened by famine. The Athenian peasantry, whose resources had been hitherto independent of the empire, were ruined and decimated; they were now reduced like the artisans, sailors and minor officials, to supporting the imperialist war from which they expected work and bread.

Plato's Socrates scarcely exaggerates when he accuses Pericles of having made the Athenians 'idle, base, talkative and greedy'. Pericles was in fact responsible for the formation of that body of indolent citizens who expected the State to feed and amuse them. The State by turns paid out their wages, or paid them for attending the theatre, or sent them to get killed on the battlefields of the Peloponnese or of Thrace. But they would not for long be willing even to defend the Athens that was supporting them. Soon there was to be no more citizen-army. To maintain the wars which were to provide their 'dividends', the citizen-shareholders of Athenian democracy were to demand the engagement of mercenary troops. Civic pride did not long survive the achievement of those democratic institutions which had been so dearly bought but which seemed to die for lack of progress.

These institutions indeed remained intact, but during the fifty years of the golden age they became fixed in a dangerous immobility. It seemed as though there no longer existed a militant class to defend and improve them. The class which had produced them had fallen into a strange inertia. It was no longer a class of producers but much rather of men who exploited those who were producing. These were the metics (citizens of other states or subjects of barbarian kingdoms, men resident in Athens), the allies and especially the slaves. A drastic divorce had taken place between the beneficiaries of the régime and those who produced for it.

This exploitation of the democracy and the empire went on in the midst of a frightful muddle, of which Aristophanes—whom one should re-read, not for the pleasure of the comedy but for the image of the people—is the surest and most clear-sighted witness. Even if he on occasion idealizes certain of his characters, the peasants for example, or if, as happens more often, he caricatures and rends them too harshly—the politicians, philosophers and judges—one thing is certain about his satire and that is that he is always attacking real faults.

If we take up the *Knights* or the *Wasps* we shall discover, behind the comic fiction, an authentic image of the new masters of the people, the successors of

Pericles, and an image of the people itself, with which these demagogues corresponded.

Here is the Cleon of the *Knights,* a greedy and flattering orator. To flatter the people in order to assure one's own power and to use that power to fill one's pockets! How far we have suddenly become removed from the Pericles of Thucydides, 'entirely incorruptible', a man who spoke to the assembled people only 'to give them the best advice'. Flattery had now become a means of government with respect to that plebeian mass whom war had rendered idle and whose demands already give a foretaste of the 'panem et circenses' of the Roman populace. Listen to the demagogue addressing the Sovereign People (I quote or summarize passages from various parts of the play): 'Demus, I love thee, I am enamoured of thee.'

> *That over all Hellas our Demus may rule, for do not the oracles say,*
> *He will surely his verdicts in Arcady give, receiving five obols a day ... ?*
> *Wait till you've heard my oracles, I pray....*
> *Nay mine foretell that over all the land*
> *Thyself shalt rule, with roses garlanded ...*
> *O Demus dear, be idle all the day,*
> *And I'll provide you free to swill, a foaming bowl—of pay.*[1]

'Take a bath, gorge and stuff yourself.... Here's some jugged hare, here are some presents.... Here's my own tunic.... Here's a plateful of wages to gobble up, and no need to work for them.' Thus, right through the play, Cleon tirelessly and methodically proposes to corrupt the people with flattery, with the bait of pleasures and money and idleness. 'I know the people,' he says, 'I know how one lays bait for it, ... and that is why it belongs to me.'

Here now is the same Cleon, flattery laid aside and as he really is. He unleashes himself like a typhoon ('the most violent of all the citizens,' says Thucydides), with a tempest of threats. Those who are truly serving the people, he denounces and causes to be punished. Why? So that he can be paid and bought off. He is a blackmailer. In everything and everywhere 'he alights upon the flowers of venality'. He demands, extorts, confiscates. Those among the rich who are his enemies, he causes to be registered for taxation.

Chorus.   *And you squeeze the audit-passers, squeezing them like figs, to try*
                    Which is ripe, and which is ripening, which is very crude and dry....
Sausage-Seller. *I denounce this juggling fellow; at the Hall, from day to day,*
                    In he runs with empty belly, with a full one hies away....
Chorus.   *Ruffian, who has deafened Athens with thine everlasting din,*
                    Watching from the rocks the tribute, tunny-fashion, shoaling in.[2]

[1] *The Knights,* trans. cited, pp. 113, 127, 135.   [2] Trans. cited, pp. 37, 41, 45.

'He gobbles up the islands as a dog licks up what is on the plate'; and offering Demus, the Sovereign People, only a small slice of nothing at all, he keeps 'the huge share of the cake' for himself. Our metaphors have not changed.

He is a greedy and thieving flatterer and boasts of it. 'I boast of my thefts,' he tells his rival. 'You don't . . . when I'm caught red-handed, I perjure myself.'

Secondary features add further touches to the portrait. Cleon is a coward (as in Thucydides), a coarse and uncultured 'blackguard', obscene and debauched. Not to speak of his repulsive physique. He is a ginger-haired man who stinks like a seal, he is a baboon. I omit other features.

Such was the most colourful of Pericles' successors. And why? Because the people had the masters it deserved. But let us first glance at that satire on the Athenian legal system, that picture of a people with a mania for chicanery and litigation—the famous *Wasps*, from which Racine was to draw his amusing comedy of *Les Plaideurs*.

The Wasps clearly brings out the necessity of multiplying the number of law-suits in order to provide a livelihood for the population of judges;[1] for otherwise it would mean starvation for this multitude who have lost any possibility of work and any taste for it.

Boy. *Father, if the Archon say*
　　　That the Court won't sit today,
　　　Tell me truly, father mine,
　　　Have we wherewithal to dine?[2]

Here then we have a class of people who can only live, and live pretty miserably, unless they have other resources, on a multitude of lawsuits. These lawsuits were occasioned by denunciations. There was a tacit but perfectly conscious agreement between the demagogues and the judges. In order to provide for this proletariat of legal officials, the politicians brought innumerable lawsuits against individuals, or arranged for them so to be brought. A system of delation reigned in the city.

[1] The Court of the 'Heliasts', or 'Dicasts', is supposed to have numbered 6000 men, elected by lot. They seem to have been divided into ten sections, or committees, and it appears that at least 500 would be assembled to try a case. The German historian Grote is completely mistaken when he states that 'the theory of the Athenian dicastery, and the theory of jury-trial as it has prevailed in England since the Revolution of 1688, are one and the same' (*History of Greece*, II, xlvi). They are utterly different, as Dr Rogers points out in his edition of *The Wasps*, pp. xxxviii–xxxix. In the Athenian system, the Dicasts were both judge and jury, that is, they were supposed to interpret the law and to ascertain the facts of a particular case. In the English system, the judge interprets the law and controls the submission of evidence; the jury decides on the facts. Moreover (another error of Grote's) the theory of jury-trial was not affected by the 1688 Revolution (Translator).

[2] *The Wasps* . . . with a Translation, etc. by B. B. Rogers, London, 1915, p. 49.

And the people, who were grateful to the point of servility to those who fed them, supported in the Assembly the policy of the men who supplied them with cases to judge. By this kind of pact each party became enslaved to the other. Aristophanes denounces the pact of mutual enslavement. The judge Philocleon, who is the principal character in the play, rightly boasts of having domesticated the demagogues:

> *Yea, Cleon the Bawler and Brawler himself, at us, and us only, to nibble forbears,*
> *And sweeps off the flies that annoy us, and still with a vigilant hand for our dignity*
> *   cares.*
> *Yet Theorus, a statesman as noble and grand as lordly Euphemius, runs at our*
> *   call,*
> *And whips out a sponge from his bottle, and stoops, to black and to polish the shoes*
> *   of us all.*[1]

But Bdelycleon (that is, the man who feels sick at the name of Cleon) points out to his father Philocleon, and with quite as much reason, that his father is a slave without suspecting it. The demagogues, who were much more cunning than the officials, got the major share of the profits. [The son points out that whereas the annual revenue is about two thousand talents a year, the judges receive only one hundred and fifty—less than a tenth. Translator.]

Philocleon. ... *And what becomes of all the rest of the revenue pray?*
Bdelycleon. *Why, bless you, it goes to the pockets of those, 'To the rabble of Athens*
> *   I'll ever be true,*
> *I'll always battle away for the mob.' O father my father, 'tis owing to*
> *   you:*
> *By such small phrases as these cajoled, you lift them over yourselves to*
> *   reign.*
> *And then, believe me, they soon contrive some fifty talents in bribes to*
> *   gain,*
> *Extorting them out of the subject states, by hostile menace and angry*
> *   frown.*[2]

The politicians however religiously observed that clause of the pact which obliged them to supply the judges with their daily ration of lawsuits—and this for the misfortune of the country. They made use of the sycophants, which was the name given to the professional accusers and blackmailers; unless they preferred themselves to exercise this most profitable of trades. The sycophants were the

[1] *Ibid.,* p. 95.   [2] *Ibid.,* p. 105.

27. The Harlequin of Italian comedy

27

28

worst parasites of Athenian democracy, and Aristophanes' comedies are full of them. Delation was rampant in Athens during the Peloponnesian war. Now because the judge had to draw his daily wage and because the quarrels of factions were envenomed in an atmosphere of approaching defeat, Athens was wholly poisoned by this dreadful gangrene.

We know that if this plague could develop to such proportions, it was partly owing to a serious defect in the judicial system. There was no public ministry or chamber for finding a true bill of indictment. The state did not prosecute: only the person allegedly injured had the right to do that. Hence, if the question arose of impeaching an act injurious to the public interest, any citizen whosoever, as part of the community, could be the plaintiff and denounce the act. Hence also that swarm of accusers, especially politicians, certain of pleasing the people by bringing as many actions as possible concerning state security. They denounced people in season and out of season. They denounced the allied cities so as to increase the amount of their tribute. They denounced the rich in order to confiscate their goods. They accused people of plotting with the aliens; they accused officials of corruption and embezzlement; they accused their fellow-citizens of attempting to set up a tyranny, and of many other conspiracies. Athens was living in an atmosphere of terror and insecurity, of which we hear echoes in Thucydides as well as in Aristophanes.

Comedy of course chose extreme cases or sometimes invented humorous accusations. It was enough to be too elegant, to wear a fringed cloak and a well-trimmed beard to draw on oneself the accusation of being an enemy of the people, an aristocrat, a monarchist. Bdelycleon points out that

> *Everywhere the name of Tyrant, now for fifty years unknown,*
> *Is than cheap salt-fish at Athens commoner and cheaper grown.*
> *Everywhere about the market it is bandied to and fro:*
> *If you wish a bass to purchase, and without a pilchard go,*
> *Straight the man who sells the pilchards grumbles from his stall hard by,*
> *'Here is plainly one that caters with a view to Tyranny.'*
> *If a leek, besides, you order, relish for your sprats perchance,*
> *Says the potherb-girl directly, eyeing you with looks askance,*
> *'Leeks indeed! and leeks I prithee! what, with Tyranny in view'!*[1]

The picture Aristophanes has painted of the Athenian people and its masters is cruelly comical and borders on the grim. The playwright has but recently been regarded as an enemy of democracy. This is an error. He was the best friend the Athenian people had, a friend who loved his countrymen well enough to tell them

[1] *Ibid.,* pp. 75, 77.

o

28. *Girls gossiping at a fountain. Detail of a Panathenaic amphora of the 6th Century*

home truths. The picture is so true even in its exaggerations that this very darkening of the colours reveals in an almost prophetic fashion what Athenian democracy was to become towards the middle of the fourth century.

In the time of Solon a great hope had arisen, a hope that too soon proved abortive: a social class had been formed in Attica, a producing class composed largely of small peasants. The city-artisans had joined it and, engaged in the production of material and cultural wealth, they had together exercised a revolutionary activity productive of new institutions.

War first, then the formation of the Athenian empire and finally its exploitation, exhausted their productive capacity and destroyed the solid bonds which united them in participating in the achievement of a great piece of work. This work was in fact disappearing. Athens no longer contained a class of citizens with equal rights and acting together in the possession of rights which were the outcome of their work. There was now only an agglomeration of individuals whose sole bond was soon to be poverty and hatred for a few men who were exploiting them. Confined within the city walls and doomed to idleness, the only thing they had in common was the sharing out of wealth acquired at the expense of an empire that was about to crumble away. They were magistrates, officials and judges by the thousand. In order to get their wages we know that many of them registered simultaneously in several sections of the Popular Tribunal so that after judging one case they could immediately go and draw wages for judging in the other sections. Their rather meagre pay was supplemented on occasion by distribution in money and kind. But, as we see in the *Wasps*, they lamented at receiving only a very mean share of the tribute from the allies, the greater part being absorbed by military expenditure or disappearing into the pockets of the demagogues. Thus the whole economy by which they were living was illusory. The tribute from the allies and especially slave-labour were the only things that gave it a concrete existence.

When the tribute vanished in the hour of defeat (404 B.C.), the citizen-body was reduced to poverty and was for long to remain in that condition. Most of them, who were peasants, did not recover their property in the country. The poorer ones emigrated. The utterly poverty-stricken sold themselves abroad as slaves or enlisted in mercenary armies. In the course of the fourth century the number of citizens was soon to be reduced by fifty per cent. A minority of wealthy parvenus appropriated the estates of the Attic countryside; small properties were swallowed up in large ones. The boundary-stones that marked the mortgages of the rich on the lands of the poor—stones which Solon had had removed in the sixth century—reappeared in the fourth. The new masters of the land now operated their farms with slave-labour; and the presence of such labour prevented the free workman from resuming his former activity. In this period the cost of a slave was very low, no doubt owing to the incessant wars which threw great numbers of people on to the slave-market. The maintenance of a slave was not costly; it cost less than that of the poor devil of a freeman, however sober he was, of necessity. It was therefore natural that among the city artisans, as in the country districts, slave-labour predominated more and more.

It is also said that the freeman's scorn of manual work led him to prefer the indolence that was financed by the State. Hunger is, alas!, a cruel necessity that dominates the choice between manual work and *farniente*. Besides, I do not see that at the date in question any such scorn existed. It is hardly attested by a few intellectuals like Xenophon and Plato, and they do not much insist on it. It was a good deal later, in the second century of our era, that Plutarch surprisingly enough declared that no young man of good family would ever wish to become a Pheidias or a Polycleitus because those artists must have been considered contemptible as being manual workers.

The numerical proportion between the free citizens and the slaves is enough to explain the predominance of slave-labour over free-labour. The number of citizens was diminishing; the number of slaves (however difficult an affirmation in such a matter may be) was clearly following an opposite direction; it was constantly increasing and seems to have reached the figure of four hundred thousand in Athens at the end of the fourth century, whereas it had been two hundred thousand towards the middle of the fifth.

In spite of this increase, of which there was only an indication at the end of the golden age, it would be a mistake to suppose that there were then no more free workers in Athens. On the contrary, the small artisans who worked on their own account were still numerous. We find mention of them in the plays of the Old Comedy and in the Socratic Dialogues of Plato which are supposed to take place at this time. The potters who still occupied the vast suburb of the Cerameicus were the most important. But it would be no surprise to learn that they were only working on half-time. Athenian economy was undergoing a grave crisis. The distant lands—Italy, Persia and Scythia—in which we are still discovering the original Attic vases of the fifth century, had begun to manufacture their own vases in the same style and on the spot, to meet local needs and sometimes even for export. And what is attested for the production of vases must be true of many other objects which, previously, had been of exclusive Athenian manufacture and which the new countries had learned to produce themselves. It was no doubt during the Peloponnesian war that Athens must have lost these markets.

All this explained, none the less, or at least did not prevent the increase in

the number of slaves in relation to the number of citizens and notably of free
workers.

The increase in slave-labour as against free labour was disquieting, though it
was not yet stifling, except perhaps on the great country-estates which again
covered the greater part of Attica. From this increase one must expect a slow
extinction of civic life, an extinction including many other factors which were only
to appear as Greek civilization slowly declined. But this does not yet concern
us. What, on the other hand, one could certainly not expect from slavery was
the transformation and rejuvenation of the economic and social structure of the
ancient city-states. The mass of the slave-population of Greece had not become
conscious of itself and of its unity. It had no plans. It did not form a class in the
political and revolutionary sense of the word. It envisaged no end to its wretched
condition except by escaping *en masse* or by the very rare freeing of an individual.
An escape of the former kind took place towards the end of the Peloponnesian
war, involving twenty thousand slaves, most of them workers in the silver-mines
at Laurium, who went over to the Spartans. But this was a reaction of misery and
not a political act in the struggle of the exploited against the exploiters.

Nothing therefore in late fifth-century society shows that slavery was or could
ever become an active factor in the renewal of a civic life that was now threatened.
Slavery simply multiplied, and it was a purely quantitative phenomenon without
any other meaning. Slavery could in fact only offer the society of free men
an image of what that society would become in the course of centuries, a
sinister image of the last degree of wretchedness. It was therefore a source, and
the most active source, of a production limited to material goods, but at the
same time a dead weight which was continually growing heavier. One must
not dream of expecting this dead weight to be an instrument of salvation for ancient
society.

So the image of misery which was to dominate the latter days of Greek civilization was now appearing on the horizon. We have a glimpse of such poverty and
also of wealth acquired by the most dishonest means, right through the *Plutus*
of the prophetic Aristophanes, a comedy which already belongs to the fourth century (388 B.C.) I may recall at this point that Zwingli, the most humanistic of the
reformers, once had the *Plutus* performed in Greek.

Chremylus, an honest peasant, an Athenian citizen living in a small village,
wonders now that he is old what he can do with his son. Must he leave him in the
country to scratch his meagre patch of ground and get nothing from it, or send
him to the city to grow fat among the scoundrels and expect the reward of his
dishonesty from Plutus (Wealth)? He goes to consult the oracle at Delphi. The
priestess does not answer his question, but tells him to follow the first man he

meets on leaving the temple. This person is a filthy and ragged beggar, a blind one, too. Really it is Plutus himself.

Chremylus follows and stops him. He decides to heal Plutus of the blindness Zeus has inflicted on him because he only rewarded just men, of whom the god was jealous. On recovering his sight, Plutus will reward the honest Chremylus and the other poor devils of villagers who, at the end of a life of poverty, have no means even of providing for their own burial.

Plutus is miraculously cured at the sanctuary of Epidaurus, and the sycophants, riff-raff and bandits who have been systematically plundering the Republic, begin to fall on evil days, to the great joy of the old true-born race of peasants.

No work more clearly reveals the importance which money had acquired in Athenian life. The very subject indicates that the problem of poverty was being faced by the masses who attended the play. 'Love of money dominates all of us,' says one of the characters. There had long been poor and hungry folk at Athens, especially since war had taken up its abode there. But what, on occasion, was said about them at the time of the *Clouds* (423 B.C.), and which might then be humorous, was no longer very fitting in 388 or else its meaning had become pathetic. It was no longer a joke to speak on the stage of people who had no coat, or bed, or blanket. There were too many of them sitting on the tiers of seats.

Distributions of corn at a reduced price or even gratis had become more and more frequent, but they were also increasingly meagre. People fought to get them. Men made money out of everything; one pawned one's furniture and military equipment. Neither the measures taken by statesmen nor the frugality of the peasants prevented the cost of living from constantly going up. Decrees which attempted to prevent an increase in the price of the most necessary products, such as salt, met with no success.

Thus in the last comedies of Aristophanes, from which these few features have been taken, a host of little facts shows that for the majority of Athenians poverty had become a source of daily anxiety and money an inaccessible dream. There is a particularly curious and interesting scene in the *Plutus*. When Chremylus takes it into his head to cure the blindness of 'wealth', an allegorical personage unexpectedly appears. This is Poverty. To drive her from the earth, she says, would be to banish the true benefactress of mankind. Poverty alone stimulates energy and procures ease and happiness. Such is Poverty's argument. No one answers, because, at this moment in history no one was in a position satisfactorily to refute the sophism. Chremylus contents himself with replying by action: he expels her and refuses to entertain her fallacious plea. But he does not fail to evoke the train of Misery, which follows close on the heels of Poverty: the scourge of lice, fleas and vermin that torment the wretched and prevent them from sleeping by repeating the words:

> *Up! up! they will shrill, 'tis to hunger, but still up! up! to your pain and privation.*
> *For a robe but a rag, for a bed but a bag of rushes which harbour a nation*
> *Of bugs whose envenomed and tireless attacks would the soundest of sleepers*
> *   awaken.*
> *And then for a carpet a sodden old mat, which is falling to bits, must be taken.*
> *And a jolly hard stone for a pillow you'll own; and for girdle-cakes barley and*
> *   wheaten,*
> *Must leaves dry and lean of the radish or e'en sour stalks of the mallow be eaten.*
> *And the head of a barrel, stove in, for a chair. . . .*[1]

and so on.

One wonders whether on that spring day in 388, when a new war was in progress and was to last for ten years and when the Athenians' favourite poet thus depicted their miserable existence, as a warning on the threshold of a century of defeats, disasters and famine—one wonders whether the people laughed very much. Why then had Aristophanes lost his gaiety? Why, unless it were because the decline of his beloved city had begun, the misery of his joyous countrymen, the misery of 'suffering brats and old women in shoals'?

Yet we must not let the sky be darkened by the clouds of continual war, of the decay of democracy, and of slavery and misery. The Greeks were tenacious of life. Ages yet unborn were to be modelled in their image. We are now at the end of the fifth century. It would be a thousand years before Justinian was to close the schools in Athens where profane philosophy was taught; a thousand years after the days when Socrates in his strange manner began to put questions to the mind of man.

With their wars and their misery and decaying institutions, but also with their arts and letters, their reason, wisdom and untiring courage, the Greeks had a career of a thousand years before them.

In the streets of Athens Socrates is questioning the passers-by; and here we see him preparing to gather in his honey.

[1] *The Plutus* . . . trans. Rogers, London, 1907, pp. 59, 61.

CHAPTER TEN

THE ENIGMA OF SOCRATES

Socrates was for his contemporaries and remains for us an enigma to which we shall doubtless never hold the key. Very strange, almost extravagant in his behaviour, he was also a man of great common sense and even strict logic; and he never ceases to astonish and instruct us, and to dispense his discoveries, his knowledge and his precious ignorance.

But the most astonishing feature of a life that was at once singular and quite ordinary, was the death that concluded it and that was full of incredible consequences. It raised a cloud of witnesses, disciples and opponents, who speak to us across the centuries, and sometimes in contradictory terms, of the importance of Socrates' words and of the truth for which he gave his life.

What was the gist of his message? Why did he die? And what truth seemed to him more precious than life itself? Here our embarrassment begins, and also a great confusion among the historians. For we must admit that the testimony of the men who claimed to be his disciples, not to speak of the witness of his adversaries, is often very contradictory. Let us enumerate them, restricting ourselves only to those who knew Socrates personally.

First comes Aristophanes who in 423 made Socrates the principal character in the *Clouds*. Socrates was forty-six at this time. He had no doubt been teaching for many years past in the squares and streets of Athens; and he was to go on teaching for twenty-four more years before the authorities thought of disturbing him and summoning him before the Popular Tribunal. Aristophanes was a comic poet and so, in accordance with the laws of the genre, he paints a highly-coloured caricature of Socrates; at the same time, this had to be such that the original would be immediately recognized. He makes his victim wear the mask of 'the learned foreign doctor', a character who, as we have seen, appears in the comedies of all the people in the world who have remained close to the primitive vein. The Socrates of the *Clouds* has certainly been simplified by the exaggeration of those comic features which he has in common with all such 'doctors'. We may, however, at least admit

that the features which the poet has exaggerated existed in embryo in the real
Socrates. Now the two essential traits of Socrates in the *Clouds* are, first, his
explanation of natural phenomena without recourse to the intervention of the
gods: thus, he explains rain and storms not by the action of Zeus, but of the clouds;
and in this sense he is, in strict etymology, an atheist. In the second place the
Socrates of the *Clouds* practises sophistry, described by the poet as the science
which enables you, in the law-courts, 'to make the weaker cause appear the
stronger'; in other words, he perverts the young men by offering them an easy way
of escaping from the penal consequences of their misdeeds, as for example adul-
tery. Now these two features of Aristophanes' Socrates—atheism and the corruption of youth—we find almost identically formulated in the action brought
against Socrates twenty-four years later. Plato dwells on this identity, while con-
testing the accuracy of Aristophanes' portrayal which he regards as slanderous.

We now come to those witnesses who were disciples and even apostles. The
greatest of them were also founders of the schools of philosophy which, in spite of
their glaring opposition, claim to derive equally from Socrates.

Plato offers his master this homage, unique in literary history, of putting the
thoughts that came to him throughout the course of nearly fifty years, into the
mouth of the man who had led him along the road of wisdom. Plato in his works
makes Socrates the author of Platonic idealism. Plato was a great poet and his
distortion[1] of the real Socrates was certainly no less important than that of Aristophanes. He also sometimes blends and confirms Aristophanes' statements as well
as contradicting them.

He was not simply a poet but an inventor of political myths, perhaps most of all
a political thinker and a man who detested Athenian democracy. A whole part of
his work implies this and he himself recognizes his temperament in the best known
of his letters. It seems therefore very probable that he imparted a political colour
to Socrates, and in an anti-democratic sense. Nothing, however, proves that
Socrates, who was a man of the people, was the first founder of the reactionary
Platonic ideology, as is sometimes too lightly asserted.

Among other witnesses are two philosophers who stood at the opposite poles of
fourth-century thought but who both made use of Socrates' name: these were
Antisthenes, founder of the ascetic school of the Cynics, and Aristippus, founder
of the hedonistic school of rational enjoyment.

Nor should we forget the abundant testimony of a disciple who was not a
philosopher but an historian or who posed as such. Xenophon was a very loyal
friend who has been excessively slighted and who was by no means as limited as
people have tried to show. Now Xenophon claims to be recording a great number

---

[1] 'déformation.'

of Socratic conversations he had heard. We should observe however that his position as a country-landowner and cavalry-leader was doubtless not such as to prepare him particularly well to give a faithful report of Socrates' teaching. He too distorts the picture of the real Socrates; but I will not undertake to say whether the politician-poet does so more or less than the comic-poet or the philosopher-poet.

Finally, one must at least mention a hostile witness, Polycrates, the author of a charge brought against Socrates, although this was not the official indictment brought before the archon but an independent piece of writing. It has not been preserved, but we have a report of it which we may regard as correct, belated though it be.

Of course these witnesses frequently contradict each other. To weigh their evidence, to choose between them, perhaps even to challenge them all—all this affords plenty of work for the scholars.

Much has been written about Socrates in recent years and nearly always to throw doubt on the value of the traditions which record his words. There are two weighty volumes by M. Magalhaes-Vilhena—theses presented in the Sorbonne—crammed with erudition and very intelligent, although filled out with passages that do not always relate to the subject. Then there is the book which at first seems more impartial but is also far more negative, of the Swiss professor, M. Gigon. This contains a meticulous discussion of the texts, and it is meticulous and relentless also in building up hypotheses which claim to reduce the whole of Socratic literature to the level of fiction. This obstinacy in taking the various testimonies of the ancients about Socrates and using them to destroy each other, is somewhat irritating and indeed suspect.

Neither of these authors denies the existence of an Athenian named Socrates who presumably lived and held forth during the last quarter of the fifth century. They do not deny the trial of Socrates or his condemnation to death. But all the rest appears to them as pure legend, myth, poetical creation, *Dichtung*,—writes M. Gigon, who uses the term 'philosophical poems' in speaking of Plato's Dialogues.

This is the thesis which compels me at the outset to devote a few moments to literary or historical criticism. At first sight the theory seems both disturbing and attractive but it is in fact never convincing.

It calls for a few observations. We must remember that thirty or forty years ago two great Platonic philologists maintained with equal assurance a theory which was the opposite of the one defended by MM. Gigon and Magalhaes-Vilhena. In the eyes of Burnet and Taylor the Platonic Dialogues, far from being myth and poetry, were nothing less than exact records, almost written reports, of authentic conversations. They were mistaken, but their view has for long prevailed.

It is moreover to be observed that the contradictions alleged to exist between the various testimonies are not as numerous as people maintain, and perhaps not much more numerous than the points of agreement which critics sometimes forget to emphasize. Thus Aristophanes, whose *Clouds* it will be remembered appeared in 423, makes fun of a Socrates who devoted himself to observing 'meteors', that is, stars and celestial phenomena in general, in the manner of Anaxagoras; and who, the more conveniently to make his observations, sat in a basket suspended in the air. Now in Plato's *Phaedo*, which was written forty years later, Socrates professes to be a disciple of Anaxagoras. The latter had studied primarily the shape of the earth, also the sun and the moon, and had not gone into ethics. Why not point out this remarkable concordance of evidence instead of preferring to stop and to point out divergencies?

There is therefore agreement between certain of the testimonies. But people ask that all the witnesses to the life of Socrates should agree about everything. They wish to regard as authentic only those facts which are attested by Aristophanes, Plato, Antisthenes, Aristippus, Xenophon and the others, that is, by all of them. Such an exigency is absurd. The unanimous agreement of witnesses regarding the same circumstances would be the most amazing thing in the world, and the most suspect. Such a thing has never been seen in any instance. Besides, these witnesses had not necessarily been present at the same conversations; they had not seen this paradoxical Socrates in the same light; they had not all known him at the same period of his life. To expect that men who differed from each other in age, in profession, in temperament and in ideas, should bear a similar or identical witness regarding anyone, would be to expect a miracle. Observe also that it is not here simply a question of testifying to facts, but to the interpretation of the facts, and, in the last resort, to the interpretation of Socrates' thoughts, those thoughts which the ancients tell us Socrates took pleasure in concealing or filling with ambiguous irony. Are we to be surprised that the country-landowner and the philosopher of idealism—Plato, that impenitent poet—or again the most whimsical writer of comedies who ever existed, or again the philosopher of enjoyment, or the philosopher of asceticism, did not always record and interpret the same facts and the same thoughts in the same way? The contrary would be surprising, or rather, unthinkable.

From divergencies and contradictions which are perfectly natural in the circumstances, are we justified in ascribing a mythical or legendary character to the Socrates whom the ancient writers present to us? Such a conclusion seems to me scarcely reasonable.

One thing appears sure, and this restores an appearance of reasonableness to the views of Burnet and Taylor, namely that the different portraits of Socrates which his contemporaries offer us, and which are all interpretations, must all bear some resemblance to the historical Socrates which will enable us to recognize him.

Can we, besides, apply the word 'historical' simply to the Socrates who was born to a midwife in 469 and who led a life enigmatic to his contemporaries and even for a long time to himself, until poison and injustice finally caused him to expire in 399? The true Socrates is the one who lives on in our memory; the historical Socrates is the one who acts on the history of thought, and on our history as men, every time we approach him through the pages of those who tell us of him. The historical Socrates and the legendary are one and the same person, a living person because an active one.

The 'legendary' Socrates existed in the lifetime, and even in the heart, of the 'authentic' Socrates, for he was strange in his own eyes. And this is also why his problem remains an examplary problem of history. One can say of all historical facts that they are always, though in varying degrees, 'constructions' of history. And yet they are facts: they act.

To pretend to distinguish two persons in Socrates is to divide his life into two modes of existence of which one is as valid as the other. This is to condemn to death for a second time the true Socrates, the one who lives in us as in all those who have known him through the witness of his disciples; because he himself wrote nothing.

This crime I refuse to commit. Criticism indeed commits it every time a critic, when claiming to discern multiple and contradictory figures of Socrates, 'variants' of Socrates, ventures so far as to imagine, in order to explain these variants, hypothetical dialogues which have been presumably lost but which he appears to take more seriously than those which have survived.

Such philologists are not serious themselves. For them Socrates is a game, a sort of puzzle of which most of the pieces are missing: these pieces they refabricate. But Socrates is not a game. He is a living being because he makes us live. The historical and the legendary man is one and the same, and that is how I shall take him, being guided in my choice of testimony by the 'impact' I receive from the various witnesses, and also by the impact that men in the past have experienced.

This is the point on which the Socratic criticism of today appears to me most at fault. It quite simply forgets what should be called the 'Socratic impact'.

But without the active presence for half a century, in the streets of Athens, of Socrates' person and teaching, and especially without the effect of his death in 399, nothing that followed could be explained. It is only the violence of the impact experienced by his disciples that explains the abundance and diversity of Socratic literature. This real impact of a real person, each man experienced in a different way, because they were all different from each other, but everyone felt it in his flesh. No poem invented after Socrates' death could have so mobilized poets, historians and philosophers, and that for centuries. Here—or so it seems to me—is a blindingly clear answer to the myopia of critics poring over living texts which they dissect as though dealing with corpses. For example, to place Plato's account of the death of Socrates—of which I may say that I have found it exercising the same emotional power over the most diverse audiences—to place this in a chapter entitled 'Philosophical poem of Socrates' seems to me an error approaching nonsense.[1] Never has such a poem been fabricated out of nothing or practically nothing.

It is time, in short, to begin at the other end and try to resuscitate the Socrates who was both historical and legendary, that enigmatic being who, the more deeply to touch us, seems often to shrink away into the absurd under the humorous mask of irony.

◎

Socrates was very fond of young men, and this makes us curious to know about Socrates in youth.

He was not an infant prodigy. It was only at the age of forty, and because he had received a sign from a god, that he became aware of his mission. Who or what was this queer mind housed in the body of a Silen, this soul passionately enamoured of something it was unaware of, this stranger named Socrates, he did not know. Graven on the temple of Apollo at Delphi, the hackneyed adage of the old Greek wisdom: 'Know thyself'—this he had read; not merely read with his eyes like an absent-minded pilgrim, but heard within his own breast as an echo to the questions that beset his early years: 'Who are you? What are you good for? What do you know? What is the use of your knowledge?' He had a soul both ardent and thoughtful, a passionate nature and the coolest reason that ever was. He longed to commit his life, but in full knowledge of what he would be doing. He had first to learn to know himself.

The poets had helped him as a child to grasp a part of his nature, but not in the way one would have expected. At school he learned the pleasant stories they told, he recited their sayings to his master; he loved those splendid voices which told of the power of the gods and the toils of men. But he did not allow himself to be beguiled by the magic rhythm of the verse. The poets spoke to him of what he most desired to know about: gods and men. He did not, however, leave them to speak alone. He questioned. 'Are you telling the truth?' he asked Homer, Hesiod and Pindar. And if he found them lying or ascribing some evil deed to the masters of the world whom he desired to be good and just, if he observed that their heroes

---

[1] *'Un contresens qui approche du non-sens.'*

were satisfied with an appearance of virtue, unworthy of an upright man, then he was angry with poetry. He rejected any false imitation of the ideal for he carried the ideal within himself and knew it to be true. The reading of the poets revealed to him, not what he was but at least what he was looking for and what he loved. This was truth.

The scientists also were in quest of truth. Many of those who lived at that time were scrutinizing the heavens, trying to understand the movement of the stars, to ascertain the shape of the world and grasp the essence that constituted it. As a young man he listened to them attentively and with confidence. These 'physicists', as they were called, would no doubt give him the key of knowledge; by explaining what the world was, they would tell him why Socrates was in the world and what he had to do there. But he soon perceived that the scientists' answer was no better than the poets' answer to the one question that had to be solved if one was to live, namely 'Who am I?' What was the use of exploring the universe if one remained ignorant of one's own nature? The gods knew how the world was constituted, because they filled it and directed its movements. It was vain and impious to try and force one's way into the secret of the Nature they dwelt in. But what scientist was going to discover the truths that concerned the human soul, with its demand for happiness and its capacity for virtue? Nature belonged to the gods, but the mind of man was his own. Eclipses and meteors do not teach us how to live. Should we not rather listen to that frail yet reasonable voice which stammers within us and which, speaking as it does in all men, suddenly acquires the force of their common consent? Socrates therefore rejected the frivolous science of those who fled from man and the service of man in order to seek, in the firmament of space, an escape from the one necessary truth. Socrates' influence which, through the schools that derived from him, was immense, contributed greatly to cause the ancients to prefer 'philosophy' to the sciences properly so-called. It was certainly a fatal thing to choose a 'philosophy' which provisionally brushed aside the sciences and limited itself to the knowledge of man. But nothing mattered to Socrates as much as that knowledge; nothing took hold of him except man's mastery over his mind—over his soul, as he put it. It was no doubt too early in the history of mankind to found moral science on precise rules. Socrates was not unaware of this; but he liked to stride across the centuries.

Now it was the workmen far more than the poets and scientists who brought Socrates towards that state of awareness he aspired to. According to him, every man had something to teach him because every man carried within himself the truth about man; but more than any other, the man of the people, the artisan bound to his trade by strict and delicate rules, was capable of this. Socrates was a man of the people; he lived in the street; he felt himself to be a born artisan (to make what?), a brother to all those who spoke the technical language of the things they made. Most of his disciples were to be young gentlemen; and many came to him only to beguile their idleness. But Socrates was a workman and the son of workmen. The midwife, his mother, was an expert in the oldest of all trades. His father was one of those stone-masons who squared, fixed and polished the blocks of which the Parthenon was built. So Socrates sought the company of workmen. To define the useful, the beautiful, virtue, the public good, he sat down in the forge, or borrowed his examples from the cobbler or questioned the labourer. All through his life, the carpenter, the mason, the wheelwright and the potter were, so to speak, to accompany his remarks and, through his mouth, to make rejoinder to the politician and the sophist. The artisans were Socrates' first masters in the art of thought. They were obliged really to know the things they talked about. They could not cheat with the material they were fashioning nor with the object they had in view. The articles that came from their hands had to perform the services demanded of them. It was necessary therefore that the artisan should learn his art and communicate his knowledge to his hands. Socrates admired the strictness of the rules which allowed of producing an object. He marvelled at the precision the workman put both into his movements and into his language. He envied such work which, through the practice of sure rules, exactly adapted a product to the use it was to fulfil. Such work was beautiful.

Socrates even took up the chisel of his father the stone-mason; but he was attracted by a different kind of material that he wanted to fashion with the same certainty, knowledge and workmanly conscientiousness. This was the human soul. He wanted to invent a technique for producing noble characters.

After a long apprenticeship, Socrates knew what he was looking for and what he was. He sought for a method that would enable him to extract from man the truth that was in man and concerned man; in short, he was seeking a science of human life. He knew himself well enough to be able to choose his trade without hesitation. So he took up the trade of his mother, the midwife. He would deliver souls of the truth they bore within themselves. He was born to be just that: a midwife for souls.

But to come to this choice, what a hard road he had had to follow through the little-known years of his youth! What obstacles of the flesh, in conflict with obstacles of the spirit, may have been encountered on a road which led only to the will for truth? One has only to look at the Faun-like face to guess what appetites other than the love of souls may have possessed him.

He loved wine; but no one ever saw this intrepid drinker drunk. He loved young boys; but no one at his trial dared maintain that he had made infamous use of them. The ardent sensuality that burned within him he converted into a violent desire to possess one thing: the truth! The face of a brute on whose magic lips the word of the spirit will alight.

The vocation he had made his own at the cost of inner struggles of which we can hardly suspect the nature or severity, at the cost also no doubt of great sacrifices, was one day clearly revealed to him by the god of Delphi. The story is well known. Socrates was already in the prime of life; for years past he had been conversing with himself and a few familiar friends. But he did not yet regard his profession as a service of the god any more than as a public service. Now one of his childhood friends conceived the notion of asking the oracle of Apollo whether there was in the whole world a man wiser than Socrates. 'There is not,' replied the god. Socrates was surprised, and in good faith, because he knew only his own ignorance. He was extremely embarrassed. Although sure that the god was not lying, he did not consider himself exempted from proving the matter. And to verify the truth of the oracle there was no way except to examine every sage of established reputation. Thus began that dialogue which he was to carry on for thirty years, conversing with the most illustrious minds in Athens and in Greece as a whole, confounding the knowledge of statesmen and priests, of poets and scientists and, on each occasion, bearing witness to the god who had proclaimed him the wisest because he alone was wise enough to recognize his ignorance.

A strange profession and a strange doctor! For thirty long years he questions, refutes, 'debunks'. For thirty years he causes everyone to be laughed at, including himself. He disconcerts, scandalizes, exasperates and sometimes bewitches.

Who could understand him in his office as public prosecutor of all Athenian, and indeed human, wisdom? Hardly one of his disciples and certainly not his own people. He knew this and did not care. He would continue without respite to snatch the mask from the face of folly, since the god so willed it. He would continue without wages and almost without hope to serve as educator of the most restive of all the peoples; because this was his way of being a citizen and of practising the true art of politics (he said there was no other) which consisted in 'making one's fellow-citizens better'.

And so he went on until his countrymen in their irritation struck him down like a gadfly that you crush because it is stinging you.

◎

Why did his compatriots condemn him to death? He bore a tender love to his people. For them he lived, for them he consented to die.

To understand the meaning of his life and death, one must follow the two paths along which Socrates and the Athenians travelled to that goal. One must live with Socrates for many years in the streets of the city he would not abandon even to save his life. One must see him through the eyes of the people he loved and who could not understand him.

Imagine yourself in the market-place at ten in the morning on any day of the thirty years of Socrates' apostolate (that is, in the last third of the century which has been called by agreement the age of Pericles, a name that Socrates would not have liked because he had no love for Pericles' Athens). The market-place is full of people. The pork-butcher is crying: 'Black puddings for sale'; the cavalry-officer holds out his helmet for the fish-wife to put some herrings in it; by the barber's shop and round the tables of the money-changers, Athens is talking and listening.

Socrates comes up. Everyone knows him: it would be impossible not to recognize the ugliest man in Athens. His broad, pug-nosed face is surmounted by the vast bare dome of the forehead. Under their heavy brows his protruding eyes gaze out like a bull's.[1] The nostrils of the least Greek of all noses in Greece are turned boldly upwards. A scanty beard barely conceals a mouth which, said a disciple, looks as though made to bite, and which—as Socrates added—is more ill-favoured than that of a donkey. And, to complete the picture, we see a massive body supported by a pair of short legs. Such was the Socratic ugliness, which Socrates himself was the first to laugh at, while undertaking to demonstrate that it was beauty itself. For if the beautiful is the useful, then who would not prefer a nose open to every wind and especially to the breath of heaven, rather than a straight, down-pointing nose which catches smells from the ground? Not a very convincing proof in the eyes of those who worshipped the Olympians or frequented the gymnasium. Some people were inclined to regard an ugliness so extravagant as a sign of the disapproval of heaven. Only an intimate detected the master's secret kinship with those ancient genii, the sardonic satyrs and Silenus the enchanter.

This unsightly fellow neglects himself. Holding the body in low esteem, a philosopher rarely takes a bath. If he haunts the palaestra, it is to retail his fooleries and not to thwart the ravages of age or the insidious spread of adipose. And what is to be said of the old cloak he carries about in all weathers, whether the north wind is blowing a squall or the sun high in heaven is forcing sensible people to fight for a place in a donkey's shadow? Socrates wears the dress of the poor; but the vulgar do not know that he is forestalling time itself; that this cloak, which the philosophers will adopt in memory of him, will one day be the frock of the Christian monk.

Socrates, meanwhile, has encountered a well-known personage in the Agora, one of the men whose speeches sway the Popular Assembly. He is a good orator, perhaps even an honest man, but the fine word of 'justice' is on his lips more often

[1] Cf. George Forsyte who, sitting in the bay-window of the Iseeum, has a 'bull-like gaze', in Galsworthy's *To Let*, Part I, Ch. I (Translator).

29. *Delphi: evening*

than would seem prudent. Socrates accosts him with the freedom that ancient manners permitted. 'My dear fellow,' he says, addressing him in some such terms,[1] 'you who counsel the people in all undertakings, whether just or unjust, would you like us—you and me—to try and discover what justice is?' Or else he says: 'Since a statesman's business is to see that the laws are respected, would you like us to define the law?' The crowd has gathered in a circle. The great man is full of assurance. 'The law? Justice? Nothing simpler!' He gives his definition. After weighing it up, Socrates finds one term in it obscure. Let us define that term. Or we might perhaps take an example from cooking or horse-breeding, or anything that everyone knows about. The dialogue goes on, it is kept close to solid earth, full of unexpected turns and clear demonstrations, severely logical even when apparently roundabout, until the moment when our fine phrase-maker, face to face with this man whose questions require only a yes or a no, is forced to break off at every new step. Now he faces the threat of being pushed into some absurd position; and so, harassed with sound logic and riddled with dilemmas, he decides to conclude hurriedly that law is really illegality; and that justice is. . . . But he prefers to give it up. Which obliges Socrates to observe that he has been discoursing to the Assembly on matters about which he does not know the first thing. The bystanders laugh, while our politician slips away. Socrates has made an enemy.

People have laughed, but now they are worried. When all is said and done, what is Socrates after? What is the meaning of this verbal massacre, this strange obstinacy in making everyone admit that he knows nothing? This even stranger affectation of proclaiming his own ignorance, and constantly declaring that if he knows one thing, it is simply that he knows nothing? Why, yesterday he was questioning people about morals, making the idlers laugh at the very respectable definitions of 'the supreme good' or 'civic duty' which someone gave him. Does not this master of irony then believe either in the citizen's virtue or in his duty?

And then his sayings about the gods are especially surprising. He declares that if we were reasonable (these are his very words), the best thing we could do would be to recognize that we know nothing whatever about the gods. He talks a good deal about a Providence and about gods who see and hear everything, are present everywhere and know our very thoughts. All right. But he speaks less often of the gods of our national festivals, the gods of our fathers, whom we call on by their ancient names. This Socrates says that these are not their real names. He accepts some of the stories our fathers have told us about the gods, but he rejects most of them on the pretext that one should place no reliance on stories in which the gods

[1] The author is adopting terms, partly imaginary, partly composite, but always in the Socratic manner or tradition (Author's note).

P

30. *Marble head of a statue of Zeus (the Boston Zeus), inspired by a chryselephantine statue at Olympia, the work of Pheidias (between 437 and 432). The marble copy dates from the 4th Century*

appear as doing wrong. But it is easy to understand that what is wrong for men to do is not necessarily wrong for the gods. In any case these stories are sacred, and if you touch them, the whole city is endangered. Socrates also says that we should not pray as we do, asking for this or that, because the gods know what we need better than we know. He himself asks Pan for 'inner beauty'. What does that mean? And then he has his own god whom he calls his 'daemon' and whose voice he hears. No one has the right to hear voices—at least, no one except the Pythia and a few others, and in their case there are priests to check or control the matter. No one has the right to talk to us about gods whom we do not know, gods who are foreign to the city. And it is all very well for him to say that he knows nothing about the gods or about other things. That is not a way of getting out of the difficulty. There are things everyone knows, things every good citizen ought to know.

Still more shocking to the average Athenian was what Socrates said about popular government. The Athenian was proud of his democratic institutions, and rightly so, in spite of certain excesses. Besides, they offered him a livelihood. Everyone, or almost everyone, occupied some magisterial post, for the space of a year, or the duration of a lawsuit, or sometimes for a day. So the Athenian was astonished at hearing Socrates criticize the way magistrates were elected, which was by drawing lots. As if this were not the only reasonable and truly democratic method of choosing the representatives of the city! Socrates is reported as having said that the Popular Assembly took its decisions 'at hazard'; or again that government is a difficult science which should be reserved to a small number of men. What then does he make of equality? One day—and this everyone heard and saw—it was Socrates' turn to serve on the committee of the Assembly, constituted as a High Court of Justice. Well, he presided over the trial in the most revolting manner. He tried to prevent our voting as we wanted to vote. We wanted to vote for the wholesale condemnation to death of the ten generals who won the naval battle of Arginusae: they had not taken the trouble to save the soldiers who were drowning, ostensibly because of a tempest which had broken over the scene of battle. Now Socrates claimed to make us vote on each case separately. However, the other presiding magistrates ended by letting us do as we wished. Socrates said that the worst thing about a democracy is that the governors always let the governed do as they wish. And a good thing too! He even said one day that democracy is a sort of tyranny. It is extraordinary how many things he says and how obstinate he is in his opinions, this man who boasts of knowing nothing.

So ran the thoughts of many Athenians, while Socrates, working in the cause of truth and in the service of his people, was laying up a store of mischief for himself.

It must not, however, be forgotten that he was not the only man then philosophizing in Athens. If his manner was more picturesque and his sayings more acute than those of other philosophers, it was easy to confuse him with the new masters who had come to Athens from Asiatic Greece or from Grecian Italy and who were known as Sophists, which then simply meant 'learned men'. We know that Protagoras, Gorgias, Prodicus and their like—men much sought after by the gilded youth of Athens who often got up before dawn to go and knock at their doors—professed to instruct their pupils in all things human and divine, in all knowledge and all wisdom, in grammar, astronomy, geometry, music and ethics, not to mention the problem of knowledge and, on occasion, how to make boots. They required cash down for their lessons, whereas Socrates deemed it shameful to sell knowledge, and said that trading in wisdom deserved the name of prostitution no less than trading in beauty. Among the many sciences they professed, the one which the sophists taught with the most brilliance and personal gain was the one most useful in a democracy where the art of eloquence enabled you to sway the mind of the Sovereign People, namely, rhetoric. Moving from city to city, half-professors and half-journalists, the sophists especially liked sojourning in Athens, the most 'advanced' democracy of the time, the city they flattered themselves on turning into the home of enlightenment. Their lectures and conferences were thronged with young men eager after novelty. Some no doubt were enamoured of solid learning, but most of them desired to learn from these illustrious masters the secret of how to dominate the multitude, a secret which was promised by noisy advertising campaigns. Did not they boast that by the gift of speech they could, if they so wished, secure the triumph of the bad cause over the good, or, according to their favourite slogan, 'make the stronger case appear the weaker'? This art of verbal combat, these 'double reasons' and 'shattering orations' which sophistry offered its adepts, were a valuable trump-card in the hands of a young politician in a hurry to make his name.

This is not the place for defining exactly what the sophists were. Our knowledge of them is imperfect and what knowledge we have is mainly derived from what their adversaries say. Whether they were really 'learned' men who showed how thought might turn on itself in order more effectively to criticize itself; or whether they were virtuosos in using an encyclopaedic knowledge for the purpose of subjecting the true to the utility of the passing moment—this is scarcely to our present purpose, as we are not pretending to show what they were, but merely to indicate what they appeared to be in the eyes of the common people. On this point there is no doubt. The people regarded them as dilettanti of the mind; ingenious but dangerous performers, instructors in the art of doubting, men who were demolishing every well-established truth, and sowing impiety and immorality on every side—in a word, as people then phrased it, corrupters of youth.

Now for the average Athenian, Socrates, that perpetual doubter whose questions paralyzed the minds of his interlocutors in the manner, as one of them said, of the torpedo or numb fish whose touch paralyzes the fisherman's hand—Socrates, who forced his followers to reject all accepted notions and simply confess their ignorance, was the prince of sophists, the most insidious of the corrupters of youth. He was also the most guilty. The others were foreigners; he was a citizen.

The Athenians were mistaken. Whatever conclusion we should arrive at regarding the sophists, Socrates was not one of them. We know that he fought them, that he judged with severity the use they made of the art of speech when they proposed to establish not what was true but what appeared to be. We know, or at least we feel strongly, that if in public Socrates generally left his interlocutors disconcerted, a prey to doubt as to a necessary kind of treatment, the Socrates of the more intimate conversations had indeed first subjected his disciples to this mental hygiene of which the purpose was to cleanse the mind of that mass of erroneous notions which indolence had allowed to collect there; but that then, if their souls thus purified still aspired to the way of truth, he practised that kind of midwifery he had learned from his mother, he helped them to give birth to that wisdom they had been unconsciously bearing within themselves. According to Socrates the doubt to which the sophists invited men was merely a convenient scepticism which allowed the individual, faced with a hundred errors, to choose the one that most flattered his personal interests. Sophistry was an art of flattery, the art of a cook who is indulging the whims of spoiled children. Socrates himself practised the medical art. The doubt he inflicted was like a cauterization to destroy the gangrened tissues and restore to the soul its native health and life-giving capacity.

If the passage of time and our knowledge of what resulted from the Socratic revolution enable us today to remove Socrates from the troop of the sophists and recognize in him an intellectual and moral greatness which they no doubt did not possess, we must on the other hand admit that it was easy for his contemporaries to be deceived, since Socrates apparently exercised the same trade as the sophists, instructing the young generation—as they did—arguing in public, like them, about politics, ethics, religion and sometimes art, and like them vigorously and subtly criticizing traditional notions of these matters.

We must take care not to be too clever. In fifth-century Athens, where people took pleasure in hearing the difficult poems of Aeschylus and Euripides, fools were not more numerous than elsewhere; probably rather less so. Other peoples in other ages have sided with the destructive thinkers, denied and sometimes condemned the great artisans of the spirit. The greater these are, the harder they are to recognize.

But it was not simply the small folk of Athens, the registered dock-worker, or pedlar, or out-of-work, who were mistaken about Socrates. Athenians of old culture and refined education were equally deceived, and Aristophanes among them, Aristophanes who had eaten and drunk at the same table with him and exchanged much talk, grave and gay, with that good companion.

Socrates had been pursuing his trade as 'star dancer to the glory of God' (to use Kierkegaard's words) for some ten years in Athens when Aristophanes, who wanted to denounce on the comic stage the evils of modern education, or simply to provoke laughter—as was his right—chose as representing the whole clique of philosophers, rhetoricians, astronomers, physicists and other star-gazers—the whole clan of intellectuals—simply Socrates. And on Socrates' shoulders he placed the opinions and sins of half a century of reflexion and research. The comedy of the *Clouds,* performed in 423, twenty-four years before the trial of Socrates, was in the view of Plato one of the distant causes, but a certain cause, of the accusation brought against the philosopher.

The *Clouds* is the story of a rich peasant who, after being ruined by his son in the city, and being moreover too stupid to play the rogue without being taught how, goes to knock on the door of the 'thinking-shop' of Socrates, that master of dirty tricks, that crafty sophist who will teach anyone, against a large fee, how to manoeuvre in the law-courts and dupe one's creditors. From the farcical lessons he receives from this caricature of a Socrates, however twisted and roundabout they may be, the fellow immediately learns contempt for the pledged word and an assurance that if the gods punish perjury, it is only when imbeciles commit it. But the son is a more apt pupil of the school of disrespect than the father. It is he who, with his cudgel, avenges morals by beating his progenitor; and morals are avenged too by the burning of the 'school for learned souls' and the destruction of that den of impostors.

The Socrates of the *Clouds* is amusing, and he must have appeared very convincing also to the spectators. So complex is the portrait that the perspicacity and cruelty of the dramatist can only be analyzed by the historian of ideas. The caricature is in places founded on the poet's very acute intuition of the most original aspects of the Socratic revolution. Thus, the primacy which Socrates ascribed to the mind over the body, the reversal of values he operated in the relation between body and soul—a scandalous thing to a people who loved physical beauty—and the asceticism which in the course of time, and as early as Antisthenes and Plato, did not fail to result from it—all this easily took on, in Aristophanes' comedy, the guise of filth and rags, the mask of emaciated faces and of half-discarnate souls divagating in the thinking-shop.

Formidable is the power of art. The character in Aristophanes' play is much closer to Anaxagoras or Gorgias or any other trader in knowledge than it is to

Socrates himself; and yet it is Socratic enough in the singularity of its language and gestures, in its ironical sallies and absurd paradoxes, to represent in Athenian eyes the only Socrates whom Athenians could henceforth recognize, the only Socrates whom they could one day condemn at the bar of the court. For it was indeed Aristophanes' Socrates who was to be arraigned before the tribunal of the Heliasts; and because the people acting as judge had the poet's fiction firmly imprinted in their minds, they did not see that it was a different Socrates who answered the magistrate's summons. They condemned the phantom which, through the power of poetry, obsessed their imagination.

It is indeed a striking fact that if two grievances can be found in the comedy of 423 against the man whom it pillories, namely that he was impious and a corrupter of youth, the same two heads of accusation are explicitly formulated in the complaint lodged against the accused of 399: that he was 'guilty of not believing in the gods ... guilty of corrupting young men'.

Socrates is impious, said Aristophanes and the Popular Tribunal, with one accord. Impious—the man who, more than any other in that Athens of the enlightenment, led the quest for God while respecting His unknown Being? The man who refused to violate the divine, whether by defining its character or dislodging it from the domain of Nature which, to the souls of the ancients, was its sacred abode; the man ever on guard against making God speak the language of human folly, the man who lent Him only the word of reason and the behaviour of justice, and who knew also how to let Him dwell untroubled in His ineffable silence? In face of the supreme mystery, Socrates displays his habitual modesty and his strict uprightness. The only thing he says he knows of a certainty about deity is that he knows nothing certain. Ignorance is here the purest witness of genuine piety. In this act of reserve, how near to God is the sage who knows nothing of Him! As near as a man can be without ceasing to be human. For he conceives of this unknown God as just and good, as the best of men might be, possessed of all wisdom and aware that only such excellence can realize it. By a process of patient self-examination he has deciphered in his own mind a law of goodness and justice, to fulfil which would bring his own destiny to perfection. This law does not exist simply in him, because in it all men recognize themselves. Who then can have rooted it in the human soul but that unrevealed God who can be no more nor less than the supreme Good?

So much for Socrates' atheism. And here is the corrupter of youth, of the young men he never ceased to love and serve.

He loved the young men for the assiduous care with which they cultivated their bodies; and even more for the promise of a soul still free to develop, like a piece of good plough-land which, when patiently tilled, yields an abundant return for the seeds that have been dropped in it: seeds of courage, justice, temperance and wisdom, of which Socrates never gathered in the earthly harvest. But did he not nurse these young men over much and train them to oppose tradition?

No doubt; because he was a real educator and no young man enters the true life of the mind without some kind of break. He wished to train up his people, to bring them to a knowledge of what was truly good and to the peril and nobility of making a choice. He wished to free them from a servile obedience to accepted notions and engage them in the free service of a truth rigorously controlled and verified; to bring them out of childhood which thinks and acts by imitation or constraint, and make them adults, capable of acting in the light of reason and practising virtue not through fear of the law or the state, but because he knew for certain that happiness is identical with virtue.

Was it to be a corrupter, to teach these things every day, to devote to such an enterprise all the thoughts of a lifetime of povery and derision? But neither Aristophanes nor the Athenians could understand the greatness of the task which the philosopher had assigned himself. What people could? So Socrates' mission was in vain. The times were not yet ripe. His life, however long, had not the dimensions of the ages that were to elapse before Socrates ceased to be an irritating puzzle and became a centre of enlightenment.

One resource, however, remained to him, a quicker way of attaining his end, of convincing a few disciples at least and so establishing in human tradition the truth as he saw it. If the days of his life had been in vain, he could still give the example of his death.

In February 399, when Socrates was seventy, a young Athenian poet named Meletus posted a charge against him in the portico of the king-archon. Was he acting in obedience to religious or political convictions; or seeking to draw attention to his own writings by a kind of indirect publicity? We do not know. He was merely the figure-head of a sort of politician-promoter who called himself a moderate democrat and who appears to have nourished a ferocious animosity against intellectuals. This man, Anytus by name, was a patriot very sincere no doubt, but limited. He does not appear—although this has been asserted—to have had any motive of personal rancour. But he was persuaded that Athens, which had suffered so severely from her recent misfortunes, would only recover her greatness when the old ways of life and thought were restored to a city corrupted by the teachings of the sophists. He, together with an orator named Lycon, counter-signed the charge brought by Meletus. The text ran as follows: 'Socrates is guilty of not believing in the gods recognized by the State and of introducing new deities into the city. He is also guilty of corrupting the young men. The death-penalty is proposed.'

We know that in 399 Athens had barely emerged from one of the most terrible crises in her history. After thirty years of almost continuous war and revolution, invasion of the homeland, the plague, the defeat of the navy, the collapse of the empire, the blockade, the surrender, the foreign occupation, the dictatorship, the proscriptions, and a civil war followed by an uncertain amnesty—Athens was emerging from this ordeal with nerves on edge. Her energy was broken, and the pride of being a great power, that pride which had for so long been made to serve for armies and bread and courage, was beaten down.

In these circumstances the men in power, of whom Anytus was one, were speaking the language of repentance and hard work. They asked the people to abandon all political ambitions, to repair the economic and financial disaster by assiduous toil, to reconstruct the farms, replant the vineyards and olive-gardens, rebuild the ships, go down into the mines and, generally, to restore industry and commerce. Hence there were to be no more intellectuals infatuated with abstract theory, no more arguments about trifles. Intellect was a luxury. Production came first of all.

In the meantime Socrates, with the few idlers who accompanied him, continued to speculate in public on 'the supreme good', to pass his comb through accepted notions, and urge his countrymen to take thought for nothing but their souls. 'My only business,' he said, 'is to go through the streets and persuade you, young and old alike, not to be concerned with your body or your material fortune as much as with your soul and how to make it better. My task is to tell you that riches do not bring virtue, but that virtue is the source of all prosperity and of all good things whether public or private.' Perhaps, in his strange intellectual language, he was right; but the least one could say of such speeches was that they did not give people bread and scarcely induced them to put all their strength at the service of the country and in obedience to government. Thus, no doubt, reasoned Anytus and the men in power.

Popular feeling went further. People did not fail to establish a connexion of cause and effect between Socrates' teaching and the national misfortunes. They saw the following connexion, for example. The defeat of Athens was a punishment from the gods who had been irritated by the impious researches of the philosophers, just as the victory of Sparta was a reward due to her respect for ancestral tradition. And there was this closer connexion: in the years of disaster two of Socrates' familiars had been men of evil genius for the city. Was not one of his familiars that wretched Alcibiades who had profaned the statues of Hermes and who along with his friends had sacrilegiously parodied the mysteries in his own house? Alcibiades who, after using fair promises to drag Athens into the disastrous Sicilian campaign, had then gone over to the enemy and used all the resources of his genius to help Sparta and Persia to ruin his own country? And then there was the other politician who had received lessons from Socrates, that atheist Critias, author of a tragedy in which the hero impudently pretended that the gods were only a useful lie, and head also of that sanguinary clique of dictators whom the conqueror had installed in power and whose police had exiled or put to death thousands of good citizens. *There* were the two men of whom it could be said: 'Socrates was their master.' It was not difficult for the politicians, whether or not they were convinced that a master is responsible for the faults of his disciples, to use these two names to whip up popular fury against the philosopher and make him the scapegoat who would bear all the former sins of Athens and expiate them by his death.

If, however, the city's misfortunes partly explain the condemnation of Socrates, we must not neglect to recall that a charge of impiety was no new thing in Athens and that, prior to the disasters we have spoken of, at least three philosophers had had actions brought against them—Anaxagoras, Protagoras and Diagoras of Melos. Certainly Athens was tolerant. In the Ville-Lumière of the fifth century the boldest opinions regarding the gods or the state could as a rule be freely advanced under various forms, and notably on the stage, without anyone's dreaming of fishing out the old laws which had been enacted in earlier centuries to protect the city's gods against impiety. Of this great liberty of thought, which Athens above all the Greek cities prided herself on, we have many proofs. We must not therefore regard Athens, on account of Socrates, as the home of some fanatical Inquisition. But it sometimes happened that, in this agreeable atmosphere of liberty, politicians with exclusively political ends in view, used a charge of impiety to silence a man whose talk was, in their opinion and in the circumstances of the day, dangerous for the community. To silence him, and nothing more. These lawsuits were employed as a kind of threat, and it was understood that the accused might escape, either by an arrangement with the plaintiff, a promise of partial silence, or by exile. So that if other lawsuits were indeed brought against philosophers, it is very important to observe that only Socrates was actually put to death. Why was this? Partly on account of the misfortunes we have mentioned, misfortunes which for a time had changed the liberal temper of Athens, and also and especially because Socrates refused to evade the blow and because, in the arguments that ensued, he did much to exacerbate the people's anger. It may be supposed that in the last resort Socrates desired to die much more keenly than his accusers desired his death.

We are at this point very near the deeper, and also the stranger meaning of his death. Once again Socrates appears as an enigma and guards his own secret. Our sources do not enable us to say with absolute certainty why he wished to die, if indeed he did wish. And, moreover, have we the right to force a secret which he never divulged to his intimate friends? Scarcely may we suggest that the philosopher desired to die so that this might be the act which bore witness to a truth he had hitherto merely taught. In any event it was here that his teaching found its accomplishment, and it was here that Socrates still touches us.

The case depended on one of the courts of the popular tribunal of the Heliasts. This court numbered five hundred and one judges chosen by lot from the citizen-body. They belonged to every social group. Sailors were not more numerous than men of the lower middle-class, whatever may have been said to the contrary. This mob of judges sat in the public square, while outside the palisade that surrounded the court, the crowd thronged as to a public spectacle. The tipstaffs had difficulty in preventing demonstrations. The judges themselves behaved as though they were on the stage; sometimes they booed the accused, sometimes they shed tears over his fate.

From such a tribunal Socrates did not expect an equitable verdict. He knew that the Athenians were still children, capricious, angry when they heard the truth and ready to purr when they were flattered. He had never spoiled them with sugared words; and on this day when he and the people found themselves face to face in the presence of Justice, he proposed to offer them nothing but an opportunity to be just and wise. He was going to put them to trial for a last time; because he regarded his prosecution as a trial—not his trial, because he had for long been ready for anything, but the trial of his fellow-countrymen.

We know little about the speeches of the three plaintiffs. The poet who was the official accuser seems to have been weak. If he had counted on an oratorical success, all he got was ridicule, at least according to Socrates' friends. The politician Anytus and the orator Lycon who supported the poet were on the other hand extremely brilliant. Their speeches were adorned with all the flowers of fashionable rhetoric and—as Socrates rallied them—so persuasive that while listening to them he was no longer very sure that he was still Socrates.

To establish good grounds for the accusation of impiety, the plaintiffs did not fail to exploit the old prejudice against those who tried to explain celestial phenomena. Now Socrates had long ago given up astronomy which he regarded as impious. But in the eyes of the vulgar a philosopher is always a man who falls into a well while gazing at the stars, and who deserves to. The plaintiffs also tried to prove that the criticism of the myths, which Socrates indulged in, implied impiety and even atheism. This, however, only demanded a beating, because mythology was scarcely an article of faith among the ancients and the Athenians were accustomed to hearing even the most pious of their poets constantly rehandling the old myths. The prosecution very clumsily attempted to support the complaint that Socrates had introduced new deities in his alleged worship of the 'daemon' whose voice he heard. But Socrates had never worshipped his 'deity'; nor had he ever

used the word 'daemons' in the plural, as the text of the accusation had it, still less
had he invited his fellow-citizens to adore such 'daemons', since he held the 'divine
voice' that spoke to him as a sign of the peculiar benevolence of deity in his regard.
But the people, who were not surprised at hearing an accusation of atheism
brought against the very man who was reproached with hearing a divine voice
within his breast, were scarce disposed to make subtle distinctions.

The prosecution appears to have directed its efforts less in respect of the charge
of impiety than of the charge of corrupting the youth of the city. Socrates, they
said, was inspiring young men with a taste for 'trifles' or 'nonsense', by which
'realistic' minds were ready enough to describe reflexion and study. He was turning them away from 'action' and particularly from taking part in state affairs. By
keeping them at his side, he was breaking up the family, in favour of which Anytus
and his friends were then displaying great zeal. He was openly teaching the scorn
of paternal authority. The false knowledge he inculcated in his disciples raised
them in opposition to the accepted wisdom and the laws of the city, in opposition
to order and tradition.

Varied as were the forms, it was always the same reproach: Socrates was teaching young men to think.

Athenian law required the defendant to undertake his own defence. There were,
however, a sort of professional advocates, the logographers, who would compose
for the accused speeches which the latter presented before the tribunal. Lysias, the
most famous of these men, offered Socrates his services. The philosopher caused
to be read to him in advance the speech that had been composed for him and which
was very nicely phrased. But he refused with a smile.

'That is a fine speech,' he told Lysias, 'but it scarcely befits me.'

'And why doesn't it befit you, if it's fine?'

'Don't you know that fine shoes and handsome clothes scarcely suit me?'

Fine phrases, in his view, were but poor clothing for his innocence.

He therefore engaged no advocate. He prepared no defence, holding that he
had worked all his life in his defence by never committing an unjust act. He
presented himself before the judges with the consciousness of an upright life
devoted wholly to the service of the city. He also felt too much dislike for formal
eloquence or even for the artifice of a speech prepared at leisure and delivered as
though it were extempore, to engage in this last dialogue with his people with a
head full of ready-made phrases and feigned replies to arguments which one would
not really have had time to weigh up. So he improvised. In the *Apologia of Socrates*
Plato has left us, probably not the exact text, but a living echo of the defence, in
which the disciple cannot have failed to retain the inspiration which had animated
the master.

The tone is conversational. One seems to hear Socrates talking with that brusque and charming familiarity that was peculiar to him. Using the right which the law gave him of arguing the case with the plaintiff, Socrates cross-examined Meletus; he entangled him in the net of his ironical dialectics, and made him fall into the trap of those sophistries which Socrates himself could handle as well as anyone else; and he reduced him to silence.

But he conversed especially with the judges, and this was a decisive dialogue between the philosopher and the Athenian people. He explained his mission, not with a view to defending his life, which was of little moment to him, but in order to incite Athens to an act of sound reason which would make the city better; to force it, in short, to perform an act of justice, not in order to defer or delay the death of Socrates, which could be no great evil for him, but to preserve the souls of his fellow citizens from the worst of all evils, which is injustice. The stake for which the defendant was fighting was the salvation of Athens. 'If you condemn me to death, it is not I whom you will be wronging, but yourselves. . . . It is not I whom I defend at this moment, far from it. I am defending you.'

This was why Socrates absolutely refused to plead for indulgence. Ordinarily speaking, accused men knew they would please the sovereign people by lowering themselves to supplication or bringing their family in tears to the bar of the court. By this kind of comedy they often contrived to touch the hearts of the crowd which composed the tribunal. But nothing could have been worse in Socrates' eyes than to owe acquittal to pity. He was not provoking his judges to any base sentimentalism, but to have the courage of being reasonable. He did not desire their compassion; he wanted to make them just. He refused to flatter their vanity, still less to cringe and beg and humiliate himself before the people, his masters; for in truth he was the master who chastises because he loves.

At this game he was risking his life. He knew it, and every one of his words was weighted with indifference to death. Though his life was in the hands of these men, he continued to riddle them with the shafts of irony, he did not change a word of his ordinary language, or an inflection of his voice. It was not a question of his, Socrates', life, but of not degrading this people; it was a question of still trying to raise them. In this last hour of his life Socrates remained what he had always been, the educator of the city.

There were murmurs buzzing round him. 'Give up, Socrates; desist. Cannot you, at your age, just rest from the frenzy of harassing people, from the rage of sermonizing? We don't wish you any harm; but do simply relax your zeal, which is now useless. Cease to philosophize in the streets; we only want peace.' Even his friends were talking like this.

He silenced them, and loftily reaffirmed his divine mission. 'I am he whom the god has given you to make you better. . . . If you put me to death, you will not receive such a favour a second time.'

The words were provocative, and unbearably arrogant. The jury kept interrupting him with their cries. Socrates stood firm. 'Do not cry out, Athenians . . . there is something divine in a man who sacrifices his goods and his life in the interest of others.'

The court rebelled against the goading. Ah! if only Socrates could make them understand the supreme good, if only he could open their eyes to wisdom, enable them to acquire it! But it was too late for persuasion; and all he could do now was to bear witness to his love for his people and his fidelity to God. 'I love you, Athenians. . . . But I shall obey God rather than you.'

This was the last dialogue between Socrates and Athens, between a people and its soul.

The judges proceeded to vote. Socrates was pronounced guilty by two hundred and eighty-one votes as against two hundred and twenty. The people had lost.

But not yet. Socrates mounted the rostrum to play the last stake on behalf of Athens. For the penalty had still to be assessed. Now the law permitted him to propose a lighter punishment than the one demanded by the prosecution. Socrates, had he wished, could at that moment have saved his life by proposing exile or imprisonment, or even a heavy fine which his friends, with Plato at their head, offered to pay for him. The court would no doubt have agreed to this lighter penalty. But Socrates would not have it. To propose any sort of penalty was either to admit his guilt or to invite the judges to commit the worst kind of injustice, namely, to punish an innocent man. He was innocent; and, even more, a benefactor of the city. Justice required not merely that he should not be punished, but that he should be rewarded. He therefore asked the judges to award him the supreme honour reserved for citizens who had deserved well of their country: to be lodged and maintained in the Prytaneum. Only in this way could justice now be restored to its place in the judge's soul.

Socrates' words, in this second speech, were more cutting than before, his appeal to the people more exacting, his witness to the mission they did not understand, more proud. He was, as it were, applying a white-hot iron to the gangrene of injustice. And when he flung out his defiance: 'A reward, or death!', he doubtless knew what the court would decide, he knew also that death was now the only means of reaching the hearts of those he had most loved.

This provocative speech, of which, at the instance of his friends, he disdainfully softened the concluding sentences, exasperated the court. Beyond the bravado of the utterance the judges could not hear the urgent and tender voice that was appealing to Athens. The earlier vote had pronounced Socrates guilty by a fairly small majority; the vote for the death-penalty was almost unanimous. What a strange court, in which very many judges were found to declare the accused innocent and at the same time worthy of death!

Socrates was a man who never gave up. His task was not finished. He rose once again to warn the people. He first addressed the judges who had condemned him. Let them beware! It is not by killing people that one gets rid of truth: on the contrary, truth renews its onslaught. One can only silence those who serve the cause of truth by becoming a good man oneself.

Then he took leave of the just judges, those who had voted for acquittal, assuring them that death could not be an evil either for them or for him. They were going to live; he was leaving them to die. But which had the better part, he or they? 'No one knows, except God.'

The knowledge of God was the certainty to which Socrates' ignorance referred, in the last resort, and this sacred name was also the last word pronounced before the people by the man who was condemned for having scorned the gods of the city.

◎

On the eve of Socrates' condemnation, the Athenians had adorned with garlands the poop of the sacred vessel which took an embassy every year to Delos, to celebrate the birth of Apollo. The law provided that, during this pilgrimage, no execution might take place to pollute the city. One had to wait until the ship returned, and if the winds were contrary, the voyage might be long. Socrates waited thirty days.

He received his disciples in prison, serenely pursuing his usual conversations. He also, in obedience to dreams which bade him be a poet, busied himself with writing a hymn to his master Apollo; though he had always thought that the philosophy which had filled his life was the highest kind of poetry.

But he had still to face the most cruel of his ordeals. His disciples, unknown to himself, were planning his escape. The scheme met with no obstacles. The politicians seemed to be regretting the turn the affair had taken, since Socrates' obstinacy had virtually forced the magistrates to condemn him. On the other hand the clique of professional blackmailers and informers, without whose connivance a plan of this kind had no chance of success, looked as though it would be well disposed. Knowing that several of Socrates' friends were well-to-do, they were amazed at not yet having been approached by them. The prison-warders, who were very friendly towards a prisoner so mild-tempered, would have been glad to receive an official order to close their eyes. Finally Crito, the oldest of Socrates' friends, had relations in Thessaly who would be overjoyed to receive the philosopher. His friends were therefore zealously plotting his escape, and without much secrecy. Everything appeared to be ready and easy.

Socrates' consent had still to be obtained, and his disciples knew him too well to count on succeeding without a struggle. All through the trial they had felt that he was demanding to die; and they now feared he would read them a severe lesson. The days passed by, a long month of intimate talks, without anyone's daring to broach the matter. But finally, having heard that the sacred vessel had been signalled off Cape Sunium, Crito made up his mind. He called at the prison in the early morning. Socrates was still asleep, and Crito contemplated the peaceful figure. He was fearing to disturb him when Socrates opened his eyes.

'What are you doing here so early?'

'I am bringing news.'

'I know what news. The day after tomorrow. . . . A dream revealed it to me.'

Then Crito, tenderly but urgently, opened the attack. He spoke of the disciples' feeling of shame, if they could do nothing for the master. He spoke of the steps which had been taken. He begged Socrates to agree, he begged him not to abandon his children and his friends. He was bold enough to blame him for such treachery. He even ventured to accuse him of consenting to a death so iniquitous merely out of weakness, and so of collaborating with wicked men in an act of injustice. Thus the old friend who, throughout his life, had surrounded the philosopher with affectionate attentions, who had piously admired without always comprehending, but agreeing by instinct—at this moment when Socrates was abandoning him to obey some blind 'daemon', suddenly rebelled against this caprice for dying, and, in order to dissuade him, uttered the worst insult that could be offered Socrates: the accusation of injustice.

'No, Socrates, you will not commit this fault. You will leave with me tonight.'

To this fervent prayer Socrates replied in a tone which at first sounds rather cold. He had made up his mind. But he wished to reflect, as was his custom. He wished to justify himself in his friend's eyes. 'Your solicitude is praiseworthy,' he told Crito, 'if it accords with duty. Otherwise, the more urgent it is, the more regrettable.' And he asked Crito to consider, according to their usual methods, whether the escape he proposed was, or was not, in harmony with the principles which he, Socrates, had taught all his life and which, now or never, it was a question of practising. He was not going to change his principles because threatened with misfortune. The essential thing was not to live, but to live well. Would two old men like Crito and himself have passed their lives in discussing imaginary things? Or did they not know that there comes an hour when principles, if genuine, must be lived?

Socrates then engaged Crito in a long debate on civic duty. Can a citizen who

has been unjustly condemned evade the sanction of the laws? Has he the right to
be unjust too? To return evil for evil, and by disobedience set an example of disorder? Should he respond to the benefits he has received from the city by destroying its laws? Certainly not. Evil is always evil, and should always be avoided.
Arguments crowded on Socrates' lips.

At last he fell silent, as he still heard echoing in his heart, like the notes of a flute,
the words which the city's laws had inspired in him.

Crito had nothing to answer; and what could the judges have said if they had
heard these words from the man they had condemned on the ground that he was
teaching scorn for the laws, and who was now dying rather than injure them?

Two days later the sacred ship cast anchor off the Piraeus. Socrates' disciples
reached the prison earlier than usual. According to Athenian custom, Socrates was
not to die until after sunset. He wished to pass the whole of this last day of his
earthly life in conversing with those he loved about death, and the hopes of
immortality which our reason may entertain.

It would be impertinent to record the stages of this debate or describe the last
moments of the sage in a form different from that which Plato has for ever made
his own. He no doubt put into his narrative many arguments that came only from
himself; but he also put into it all his love for his master, and this is enough to
authenticate the narrative, if not the demonstration. The serene death of the master
crowned the disciple's faith in his immortality. With an intrepid love of truth,
Socrates faces the problem set by the approaching dissolution of his body. The
immortality he seeks is not a pretty lie with which it would be pleasant to delight
the imagination, but a knowledge he wishes to establish on the basis of reason. He
joyfully receives all the objections presented by his fellow-seekers because they
oblige him to consolidate his proof, and correct any error he may have committed.
And if at the end of the colloquy, when all has been weighed up, the felicity beyond the grave of the soul of the righteous man appears only as a 'noble risk',
this modest assurance is enough, at the moment of the departure, to fill him with a
serene expectation.

Who knows? Maybe one must be cured of life, to be cured at last of ignorance.

'How shall we bury you?' Crito had asked.

'As you like,' replied Socrates, scarcely able to repress a smile. 'That is, if you
can catch me.'

Good Crito! He gave the name of Socrates to the corpse he was presently going
to see. He was asking something which he should have deemed immortal how he
was to bury it.

'You ought to know, Crito, that to speak inaccurately is to do harm to people's
souls.'

31. *Olympia: ruins*

So we must not speak of Socrates as dead, but know, if we have understood him, that the dissolution of his body did not mark the end of his life but the beginning of another life which he was to lead in the souls of his followers. These faithful souls were not simply the temple of a cult to his memory; they were the scene of a new birth, the throne of his being, obstinate in pursuing socratically, even if it were to combat the reasons advanced by Socrates, that great adventure—the quest of knowledge.

BIBLIOGRAPHICAL NOTE

THE reader will find below a list of the principal works and articles consulted or used by the author in this second volume of *Greek Civilization*. The Greek texts, which are the most important source, are generally not indicated.[1] The author has not on the other hand felt free not to mention his own works, as he has borrowed from them more than one page of the present volume.

CHAPTER I

C. M. Bowra, *Sophoclean Tragedy*. Oxford, The Clarendon Press, 1944.

André Bonnard, *La Tragédie et l'Homme*. Neuchâtel, La Baconnière, 1950.

Max Pohlenz, *Die Griechische Tragödie*. Leipzig, Teubner, 1930.

Heinrich Weinstock, *Sophokles*. Leipzig, Teubner, 1931.

CHAPTER II

J. Charbonneaux, *La Sculpture grecque archaïque*. Lausanne, La Guilde du Livre, 1938.

J. Charbonneaux, *La Sculpture grecque classique*. Lausanne, La Guilde du Livre, 1942.

Elie Faure, *Histoire de l'Art, L'Art antique*. Paris, H. Floury, 1909.

Henri Lechat, *La Sculpture grecque*. Paris, Payot, 1922.

Henri Lechat, *Phidias et la Sculpture grecque au Ve Siècle*. Paris, Librairie de l'Art ancien et moderne *n.d.*

A. de Ridder and W. Deonna, *L'Art en Grèce*. Paris, La Renaissance du Livre, 1924.

Max Wegner, *L'Art grec*. Paris, Editions Charles Massin, 1955.

CHAPTER III

J. D. Bernal, *Science in History*, London, Watts & Co., 1954.

Jean T. Desanti, *Remarques sur les Origines de la Science en Grèce*. Paris, *La Pensée* No. 66 mars–avril 1956, pp. 86 *ss*.

Benjamin Farrington, *Greek Science*, Vol. I, *Thales to Aristotle*. Harmondsworth, Middlesex, Penguin Books, 1944.

Abel Rey, *La Jeunesse de la Science grecque*. Paris, La Renaissance du Livre, 1933.

Arnold Reymond, *Histoire des Sciences exactes et naturelles dans l'Antiquité*. Paris, Librairie Albert Blanchard, 1924.

[1] In the Swiss edition. They are indicated in the present translation (Translator).

Q

32. Laconian landscape: Bee-keeping near Sparta

Maurice Solovine, *Démocrite*. Paris, Félix Alcan, 1928.

George Thomson, *The First Philosophers*. London, Laurence & Wishart, 1955.

V. E. Timochenko, *Le Matérialisme de Démocrite*. Paris, *La Pensée* No. 62 juillet-août 1955, pp. 50 *ss*.

CHAPTER IV

The same works as in CHAPTER I.

CHAPTER V

Jaqueline Duchemin, *Pindare poète et prophète*. Paris, 'Les Belles Lettres', 1955.

Pindare, *Odes*, Version Willy Borgeaud (avec commentaires). Lausanne, Rencontre, 1951.

Andre Rivier, *Mythe et Poésie, leurs rapports et leur fonction dans trois épinicies de Pindare*. Paris, *Lettres d'Humanité*, IX, pp. 60 *ss*.

Marguerite Yourcenar, *Pindare*. Paris, Grasset, 1932.

Ulrich von Wilamowitz, *Pindaros*. Berlin, Weidmann, 1922.

CHAPTER VI

Hérodote, *Histoire*, Traduction de P.-H. Larcher. Paris, Musier, 1786.

Hérodote, *Découverte du Monde*, Version André Bonnard. Lausanne, Rencontre, 1951.

W. W. How and J. Wells, *A Commentary on Herodotus*, Vol. I. Oxford, The Clarendon Press, 1912.

Charles Parain, *L'Entrée des Scythes*. Paris, *Lettres Françaises* No. 633 of 23.8.56.

S. I. Rudenko, *Der zweite Kurgan von Pasyryk*. Berlin, Verlag Kultur & Fortschritt, 1951.

CHAPTER VII

Louis Bourgey, *Observation et Expérience chez les Médecins de la Collection hippocratique*. Paris, J. Vrin, 1953.

Hippocrate, *Oeuvres complètes* (Texte et traduction, avec commentaires medicaux) par E. Littré. 10 vols. Paris, J.-B. Baillière, 1839–61.

Hippocrate, *Oeuvres médicales*, d'après l'édition de Foës. 4 vols. Lyon, Aux Editions du Fleuve, 1953–4.

Gaston Baissette, *Hippocrate*. Paris, Grasset, 1931.

J. Bidez et G. Leboucq, *Une Anatomie antique du Coeur humain*. Paris, *Revue des Etudes grecques*, 1944, pp. 7 *ss*.

A. Castiglioni, *Histoire de la Médecine*. Paris, Payot, 1931.

Ch. Caremberg, *La Médecine dans Homère*. Paris, Didier, 1895.

B. Farrington, Cf. bibliographie ch. III.

A. J. Festugiere O.P., *Hippocrate, L'Ancienne Médecine*. Paris, Klincksieck, 1948.

W. Jaeger, *Paideia, Die Formung des Griechischen Menschen*, III. Berlin, Walter de Gruyter, 1947.

Dr Charles Lichtenthaeler, *La Médecine hippocratique*, I. Lausanne, Gonin frères, 1948.

CHAPTER VIII

Q. Cataudella, *La Poesia di Aristofane*. Bari, Gius. Laterza, 1934.

Francis Macdonald Cornford, *The Origin of Attic Comedy*. London, Edward Arnold, 1914.

Pierre-Louis Duchartre, *La Commedia dell'arte et ses enfants*. Paris, Editions d'art et d'industrie, 1955.

Paul Mazon, *Essai sur la Composition des Comédies d'Aristophane*. Paris, Hachette, 1904.

Gilbert Murray, *Aristophanes a Study*. Oxford, The Clarendon Press, 1933.

Octave Navarre, *Les Cavaliers d'Aristophane*. Paris, Mellottée, 1956.

A. W. Pickard-Cambridge, *Dithyramb, Tragedy and Comedy*. Oxford, The Clarendon Press, 1927.

CHAPTER IX

W. Deonna, *L'Eternel Présent*. Paris, *Revue des Etudes grecques*, 1922, pp. 1 *ss.* et 113 *ss.*

Victor Ehrenberg, *The People of Aristophanes*. Oxford, Blackwell, 1951.

Claude Mossé, *La Formation de l'Etat esclavagiste en Grèce*. Paris, *La Pensée*, No. mars–avril 1956, pp. 67 *ss.*

Lucien Sebag, *La Démocratie athénienne et la guerre du Péloponèse. Ibid.* pp. 114 *ss.*

R. F. Willets, *The Critical Realism of the Last Play of Aristophanes*. London, *The Modern Quarterly*, Vol. 8, pp. 34 *ss.*

CHAPTER X

Georges Bastide: *Le Moment historique de Socrate*. Paris, Félix Alcan, 1939.

André Bonnard, *Socrate selon Platon*. Lausanne, Mermod. 1945.

Olof Gigon, *Sokrates, Sein Bild in Dichtung und Geschichte*. Bern, Francke Verlag, 1947.

V. de Magalhaes-Vilhena, *Le Problème de Socrate. Le Socrate historique et le Socrate de Platon*. Paris, Presses universitaires, 1952.

V. de Magalhaes-Vilhena, *Socrate et la Légende platonicienne*. Paris, Presses universitaires, 1952.

INDEX